Mahalla - Traditional Institution in Tajikistan and Civil Society in the West

STUDIES IN SOCIAL SCIENCES, PHILOSOPHY AND HISTORY OF IDEAS

VOLUME 7

PETER LANG
EDITION

Saidbek Goziev

Mahalla – Traditional Institution in Tajikistan and Civil Society in the West

PETER LANG
EDITION

Bibliographic Information published by the Deutsche Nationalbibliothek
The Deutsche Nationalbibliothek lists this publication in the Deutsche Nationalbibliografie; detailed bibliographic data is available in the internet at http://dnb.d-nb.de.

Library of Congress Cataloging-in-Publication Data
Goziev, Saidbek, 1983-
Mahalla : traditional institution in Tajikistan and civil society in the West / Saidbek Goziev. -- 1 Edition.
pages cm. -- (Studies in social sciences, philosophy and history of ideas, ISSN 2196-0151 ; Volume 7)
Includes bibliographical references.
ISBN 978-3-631-64724-0 (Print) -- ISBN 978-3-653-04345-7 (E-Book) 1. Tajikistan--Social conditions. 2. Social institutions--Tajikistan. 3. Social structure--Tajikistan. 4. Islam--Tajikistan. 5. Civil society--Tajikistan. 6. Collectivism--Tajikistan. 7. Individualism--Tajikistan. I. Title.
HN670.25.A8G69 2015
306.09586--dc23
2014044004

This publication was financially supported by the Central European Educational Foundation, Warsaw.

ISSN 2196-0151
ISBN 978-3-631-64724-0 (Print)
E-ISBN 978-3-653-04345-7 (E-Book)
DOI 10.3726/978-3-653-04345-7

Peter Lang Edition is an Imprint of Peter Lang GmbH.

Peter Lang – Frankfurt am Main · Bern · Bruxelles · New York · Oxford · Warszawa · Wien

This publication has been peer reviewed.

www.peterlang.com

To My Parents: Kudratullo and Zahfaroy
and my Uncle Bahrullo

ACKNOWLEDGEMENTS

This dissertation would not be possible without the help of many. First, I am greatly indebted to my supervisor, Professor Andrzej Rychard for his patience, intellectual guidance and numerous remarks on this work. I am also very grateful to Professor Stanisław Zapaśnik for his advice, constructive criticisms and insightful comments. I have learned much from his lectures and our meetings and will always be grateful to him. Additionally, I extend my gratitude and appreciation to Professor Jolanta Sierakowska –Dyndo for being generous with her time in reading this dissertation, and her helpful comments and suggestions.

I would like also to thank Dr. John Fells, Mrs. Joanna Płoszajska and the entire pedagogical staff and students of the PAS Graduate School for Social Research (GSSR). I am grateful to the GSSR for providing both the scholarship funding and opportunity to pursue this PhD study in Warsaw.

To my parents, I express my deepest love and gratitude for always supporting me in every way and having great faith in me. I also thank Andrew Korybko for assisting with editing and proofreading this dissertation. Additionally, I thank Avraz Alduski, Mariusz Marszewski, Baktybek Kainazarov, Dhibian Shaamam Hasan, Chrsitoph Wirth, Isa Yusuf Chamo and all my friends for their support and assistance.

TABLE OF CONTENT

Introduction

My thesis topic focuses on first, understanding the function of *mahalla* — a traditional social institution in Tajikistan, which fulfills an important life-long role in promoting and preserving the cultural values of Tajiks, and second, on justifying the equivalence of mahalla to the concept of civil society in the West.

In this dissertation, I will search for an answer to the question why the traditional institutions in Tajikistan, especially mahalla, are inadequately involved in the development process or even at times, are dismissed from it. In my opinion, mahalla, as a social institution, is open to economic and political transformations because its structure is dynamic and flexible The centuries-long history of mahalla manifests its vitality in various political and economic fields, albeit it also demonstrates how mahalla upholds values by carefully protecting them and discouraging change.

An historical sketch of mahalla illustrates the process of its development and adaptation throughout the pre-Soviet, Soviet and post-Soviet eras. Its survival during the anti-religious and anti-nationalist propaganda launched by the Soviets is an evidence of the inrootedness of mahalla into the social fabric of daily life. As a social institution, mahalla sustains its own unwritten rules and codes of behavior, that altogether are based on cultural values. This reflects the peculiarity of Tajikistan, and leaves open the hope that mahalla can be used to implement various changes to enhance the lives of the Tajiks.

The structure of the dissertation is organized in such a way as to reach the above formulated aims. In the first chapter, I will work to explain the differences between the Western and Eastern cultures. On the basis of the scientific literature that I had been reviewing, I examined the opposing differences between these cultures: individualism- collectivism. I will work to justify that individualism is still an alien concept to Tajik society, whereas the spirit of community and collectivism have been ones of the prior hallmarks of Tajik culture throughout all its history.

In the second chapter, I will provide general information about mahalla and its history, structure and functions that are performed in relations to its members. As a part of this chapter, the description of informal institutions of Tajik society such as avlod, qawm, jamomad, mashwarat and gashtak are touched upon[1]. Due to their existence, the structure of Tajik society is different from the structure of all Western societies that I have studied. All these institutions play an important role in the life of every Tajik. The strength and power of these institutions show that they have significant sway on the economic conditions of the mahalla, and they can counterpart any unfavorable policies initiated by the state authorities. The third chapter contains general characteristics of civil society in the West and a discussion of some theories concerning this concept. Particular attention is devoted to the views of Piotr Glinski.

In the fourth chapter, I will pursue answering such central question, "Can mahalla be considered a counterpart to the Western concept of civil society?". Subsequently, I discuss the views that might preclude the recognition of mahalla as civil society institution: referring to Robert Putnam's point of view: the civil society cannot be embodied in a hierarchic society, and modernization theories stating that in the process of modernization, the traditional social institutions should be eliminated and replaced by new ones so in the case of Tajikistan it would be NGO's replacement of mahalla.

Addressing to the view that mahalla is the equivalent of Western civil society, I will justify characterizing mahalla as a public benefit and point to cultural factors that produce a significantly higher social capital than is possible in Western society. At the end of the chapter, I will analyze the role of mahalla as a mediator between its members and the state administration. In the final portions of this chapter the specific attention is to be paid to justifying the view that through an appropriate legal basis, mahalla could be utilized as an instrument to bring Tajikistan closer to the notions of Western democracy.

In the West, with exception of Poland, mahalla has not commonly been the subject of scientific research. In Poland, several texts concerning mahalla were published. The texts were based on actual Polish field studies. I am pleased to say that my personal views about the social role of mahalla fall fully in line with assessments of Polish researchers. I see this as confirmation that my belief about mahalla being used as an instrument of political transformation is not idiosyncratic, taking into account the fact that the author is an ethnic Tajik.

---

1 The meaning of these concepts will be explained later in the work.

Methodology of data collection

1.2.1. Hierarchy of data sources

During my research, I used several tools and methods to deepen the understanding of the subject and to collect a diverse array of data for explanation and analysis. This paper will present data sources and discuss the chosen methodological topics related to the data collection process. These methods include:

reading ethnographic literature concerning mahalla and reviewing the archives of mahalla;
- the conducting of interviews with members of various mahallas and representatives of the international aid organizations working in Tajikistan;
- an analysis of publications concerning traditional institutions in Tajikistan;
- a participant's observation of life in mahalla, based on the author's own experience.

1.2.2. Analyses of historical and ethnographical literature concerning mahalla

For the reason of existing several sources of data, it would be logical to think about hierarchy of the sources of this dissertation. The ethnographic and historical literatures provided the core of the research. It would have been impossible to write about this subject without knowledge about the history and the creation of the traditional institutions, especially mahalla. The main sources concerning the history of mahalla are Narshakhi's book, "History of Bukhara", Sukhareva's book, "*Квартальная община позднефеодального города Бухары* (Quarterly community of late feudal city Bukhara)" and Sadriddin Ayni's books concerning the daily life in the mahallas of Bukhara.

It should be noted that there is almost a complete absence of Western sources on mahalla. As I have stated above, it has not been the subject of scientific research, except in Poland. In my dissertation, I have referenced Arabic, English, Polish, Russian and Tajik sources. The papers written by Western authors were useful as instrument in such degree to prevent the appearance of any possible pro-Tajik bias in my research.

1.2.3. In-depth interviews with mahalla members

To collect primary source data, I conducted a focus group and semi-structured interviews with key informants (mahalla members, members of council of elders and Rais- the head of mahalla), and also performed an analysis of secondary sources. The data received was mostly qualitative, which added some peculiarity to the description of the results of the study. I hope this method helped me to receive answers to the hypothesis mentioned in the introduction. I also prepared questionnaires for the semi-structured interviews with the key informants – head of mahallas, members of mahalla, mulla and council of elders. I had open interviews and was a participant observer in different parts of Tajikistan: Badakhshan autonomous region (mountainous province in the east of Tajikistan), Dushanbe (capital city), Hisor[2], Fayzabad[3], Shahrinaw[4], Tursunzoda[5] and Sughd region (northern part of Tajikistan). I had conducted 60 interviews, however, I only have recorded 25 of them. I had 15 interviews with different mahallas in Hisor region, five interviews in Dushanbe, and three with people from the Sughd Region and two in Gorno-Badakhshan (Autonomous Province). The questionnaire and the subjects of the focus group interviews are included in the appendix that provides an opportunity for a detailed review.

As it was mentioned before, I did not record all interviews. However I had used all of them in my dissertation. I chose these regions because of the complexity of geographical, economic and identical factors. Further in my dissertation I will give more information about differences between regions in Tajikistan. Additionally, in some regions mahalla includes all traditional functions and some mahallas are less traditional.

I conducted my field research during summers of 2010, 2011 and 2012 while on vacation in my home country. The 10 interviews of the 25 total were con-

2 Hisor Region (also transliterated as Gissar in Russian or Nohiyai Hisor: Ноҳияи Ҳисор in Tajik) is a region in the Region of Republican Subordination, in Tajikistan, located between Varzob region in the east and Shahrinav region in the west (ap. 22 km from Dushanbe).

3 Faizobod region (in Tajik: Ноҳияи Файзобод) is a small region in the Region of Republican Subordination. It is located about 60 km east of the capital Dushanbe. It borders with Vahdat region from the west and the north, the Roghun district from the east, and the Khatlon Province from the south.

4 Shahrinaw district (in Tajik language: Ноҳияи Шаҳринав) is a district in the Districts of Republican Subordination in Tajikistan. The region is located between Tajikistan's capital Dushanbe and Uzbekistan. Shahrinaw has borders with Tursunzoda in the west, Hisor in the east, and Rudaki (former Lenin district) in the south. It is approximately 48 km west of Dushanbe.

5 Tursunzoda region (Tajik: Турсунзода,) is the westernmost region of the Regions of Republican Subordination (RRP). It borders with Uzbekistan in the west and is enclosed by Tajikistan's Shahrinaw region from the other directions (ap. 60 km from Dushanbe).

ducted at participant homes, 8 were conducted in mosques after prayer, 4 were in teahouses and 3 were in offices. The average time of my interviews lasted from 1 to 1.5 hour. At the same time interviewees were not in hurry. Beforehand, I arranged time to do my interview comfortably to last at least one hour. Most respondents proposed to conduct interviews at their homes. As previously mentioned, eight were conducted in mosque after prayer.

I selected participants according to the following criteria: social status and position of influence in the life of mahalla (for example, the head of mahalla, vice head of mahalla, member of council of elders). Moreover, the majority of my respondents are highly educated. Thus I selected mahalla members with high education and who are very active in everyday life. As for gender characteristics – 20 respondents were men and 5 were women in the main group. The representation of women is much lower because men publically participate in everyday life of mahalla, because women are occupied with family issues[6].

Concerning religious belief, all of my respondents without any exception declared their belief in God, and stated they were Muslims. When asked about religious practice (praying five times a day- namaz), I found out that most of them conducted regular namaz (five times a day). Most of them visited mosque at least once a day (some of them from one, two up five times praying in mosque). Only 3 of my respondents from two regions participated in prayers only during Muslim holidays and funerals. Mostly all of them regarded religion to be a significant part of Tajik culture and almost all of them used verbal references to God during our conversations. They all agreed that Islam has to be revived among Tajiks and that it is a basis of moral and traditions. It should be noted that at the same time, they opted for separation of religion and politics.

My advantage is that I am a mahalla member who had been living for 23 years in mahalla. I have participated in the daily life of mahalla, and in rituals like weddings, funerals, mahalla meetings, jamomads, gaps, holidays and many others. Being a member of mahalla in this study provides me with rich background information about the psyche of average people, both in the private and public spheres of life. In general, being an actual member of mahalla bestows the researcher with enormous benefits.

As I mentioned above, I conducted 15 interviews in the region where I was born and raised. I was a member of mahalla and I participated in its daily life. The inhabitants of the region know me well. It was an advantage that the inter-

6 The issue on role of women in Tajik society will be detailed discussed in the separate subchapter.

viewees knew me, as typically most people in mahalla do not trust foreigners, thereby making it very difficult for some researchers even to have a chance of conducting some interviews. I am from their mahalla and their region, which enabled them to openly agree to be interviewed. Firstly, not a single candidate refused, and I could easily reach every respondent with whom I wanted to speak. All interviewees reacted positively to the interviews and they freely provided their answers without any hesitations. Secondly, it should be noted that in all interviews, there was a professional distance between the respondents and me, as a researcher, even regarding such respondents who knew me very well. During the interviews, when the respondents entered into the role of an interviewee, their conversation became more stiff than usual.

1.2.4. Participant observation of daily life of mahalla and mahalla meetings (majlis)

As it has been previously stated, I was raised in mahalla and I am very well aware of its culture. As a part of this cultural upbringing, I had a lot of opportunities to participate in wedding ceremonies, funerals, davras or gashtaks, hashars, solving conflicts among neighbors and in mahalla meetings (majlis). During the performance of one of my interviews, I attended one mahalla majlis, where they hold an election to select the head of the mahalla. I was focused on the clarity and faithfulness of the democratic process of decision-making, so I analyzed the voting procedures of the informal mahalla meetings.

In my research, I used the principle of methodological relativism, which means that in researching another culture, one should not describe its social institutions and behavioral patterns through the perspective and experience of one's own culture. Cultural relativism is an approach to comparative analyses of the cultural differences. The key word relativism stresses the variability and non-similarity of traditions and moral issues experienced by the cultures. The relative, ambiguous character of the factual and value judgment differs between cultures, putting them into perspective of the providing different values on the same theme while not necessarily providing an opposite values on the same theme.

In addition, there are two ways that a judgment might be relative to a culture. Firstly, its truth (or falsehood) might be relative to the culture. That is, the judgment might be true in a relative rather than an ordinary, non-relative way. Secondly, the judgment might be true in an ordinary way but be relative to a culture through a tacit reference to the culture. In the first case, the relativity of the judgment derives from the relativity of moral truth. In the second, the relativity derives from the content of the judgment. The two cases differ sharply, but this is not noticed, much less appreciated, in the classic sources for relativism[7].

The issue of judgment, the expression of attitude towards particular phenomenon or situation, alters in different cultures for the reason that the starting points are different, i.e. traditional background, morality and types of behavior.

The paradox of my situation lies in the fact that I am a Tajik who has experienced Western culture with my own eyes, and who must now relate to the cultural experience where I was raised. I hope I have gotten to know Western culture well enough to allow me to distance myself from the cultural concepts and beliefs with which I was raised. In my case, using the principle of methodological relativism is an attempt to look at my own culture as though it were foreign. In attempting to watch Tajik culture from a different perspective, I am still conscious of the values it represents for me. However, I hope that this awareness does not damage the quality of my descriptions.

7 Tilley, J.J. (2000). Cultural relativism. In Human Rights Quarterly, Vol. 22, Nom. 2, May, p. 3.

Chapter 1: The cultural differences between the East and the West. (Western individualism versus the Eastern spirit of community)

East is East, and West is West; and never the train shall meet[8].

In this chapter, in order to represent the content of the research work, I need to clarify the understanding of the Western and Eastern cultures. The opposition East-West is used in social science to describe the crucial differences between the Western and Eastern cultures. These concepts are the contractual; the boundaries of the East and West can be determined only arbitrarily, albeit for the researcher of culture they actually exist. Chronically, the cultures of the East and West have begun to be considered as absolutely dissimilar from each other in the period of Middle Ages. Furthermore, it has been popularized that each of these cultures is developing in own way. It needs to be noted that ever since the Middle Ages, our knowledge of the cultural differences between the two has significantly deepened.

It is necessary to underline that the concepts of Eastern and Western cultures – I deal with in my work – are arbitrarily. I am conscious of the ethnical diversity met and experienced in Europe. In my opinion as representative of Asian country, the cultures of Asia are of more multiplicity. However, I cannot overlook the fact that there are certain categories of common sense typical and week-circulated in all cultures inhabiting the West. The concepts of the human as a separate and independent individual and individualism are the good example to apply to. Moreover, these concepts are the prolific field for the comparison between East and west since they are not highly present an developed in any culture determined in my work as the Eastern one. In this context the Asian cultures might be characterized by a certain category of thinking, opposite to individualism – collectivism.

At present, using the evident counteraction of individualism versus collectivism one becomes prepared to understand the cultural factors that are the causes of the differences in the behavior of people from the East and West. Arming with this paradigm, the general hopes in the possibility of the successful com-

8 Kipling, R.(1940) The Ballad of East and West. In *Rudyard Kipling's Verse*. Definitive edition: London

munications between Eastern and Western cultures, and erasing of the possible conflicts are raised. Hall E.T & Hall M.R. noted: "An understanding of different cultures may well be our own most important asset in meeting the challenges of our times, both abroad and at home."[9] So it might be inferred that every culture has created its specific patterns of behavior that have been recorded by religious beliefs, linguistic systems, and ethnic stereotypes, and have been transmitted through tradition.

Many cultures in the East, in general, and modern-day Tajik culture in particular, existed due to the ideal bond of individuals imitating the closest ties connecting members of the family. This among other things creates a completely different attitude to the law. As I will explain later in the case of conflict between family and neighbors, it is precisely the neighborhood community that plays a conciliatory role, and in such cases, as a direct result people rarely appeal to the courts. In contrast, the so-called American credo implies that the ideal bond between people is grounded on contract. In any case, in all Western countries the vast majority of these conflicts are resolved in the courts. Until the occurrence of the strengthening of contacts among the Western societies and the societies of Central and Eastern Asia, civil rights did not exist. Personally, I am as a native of Central Asia, during my first arrival to the West has really experienced a culture shock[10]. The ideal bond between people mentioned above imposes the certain rules of courtesy even on those who are total strangers, for example, a random person on the street. For instance, it is an unpleasant surprise for anyone from my region of Asia to hear a Western counterpart unceremoniously asking a passerby about directions without even saying "good day"[11]. I have heard this experience repeated quite often among Asians whom I had met in the West. Rather, this did not lead them to a negative evaluation of their own Asian culture.

---

9 Hall, E. T., & Hall, M. R., (1990). *Understanding Cultural Differences: German, French and Americans*, Yarmouth, ME: Intercultural Press, P6.

10 Culture shock is a concern, a feeling of frustration, an isolation and an anger that is experienced when someone is placed in a new cultural and social environment. Some people believe that culture shock occurs only with extreme changes when going from one country to another, however it can also be experienced closer to home, for example, when a person traveling within his country from one city to another. According to some scholars, even the most open-minded and culturally sensitive people do not have an immune to culture shock.

11 In most Asian cultures, it is culturally accepted before asking someone of something to say 'good day' and ask about one's health, and only later to begin asking the intended question (for example the address of street or house).

This is one of many possible examples that I could provide, such as the adaptation to another culture being a source of suffering and confusion. It is possible to learn the ways of life of another culture, however, it is much more difficult to accept its intrinsic intellectual and emotional components, especially when they stand in stark contrast with one's own ingrained habits.[12]

For furher discussion, it is relevant to refer to Tu Wei-ming, a well-known researcher at Harvard University, who has elaborated four basic differences between Western and Eastern civilizations. In his views, the primary source of this difference is religion:

1) In the Christian religion, and particularly in Protestantism, the individual is treated as an isolated being, a specific nomad, who can be existentially separated from other human beings, and who possesses an autonomy that provides the independence in relations to others. Contrastingly, according to Confucian thought, the individual is recognized as a certain point of intersection in the networks of social relations. Personal identity is built solely on the basis of these relationships with others. The ideal man is someone who fully understands his relationship with others and is aware of his associated responsibilities.[13]
2) In Western thought, under the influence of Protestantism, the rights of individuals become valuable and highly accentuated. The ideal of the rights of an individual is an autonomous, the ideal that might be encapsulated in the popular phrase: everyone best serves his own interests. In this respect, the institutions of social life are created with the intention to guarantee the individual the rights of the realization of his own interests. This gives him the opportunity to defend them whenever it is deemed that it is indispensable. For instance, in contrast to Confucianism the accent is put on the individual's responsibilities toward others and toward the community. Individual must be sensitive to the feelings of other people surrounding him, and not in the last degree, he must be capable to harmonious cooperation with others in a group. Thereof, an individual must restrain his own selfish ambitions and their various manifestations. As such, individualism in Asia is morally condemned, and any manifestation of individualistic attitudes meets the condemnation of the environment that lowers the prestige of the individualistically-minded

12 Guanipa, C. (1998) Culture shock. Department of Counseling and School Psychology, San Diego State University.
13 Gawlikowski, K. (1999) *Indywidualizm a kolektywizm.* (Individualism and colectivism)Warszawa, IFIS PAN.

individual.[14] It is inferred that the theorems of Wei-ming Tu defy the belief derived from Christian traditions – one that is still present in Western liberal culture today – that Western ideals are universal, and are to be accepted by all people regardless of their endemic culture. It is a peculiar form of ethnocentric arrogance, the source of such phenomena as missionary and colonial mentality. As Edward Said[15] suggested in his famous book *Orientalism*, Western social sciences still lack recognition that many of their concepts, categories, and theories are not universal, but refer only to their own societies. As noted by Steven Sangren: "many truths about the nature and the human race, what "we" Europeans or Westerners regard as eternal and universal, they are essentially just cultural constructs, categories, language and thought, having its own history of development and are the product of social processes[16]".

3) Regarding Western culture, the range and ritual of social life is limited, while the freedom of the individual is highly promoted. The individual is praised as having a considerable degree of freedom of choice in every aspect of conduct. These are the causes- noted by many sociologists - that result in the collapse of relationships in the West and the emergence of the atomization of society. In its turn the Eastern highly ritualized cultures, the social interaction of every aspect of life are determined by rigid rules and definite standards. Deviations from them are not tolerated. This gives the comfort of certainty, as in every situation, someone knows how he should behave, and there is no difficulty with understanding your partner's behavior since they both apply to the same rigorous standards of behavior. The Western system is based on pluralism, and, therefore, on the high degree of tolerance of deviant social behavior, whereas, for instance, the Eastern Asian system is characterized by uniformity and very low tolerance for behaviors or views "deviating from the norms.[17]"
4) In the West, as the author defines it, there is an adversary system, in that partners treat one another with mistrust suspecting of the evil intentions from the other side, and assume hostility toward one another. Asia, on the other hand, is dominated by a sense of co-membership and structure as a "community of trust" (fiduciary communities) termed by Tu Wei-ming In the first model, individual rights are guaranteed and protected, thereby stimulate and encour-

14 Ibid
15 Said, E. (1978). *Orientalism*. New York
16 Ibid.
17 Gawlikowski, K. (1999) *Indywidualizm a kolektywizm*. (Individualism and collectivism)Warszawa, IFIS PAN.

age competition. Contrarily, the second model emphasizes the common interests, values and trust, and also subordinates the belief to the leader, who works for the good of the whole group. This results in the certainty of individual that each of community members will zealously performs the duties and tasks assigned to him. The first model emphasizes the role of law for shaping interpersonal relations, based on the idea of the equality of partners and their interests. In this model, compromise is highly valued even in the domain of morals, because even moral values can be the object of justice. Though there are differences between individuals in position and prestige, they have a fluid and often temporary character. Hence, man must live in a constant struggle to attain a higher position. In the Asian system, there exists a rigid hierarchy between groups and in mutual relations within each group. Each of the individuals, therefore, has a designated place and duties determined primarily by age, seniority, kinship structure, place of origin and etc[18].

I have quoted Tu- wieng's view that covers the Confucian civilization, however, the characteristics of man and society present in that civilization are also applicable to the Tajiks. In a similar way with the similar arguments strengthening the position I could describe the Tajik society. However, there can be pointed out one slight difference. Contrary to Tu- wieng views, Asian Muslim society has always demonstrated tolerance and not only in relation to religion. It can e found out in the scientific literature describing in in-depth the institution of Millet in Ottoman Turkey. The religious minorities living there enjoyed the right to practice their own religion, to establish the significant degrees of their own authority, and most likely even have been encouraged to develop their own particular ethnic culture. As Will Kymlicka[19], a Canadian political philosopher, states that Turks created a model of tolerance that was higher than anything that existed in the West.

In the case of Tajikistan, I consider the level of tolerance to others people to be higher than in different religions. According to my both rural (mahalla) and urban (life in the capital) experience, I can say that people mostly have positive attitudes towards practitioners of other faiths. I have also quite commonly heard from the Westerners come to Tajikistan speaking about the respect that is bestowed upon their religion here. Obviously I cannot answer from the behalf of

18 Ibid.

19 Kymlicka W., (1993) Two Models of Pluralism and Tolerance: David Heyd (Ed.) In *Toleration. An Elusive Virtue*. Princeton University Press: Princeton.

all Tajiks: I am writing from my own personal observation. People often use this Tajik proverb on religious tolerance:

> *Iso ba dini khud Muso ba dini khud* (Jesus to his religion and Moses to his)

It means that everyone should have the highest respect for other's religion and faith. A person's faith is above all a matter of individual's choice, and nobody should interfere in it.

1.2. Western spirit of individualism versus Eastern spirit of community

The concepts of collectivism and individualism relate primarily to two contrastingly different, and perhaps totally opposite, ways of living that underpin the social life and the corresponding institutions, cultural forms, types of mentality and value systems. They mark the various categories of thought and value systems, and they are symbolically located and expressed in the institutions of society and patterns of behavior. In the social sciences, individualism is usually characterized as a concept that must maintain such defaults as autonomy of the individual, emotional independence, personal initiative, privacy, and the clear awareness of the "I". Every individual has own interests, and consequently, own rights for implementing them. Thus, the life of the individual is expressed by the assertion that each person will act to better for own self-interests. In contrast to individualism, Asian collectivism is based upon the conviction that the individual as a being cannot be ontologically separated from the group. In Asian societies, there is no such value as human autonomy, so in all important life situations, the individual must submit own will and opinion to the authority. It is expected that the individual acts in line with the public opinion represented by the collective group, and they are denied the right to possess their own opinion in this regard. According to many authors in the West, the individual in the collectivist society is characterized by emotional dependence, group solidarity, and the tendency to comply with the decision of the group[20].

This is undeniable fact that the rivalries exist between people (even among the closest family members) in individualistic societies, and capitalism's rules of economic behavior are governed by a competitive drive. In collectivist societies, however, relations between individuals follow the same sentiments as those demonstrated between relatives. This results in all the behavior of the society be-

---

20 On this theme see also: Birnbaum P.& Leca J.(1990). *Individualism. Theories and Methods*. Clarendon Press: Oxford.

ing subordinated to the principle of social harmony.[21] George C. Lodge and Ezra F. Vogel in their comparisons of the model of individualistic and collectivistic societies characterize differences between them:

In the first model, the individual exists as an atom, meaning that he/she is independent from others in the whole of society which is considered as the sum of its parts and the interactions between individuals determine the existence of an institution of social life and the binding of its values. In collectivistic ideology, society is understood as a being that exists not only as the sum of its parts, with each having its own needs and priorities; society is understood as being ontologically prior in existing to the individuals living in it and is the only source of values. These two ideological types should be, in their opinion, regarded as some extremes, between which one can locate all kinds of ideologies, sometimes competing with one another in the same country. In an individualistic ideology, as they indicate, the emphasis is on individual rights, particularly in the sphere of ownership, and it is idealized that the state must be but a limited authority acting as - liberals preached at that time - the night watchman. The present authors also underline, however, that with individualistic systems, one can also find different forms of collectivistic activity.

Another aspect of this issue – that might be interpreted as a negative side-effect – are actions and aspirations of an anti-systemic character frequently met: such as youth gangs and criminals, religious sects, supporters of local nationalisms, clubs, etc. The rebellious individuals can also be found in systems based on the ideology of communism. So as it is underlined by these authors, in every society, regardless of the culture, there can be found the individuals striving to extend their own independence and liberation from the pressing society and its culture.[22] In this respect, according to Lodge and Vogel, the differences of culture and ideology can be observed not so much as the values attached to the individual or a community, but rather as a way of defining, experiencing and creating individual and collective personality.

Various self-evident truths about the individual, his/her rights and dignity, basic needs and aspirations, as well as about the nature of human communities, taken from Western civilization, are in turn the products of Western type of cul-

---

21 Reykowski, R. (1999) (*Kolektywizm i indywidualizm jako kategorie opisu zmian społecznych i mentalności*) Collectivism and individualism as a description of the categories of social change and the mentality. In *Indywidualizm a Kolektywizm*. IFiS PAN, Warszawa.

22 George C. Lodge and Ezra F. Vogel (1987) Ideology and National Competitiveness: An Analysis of Nine Countries

ture, formed on the basis of the Christian religion and Greco-Roman heritage. As another author writes, "other civilizations may adopt different assumptions of the human condition and to form other types of subjectivity, both individual and collective".[23]

Returning to discussion on collectivism, in the view of Lodge and Vogel, an important feature of the collectivist conception of the world is the assumption that the group as a being is primary and the individual is secondary, that the group is self-existent, while an individual cannot exist outside the group, and is ontologically dependent on it. The group is responsible for the individual; it is the source of the criteria of good and evil. The individual is obliged to act on behalf of the group and for own benefit. Relationships with others are fundamentally different depending on whether or not they are members of the group. Under collectivistic ideology one happened to be a member of one group, at once the relationships are to be based on the principles of emotion bond, while when engaging with others outside of the group, the basis is competition. In general, the main values are mainly of social orientation: harmony, solidarity, obligation and responsibility, and a sense of shame, all of which are applied to intra-group relations[24]. From the anthropological viewpoint, man recognizes himself as a confident member of the whole society, wherever it is the family, clan, nation, religious community, etc., and understands that his/her destiny is integrally linked with the fate of the whole, thereby totally and deliberately subordinates to the group.

An important feature of an individualistic conception of the world is the approach to social life as being the result of the interaction between people forming their own beings. The individual is responsible for oneself, he/she alone determines what it is good or bad, or, in another interpretation, recognizes what is good and evil. Relationships with others are based on the principles of exchange, cooperation or competition. Henceforth main values are of individualistic orientation: autonomy, reliance, privacy, personal control, etc. The man recognizes himself as a separate, autonomous being who creates own fate and determines the relationships with others. This characteristic indicates that the collectivistic and individualistic principle of social life is completely opposite to one another. This thesis has important implications when it comes to interpretation of the processes of social change.

---

23 Sangren, P.S.(1997). *Myth, Gender and Subjectivity.* National Tsing Hua University: Hsin-chu (Taiwan)

24 George C. Lodge and Ezra F. Vogel (1987). *Ideology and National Competitiveness: An Analysis of Nine Countries.*

As illustrative definitions, for instance, Hofstede defines *individualism* as a focus on rights above duties, a concern for oneself and immediate family, an emphasis on personal autonomy and self-fulfillment, and the basing of one's identity on one's personal accomplishments.[25]Polish author Reykowski in his work *Kolektywyzm i indywidualizm jako kategorie opisu zmian społecznych i mentalności* (Collectivism and individualism as the categories of the description of social change and the mentality) defines collectivism as the category which applies to societies where people from birth to death are integrated into strong, cohesive groups throughout their life, caring for them in exchange for unconditional loyalty. He came to the conclusion that individualism is dominated in Europe (the western part), North America, Australia, and that collectivism resides in Asia, Africa and South America. According to him, for most people of the world, collectivism is the natural form of life and interpersonal relationships.[26]

The idea of individualism penetrates many concepts of Western culture and social science theories as well. Although the term individualism appears in the scientific literature, however, not all authors of numerous publications have defined the term as such. It is well known to me that there is only one sociological work, which is authored by Steven Lukes, that tries to explain the concept of individualism. His book, *Individualism*[27], has been published in 1973. According to Lukes, the notion of individualism for the first time has been appeared in work of Joseph de Maistre, the French conservative thinker: he used the concept of individualism as an important element of his critique of the French Revolution. In de Maistre's view, individualism meant anarchy in politics, Protestantism in religion, and selfishness in morals. Unlike in France, the notion has enjoyed a positive meaning in other European cultures. Over time, individualism became so coherent as a part of common sense of the people of Western cultures, that as it is observed by many researchers today, individualism is the *differentia specifica* of this culture in relation to the other cultures in the world[28].

---

25 Oyserman, D., Heather M. Coon & Kemmelmeier, M (2002). *Rethinking Individualism and Collectivism: Evaluation of Theoretical Assumptions and Meta-Analyses*. University of Michigan

26 Reykowski, R. (1999) (*Kolektywizm i indywidualizm jako kategorie opisu zmian społecznych i mentalności*) Collectivism and individualism as a description of the categories of social change and the mentalit. In *Indywidualizm a Kolektywizm*. IFiS PAN, Warszawa.

27 I use edition of Lukes, S. (1990). *Individualism*. Basil Blackwell Ltd: Oxford

28 Ibid.

Lukes inquires about the variety of connotations the term individualism brings in relation to different spheres. [29]For him, the concept of individualism is a complicated and multisided one. The understanding of individualism requires reference to the domain of religion, history, morality, philosophy and sociology. Lukes distinguishes five basic axiological ideas that form the component of individualism: the dignity of man, autonomy, privacy, self-development and the abstract individual.

The first element of individualism is an idea of human dignity as a supreme moral value. Regarding Western culture the very idea of human dignity is inspired from the Christian religion. In Christianity, the human species surpass over other species in the world of nature. The dignity as an unique characteristic of man is proclaimed by God. The Old and New Testaments of the Bibl argue that God has created man as the highest and the perfect being. Due to this privileged status – bestowed from God- man is distinguished other species in the hierarchy of living things. However, the idea of human dignity in Christianity has been recognized to man as a species, not to man as a single human being. In the Middle Ages, the vision of the special dignity of man has been overshadowed by the doctrine of original sin. One of the consequences of sin is social inequality. Until the seventeenth century, Christian theology, as a consequence of original sin, has explained human variation in terms of the value afforded to them because of the approaching state. It is considered as one of the merits of the Renaissance that the idea of dignity of man has been reaffirmed with new force and significance. This idea has constituted the leitmotif for the humanists: for instance, Petrarch has pictured man's soul as something incomparable with whatever in the world, and Gianozzo Manetti and Pico della Mirandola has praised man as the greatest creature with various possibilities and potentials for perfection. It should be remembered that the Renaissance writers resolved that the value of the dignity of man lay in the species as a whole, not in the individual.

In Lukes opinion, only in the XVIII century thinkers have appeared to hold a different vision of human dignity. In Modernity, this idea of individualism has met objections and even total rejections. One of the first to treat nature of human being without the extremes of overall praise or overall critique with moderate admire is Jean-Jacques Rousseau, to whom man is the real subject of dignity that cannot be served as an instrument for others in society[30]. The idea of the dignity of man has primarily been enshrined in the American Declaration of the Rights

29 Ibid.
30 Ibid.

of Man. However, as Lukes emphasizes, this document does not specify whether human dignity is understood as a species or an individual. The same could be said for the Universal Declaration of Human Rights (UNDHR) adopted by the General Assembly of the United Nations in 1948.

> As it was declared in Article 1 of the UNDHR:
> All human beings are born free and equal in dignity and rights. They are endowed with reason and conscience and should act towards one another in a spirit of brotherhood.[31]

In Lukes view, the contemporary idea of the dignity of the man comes from Immanuel Kant, who has been the first in European philosophy to declare that man, understood as a human individual, should always be treated as an end, never as only a means to an end. This Kantian view has entered into a third formulation of the categorical imperative. Additionally, a great number of modern thinkers have developed and defended this Kantian view in different ways. For instance, in the writings of the young Marx, the belief is presented that the individual is the highest value, and therefore should always be seen as an end, with society always being used as a means for his betterment. Lukes concludes:

> The idea of the dignity of the individual has the logical status of a moral (or religious) axiom, which is basic, ultimate, and overriding, offering a general justifying principle in moral argument[32].

In my view, the idea of the dignity of man (understood as the idea of the dignity of the individual) is the basis for the idea of democracy, democratic state institutions, the idea of the state of the law, and the guarantor of the right of access to reliable information.

The second basic idea in Lukes' opinion is autonomy, according to which man can independently create goals for his life separate from the will of society, and can also independently select, leading to their completion, various means to achieve those ends. For example, the acceptance of this idea is confirmed in the folklore tradition of Western society, which asserts that every person acts according to own best interests. The idea of autonomy is the basis for the modern ideas of individual rights and freedoms in society and politics.

The author of the idea of autonomy, as Lukes believes, is Saint Thomas Aquinas, a Medieval philosopher. In this view, Thomas Aquinas has been the initial to declare the view that an individual has the right to refuse and to execute

31 Universal Declaration of Human Rights adopted by General Assembly resolution 217 A (III) of December 10, 1948" Retrieved from http://www.un.org/en/documents/udhr/index.shtml#a1, 25 December, 2010.

32 Lukes, S. (1990). *Individualism*. Basil Blackwell Ltd: Oxford, p. 51.

commands issued by the person standing above him if it is not compatible with the voice of his conscience. Protestantism is responsible for spreading and cementing the idea of autonomy on the religious ground throughout Western culture. In acute contrast to Catholic dogma and practiced religious rituals Martin Luther has revolutionary declared that the man does not need the Church to act as a mediator in religion. Everyone can establish direct contact with God by meditating on the content of the Holy Bible. Furthermore, Luther has protested against the idea of the necessity of confession for the similar reason that man is able to properly assess own actions in the light of the knowledge that he achieved from God. If one truly regrets the sins to have been committed, one must hope on God's forgiveness without the need for absolution. In this way, Protestantism has strengthened the belief that every individual is unique and is thereby responsible for own actions. According to Lukes, Spinoza and Kant have contributed significantly to the development of these ideas.

Spinoza, in his work *Ethics*, understands freedom as a function of knowledge, with freedom being defined as the understanding of the necessity. On the other hand, Spinoza also considers freedom in a literal sense: when man is not under restraint to move anywhere, and he plans his direction based on own prerogatives. In this regard, the external circumstances are literal: the lack of the opportunity to move, punishment in the form of prison, and as the highest form, servitude, are all the causes of the absence of freedom. In the epistemological sense, freedom implies that the mind is not dependent on passions to make decisions. Likewise, passions are emotionally strong factors to prevent man from thinking in a free way and being aware of the causes of things. "This is that human freedom, which all boast that they possess, and which consists solely in the fact that men are conscious of their own desire, but are ignorant of the causes whereby that desire has been determined"[33]. However, only the release of passions allows man to get on the road to truth. Man is free, in Spinoza's belief, not merely in that he is not impeded in planning, but his direction - and is more – that the man is free when he is the possessor of truth, which in turn reaches from the highest level of knowledge - the knowledge of God.

In my interpretation, the best expression on the idea of autonomy belongs to Sir Isaiah Berlin. In his work *Two Concepts of Liberty*, Berlin manifests the high rhetoric of the autonomous individual:

> "I wish my life and decisions to depend on myself, not on external forces of whatever kind. I wish to be the instrument of my own, not other men's, acts of will. I wish to be

33 Lukes, S. (1990). *Individualism*. Basil Blackwell Ltd: Oxford.

a subject not an object; to be moved by reasons, by conscious purposes, which are my own, not by causes which affect me, as it were, from outside".[34]

The idea of autonomy becomes a central value for liberalism. The nineteen-century philosopher John Stuart Mill has been aware of the threats that the industrial society causes to the autonomous individual. Later author has expressed a growing feeling of concern because of the alienation and manipulation from the side of the bureaucratic state institutions and corporations which deprive individuals from their autonomy, as a result, this deprivation transforms man into a tiny cog in the larger mechanism of society. This view has been enriched and sustained by such twentieth-century thinkers as Erich Fromm and David Riesman. Where for the former, man in industrial and market society was "dehumanized", adjusting their personality to economic possibilities, such as worrying about the possibility to be employed successfully in the market, for the later – who strengthens Fromm's concern – man's freedom of choice was reduced to the dilemma of whether or not to conform. Lukes several times in his book notes that the idea of autonomy that is central for the morality "of modern Western civilization, and - as highlights - it is absent or under-stressed in others (such as the many tribal moralities or that of orthodox communism in Eastern Europe today[35])" [36]. This is a cornerstone element for the concept of individualism that holds the religious and socio-political aspects. However, in contrast with the first unit-idea- the dignity of man – it is less general and overriding.

The third basic-idea is idea of privacy. This idea implies the existence of the areas of personal life, which man has the duty and right to treat as exclusively their own and to which other people may have access only with man's consent. Lukes, after Hannah Arendt, reminds one that the idea of the value of private life has been completely alien for the ancient Greeks. The individual in ancient Greece has only been seen as a full man if he has participated in the life of the Polis. As Lukes further underlines, a private man in Greece has been called an idiot. Another issue concerns the possibility of participation in the life of the Polis that has been available to free men while the slaves, foreigners, and women have predominantly been centered within the affairs of the private life, i.e. the household. Moreover, the realm of political and public life was a realization of man's freedom and the symbol of class position and the privileges associated with it.

---

34 Berlin, I. (1969). On Two Concepts of Liberty. In *Four Essays on Liberty*. New York: Oxford University Press, p. 131

35 The word "today" must be addressed to the date of first publishing of the book.

36 Lukes, S. (1990). *Individualism*. Basil Blackwell Ltd: Oxford, p. 58

In later Antiquity, the idea of individual private life appears as a problem of the soul in relation to its search for God. This aspect of the idea has constituted the subject of *The Confessions* by Saint Augustine. Augustine certainly has been familiar with the works written by Epicure that focused on happiness as the best aim of man's life, i.e. private life, and definitely also benefited from the considerations of Mark Aurelius, Cesar-philosopher, who has been haunted by the dilemma of reconciling his personal stoic-oriented views with the duties performed in public life[37]. In turn, Augustine, in a frank and open manner, describes the route of the soul searching for God. In Lukes view, Augustine's work is the first in the Christian tradition to provide a description of the inner life of a man who is searching for true faith.

According to Lukes, the idea of privacy present in contemporary Western culture is relatively not so old one. As it has been pointed out that the spreading of the belief that there is a specific sphere free from public interference has tightly been connected with the development of liberalism. In liberalism "the boundaries of this private sphere lie, according to what principles they are to be drawn, whence interference derives and how it is to be checked"[38]. This manifestation of liberalism mostly contributed to the spread of the belief that private life is something quite natural, and it is only correct for it to be respected in society[39].

As Lukes states, the birth of liberalism is inseparably linked with the idea of the freedom of man's private space from the interference of the public space. Lukes illustrates his opinion by reference to John Stuart Mill, a British philosopher of the 19th century who considered as a classic author of liberalism. In Mill's work, *On Liberty*, he defines privacy as "a sphere of action in which society, as distinguished from the individual, has, if any, only an indirect interest; comprehending all that portion of a person's life and conduct which affects only himself"[40]

Constitutive for the emergence of private space is the idea of autonomy and human dignity, of which the individual has the possibility to manifest these ideas in the social freedom of belief that orders his conscience and opinion. The individual may, therefore, expect to encounter no serious obstacle in society, acting in the belief that each person is behaving in the best way to satisfy own interests. However, as I have mentioned before, it creates a situation in which the indi-

37 *The Mediations of the Emperor Marcus Aurelius Antonius* (2008). Hutcheson F., Moor J. (Trans.). Moor J. & Silverthorne, M. (Ed.). Liberty Fund: Indianapolis

38 Lukes, S. (1990). *Individualism.* Basil Blackwell Ltd: Oxford p. 62

39 Ibid.

40 Ibid.

vidual puts own interests above the interests of the community (social duties, citizen's obligations, and etc.). [41]

The forth basic idea termed by Lukes is the idea of self-development. This idea has predominantly been popularized in Romanticism. The idea of self-realization implies that every human as a unit has only proper strengths, abilities, and obligations to develop them. This view is precisely contained in the concept of *bildung*, used by the early German Romantics. The first thought that every individual is unique has been uttered by Rousseau in *Les Confessions,* where he wrote "I am made unlike anyone I have ever met; I will even venture to say that I am like no one in the whole world. I may be no better but at least I am different".[42]

The idea of *bildung* is met and is elaborated in the works of Friedrich Schleiermacher. He has declared that each entity represents all humanity in one another, if one develops his abilities and others do the same, so one can contribute to the development of the whole human species. Wilhelm von Humboldt has preached similar ideas. In his opinion, the duty of every man is to allay strength and ability in the most harmonious way. This is what he has considered to be the highest ideal of a man. Karl Marx has put the idea of self-development in a political context. In the utopia-like consideration on the last phase of human development he has urged that in communism man will be free from alienation and will be endowed with the opportunity to develop his individual nature. In this regard communism is seen as a special kind of society of "free individuality, based on the universal development of individuals and on their joint mastery over their communal, social productive powers and wealth"[43]. Karl Marx also emphasizes the idea of self-development and the uniqueness of every individual. As John Stuart Mill highlights, self-development is a strategy for the perfection of an individual's nature, it is the duty of every man as an end- in-itself.

The fifth element of individualism is labeled by Lukes as the abstract individual. This idea is a characteristic feature of Western thinking about man and society. Lukes traces out the tradition since Hobbes and later Kant, considering the man in abstract way as a being born with given interest, needs, aims, etc. Such an approach in social science let one to treat society as a construct created by the interaction of individuals. The antithesis to this tradition belongs also to Marx, who has undermined faith in the natural origin of the individual by pre-

41 Ibid.

42 Rousseau, J.-J. (1947). *Les Confessions.* Paris, p. 33.

43 Marx, K. (1953). *Capital.* p. 76

senting it as a product of social factors, and has underlined the role of the state in the process of its formation.[44]

For Marx, as Lukes writes, the eighteen-century perception of man's nature as independent from the society and obtaining natural rights is no longer valid and is false. Marx follows the development of human nature in history. In his opinion, it is formed in the process of social development and varies in different stages of the process: the first union of man is family, later the clan, or enlarged family, appears, and as the highest form - a community, or an amalgamation of the clans. In all of these stages, man has been compelled to co-operating with others because of the evident dependence on the goods produced by others. Moreover, for Marx, man is not merely a social animal (in Aristotle's terms a *zoon politikon*), but rather, so to say man is a animal who needs a socialization becomes, who becomes an individual exclusively in and due to society.

As Lukes stresses, such grand nineteen-century thinkers as Hegel, Marx, Saint-Simon, Auguste Comte and the rest of the positivists have tended to overcome the abstract vision of the individual, and as a result – what is explicitly visible in sociological thoughts – the concept of the individual has turned to become intensely linked with social background. "The individual apart from the community is an abstraction"[45].

For instance, according to views of Stanislaw Zapaśnik, who adds more reflections in the discourse on genesis of individualism: the modern idea of "I" as a unique and autonomous consciousness center, subject to own thoughts, feelings, and acts of will, is genetically derived from Christian ideas on the soul as the fundamental source of the individual being. However, Zapaśnik further urges that individualism is constituted by more ideas than those mentioned by Lukes and thus he differs in views with Lukes on the origin of the modern idea of human dignity. It is true that Christianity has promoted the ancient Greek's belief in the special dignity of man in nature and that this transformed view was presented to European culture en masse. In a general perspective, this value of human dignity is entitled to all species. However, human beings have no other value than that of being represented by a community to which they belong. The value of dignity is, therefore, entitled to man as a species in its entirety, not to man as an individual human body. Thus, human dignity has no other value than that of social status[46].

---

44 Lukes, S. (1990). *Individualism*. Basil Blackwell Ltd: Oxford, p. 62

45 Bradley, F. H. (1927) My Station and its Duties. In *Ethical Studies*. Oxford, p. 171.

46 Zapaśnik, S. (2006). *Walczący Islam w Azji Centralnej:* Problem społecznej genezy zjawiska (Fighting Islam in Central Asia: the social problem of the origin of the phenomenon). Wrocław.

Only at the end of the eighteenth century, in the development of the ideas that make up the notion of individualism in Western cultures, there has happened a change in the concept of human dignity. It has begun to be interpreted as an inalienable value assigned to each human individual on the ground that it is common to all human species. Certainly, there is no doubt that without the idea of dignity as the source of the inalienable rights of the human being, democracy would not exist, there would be no human rights, nor any of the social and political institutions created in order to ensure the presence of this value in the life of society.[47]

In the United States, at the end of the 1970s, the ideas constituted the core of the concept of individualism have been associated with the autonomy of individuals contributed to the transformation not only in the sphere of freedom in politics and economic, but also in the sphere of ethos. As a negative side-effect, they have led to the crisis of Protestant ethic, to the changing and re-evaluation of the family models, to the crisis of authority, etc.[48] As American sociologists have been observing, the individuals demand rights from the state but in the same time they forget own obligations towards that very state. For the same reason, when one observes the upbringing of children in Western societies, so to say liberal approach to bring up children, the accent is placed on the rights of children in the family, rather than on their responsibilities towards the parents and members of the family.

In Europe, individualism is not homogeneous and accepted by all, it differs in dependence on historical terms. It is possible even now to meet Europeans for whom the idea of individualism is still an alien idea. The ideas -constitutive for individualism- have been formed another way in different countries depending on historical conditions. But everywhere the ideas of human dignity and individual autonomy are reflected in legislation, judicial procedures, and social institutions, which increasingly emphasize the primacy of individual interests over the interest of the group, the right to entirely choose one's own way of life, lifestyle, etc. It is worthwhile to mention that the voices of Western intellectuals warn against the dangers of deep changes in society caused by the development of individualism. These intellectuals are, therefore, able to raise individual inter-

47 Tangad, O (2009) *Przemiany ustrojowe w Mongolii a kategorie tradycyjnego myślenia w kulturze* (Political changes in Mongolia and the categories of traditional thinking in the culture).

48 Yankelovich D.(1981). New Rules. Searching for Self-Fulfillment in a World Turned Upside Down, New York.

ests above those of the public domain by understanding the anxieties associated with individualism[49].

In my opinion, the ideas of autonomy, privacy, and individual self-fulfillment are alien to the Tajiks and perhaps other Asian nations. The representatives of Eastern culture otherwise understand such concepts as dignity. Every person in the East has the right to expect respect for oneself from others, and this right is one of the most important aspects of life in the societies of the East. But this expectation is based on a different set of values than that of the Europeans. Eastern dignity is understood as respect toward an individual's age and position in society. In relation to other ethnic groups, dignity symbolizes the value of one ethnic group within an ethnic hierarchy in a concrete society, for example some Tajiks are wearing a head cover (*tubeteika*) typical in one region with dignity of own region and respect that in the rest regions the other cultural attributes are to be met. I should also emphasize that human rights in Asia are interpreted as the rights of the groups rather than the rights of individuals.

The daily behavior of the Tajiks in preserving respect for others begins in the family. Every member has own place in the family hierarchy. Parents have the highest status and children have to respect them. Tajiks, as well as other Asians, treat children with great care and understanding. They do not scream at them nor beat them. Children adapt the patterns of behaviors that they witness being expressed by other members of the family. They live in the neighborhood community where there is a communal control over their behavior. When children behave in an inappropriate way, other members of the community immediately notify the parents about it. This is because in Tajik culture it is believed that parents are responsible for the behavior of the children. Respect for older people is one of the basic characteristics of Tajik culture. There is no rivalry between children and parents nor between any members of the family. Particularly, the responsibilities of all family members, especially their mother and sisters, are emphasized in the education and upbringing of the children. Upon entering primary school, children begin to help the family and take part in the performance of household duties, including, in some cases, hard physical work. Child upbringing and behavior patterns in the Tajik family are the consequence of the presence of the spirit of collectivism in Tajik culture, which acts as a barrier to the social penetration of the basic tenets of

---

49 Tangad, O. (2009) *Przemiany ustrojowe w Mongolii a kategorie tradycyjnego myślenia w kulturze* (Political changes in Mongolia and the categories of traditional thinking in the culture).

individualism and in cultural level the ideals learned children in family rearing fits the model of traditional society.

Collectivism

In the Eastern cultures - that can be described as collectivistic cultures - the individual as a being cannot be separated from the group. Therefore, he has no identity other than as a member of the family and the social group to which he belongs. Because of these conditions, the individual is connected with family, neighbors and the wider community in a different way than that of his Western counterparts. As Liu Qingxue writes:"Asians tend to be more aware of the connections they have as members of their social groups, and therefore, they tend to be more conscious of the consequences of their actions on their members of their groups"[50].

In general society strengthens its firmness and stability on the basis of promotion of the ideals and values of collectivism. The most precious values are such values as honesty, justice, and trust. Communities preserve the tradition of the society, as well as ethical and religious values. These ideals and values are permanent components of the ethos of the society because the consistency of the group depends on them. Every individual trusts in group's decisions and the level of trust is very high within communities. Members of the collectivist communities, on the contrary, to individualist ones, work and think not about themselves, but about the other members of the community. Thus, so to say vector of trust might be noticed: individual relies on the members of family, family relies on support from community, when communities serve as guardian and supporter of the religious and cultural values altogether contribute in the preservation of society and nation as such.

In Tajik culture, individuals are always seen as part of society, whose existence as a being in the ontological sense cannot be separated from society. In such a way individual in moral behavior must also be subordinated to the public. Man's moral duties, therefore, depend entirely on the place in which he lives: the community of mahalla is located in a particular quarter and in the streets. These obligations are regarded as duties inherited throughout generations. Thus the act of disobedience is severely condemned and results in man's placement outside of the community, and in the past, such situations were equal to death. Individual

---

50 Liu Qingxue (2003). *Understanding Different Cultural Patterns or Orientations between East and West*. Shijiazhuang Mechanical Engineering College Hebei, China. p. 25.

has no right to manifest the autonomy because there is no such idea of autonomy in culture. Individual supports the code of morality inherited from the community where he/she is living, and consequently conducts in the same way. He/she does not separate own interests from those of others among whom is living. He/she is not conscious of having sacrificed his interests and ambitions. But he/she is not alone in his life, for in daily life, the fellows show support to realize his/her wishes and interests.

In Tajik society, there is no place for a private existence, which Lukes defines as "an area within which the individual is or should be left alone by others and able to do and think whatever he chooses – to pursue his own good in his own way, as Mill put it"[51], while regardless of the ideal of the culture, the individual interacts with others in the spirit of mutual help, solidarity, and brotherhood. These ideals are also promoted by the religion of Islam. The first Muslim community- *ummah*[52] has been based on ideal of brotherhood and mutual support. In the early centuries of Islam, the principle of unifying people in society has been religion, not race. A neighbor sharing the same faith has been treated as a brother. Today the religious idea of a developing bond with others is still alive, with such a bond being built on the type of feelings typically exchanged between members of the immediate family. In this regard, calling a friend or neighbor a 'brother' expands ties of family, and become a momentum in time and space when individual becomes defeated by collectivism.

According to Triads Bontempo, we can differentiate all cultures by the power of social strength that gathers individuals into social entities. Individualism puts the individual above the group, while collectivism emphasizes the value of the "we" identity over the "I" identity. Collectivistic individuals think of themselves as a piece of the community (family, community of neighbors, friends, traditional social institutions and etc.), their actions also renounce self-interest in favor of totally ordering own behavior around others, duties, and obligations of the community. Therefore, due to the fact that they have an identity "we", the members may cooperate in achieving the common good for the community and in this way to complete the community's duty.[53]

---

51 Ibid., p. 59

52 ***Ummah*** is from Arabic أمة and means community or nation, but in the context of Islam, the word *ummah* is used to mean commonwealth *of the Believers* (*ummat al-mu'minin*), and thus the whole Muslim World.

53 Vahid, A. Z; Jayum A& Lee Y (2010). *The Epistemology of the Concept of Civil Society in the West and Iranian Interpretations*. Canadian Social Science Vol. 6 No. 4

For instance, Trice and Beyer describe collectivism as a feature "belonging to a culture (that) involves believing what others believe and doing as they do – at least part of the time".[54] The people in collectives or in communities learn everything from their families, later from neighbors, friends. In moral sense they have to follow their traditions, ethics, customs, and religion. In behavioral sense to follow father and mother's steps then the patterns imposed from outside. The aforementioned authors provide as an example the Asian immigrants in the United States. They have accepted American–style organizational culture, however, in their relations in their social environment, they preferred to retain the values of own national culture.[55]

Triads Bontempo accentuates that the ties connecting people in collectivist cultures are more sustainable than those in individualistic cultures. The main vital connections in collectivist cultures are vertical (relation between parents-children), while in individualistic the most important are horizontal (spouse-a spouse, friend-friend). In collectivist cultures, there is a stronger control of parents in relation to their children, and the interdependence between them is regulated by communal norms. Parents have to bring up and educate their children according to the rule of society, and they have to teach them the traditions and moral obligations of the community. By not doing so, they will not be respected among the other community members[56].

As I have been written above, in individualistic cultures in regard to the educational processes, the pressure is placed upon the shoulders of the parents, not the reverse. The parents' obligation lies in bringing up the child and teaching them the rights of the autonomous being, which, therefore, will allow the child to take care of their own self-interests as their reach adulthood in effective way. In collectivist cultures, the idea of privacy is not such heralded as it is in individualistic cultures. Typically, social interactions place a stronger importance on people than on the objective of the social contact's initiation. The reverse is present in individualistic cultures. As it has been mentioned before, it is a custom in collectivist cultures to stop and to talk with someone in a secluded place. In accordance with Muslim tradition, for example, when initiating contact with

---

54 Trice, H. M., Beyer, J. M.(1993). *The Cultures of Work Organizations*. Prentice Hall, p. 5

55 Alkhazraji, K. M., Gardner III, W. L.(1997) The Acculturation of Immigrants to U.S. Organizations. In *Management Communication Quarterly*, p. 217-265.

56 Triands, Bontempo, Villareal, Asal &Luca (1988). Individualism and Collectivism: Cross-Cultural Perspectives on Self Ingroup Relationships. In *Journal of Personality and Social Psychology*. Vol. 54, No. 2, pp. 323-338.

a stranger with the intent of asking for directions, it is the social responsibility of the initiator to greet the stranger and to ask him about his health and family first, prior to asking for the requested directions. In individualistic cultures, such contacts place a greater emphasis on social distance and independence.

People frequently have greater social mobility in individualistic cultures, in that they have greater freedom to join and exit from new social groups. They can make 'friends' with ease, but it is rare for these friendships to foster into close and meaningful relationships. The individuals remain friends until their mutual business has concluded, and they often easily forget one another after that. In collectivistic cultures, people have less social maneuverability in finding new friends, but it is the norm that once they are befriended with someone, they will remain true friends for whole life. Thus in Eastern countries, it is expected for friends to call one another 'brother': for the reason that the similar emotional component constitutes the relations and obligations in the friendship.

Eastern cultures usually stress group harmony. The standard of collective life does not allow for the emergence of conflicts between members of the group. A member of the community tries to avoid entering into conflict with the other members. Some forms of competition between people are extremely undesirable in collective societies. However, if the conflicts do occur, they are solved by the head of the family or the head of the community, who work in tandem with the elders to solve and decide the communal conflict. In collectivistic communities, the most significant opinion comes from the *aksakal* (literally, 'silver beard', due to this person's old age), who has the most respect and authority in the society. Overall, the appearance of conflict undermines the important communal values of trust, family honor, and protection, of which are all held in the highest regard.

It is necessary to note that in traditional communities, the values of respect and trust for parents, family, and the community prevent the emergence of the belief that the individual has interests that divert from those of the group. The individual is not thinking about himself and his profit. The motive for his actions is always to seek the good of the family and the good of the community. For example, the earnings of Tajik migrant workers in Russia are not shared equally among individuals but are dependent on the number of children in the family. The individual tries to do everything for his family and community. Every profit is common in such society regardless division on what is for family needs or community needs. The situation is different in individualistic cultures. The individual is seen as independent of the group and acts accordingly. Respect for personal autonomy does not allow for the condemnation of the individual if he works towards selfish motives – until his selfish actions induce harm in others – and he is always guided by personal self-interest. The individual views his career and future endeavors as separate from the group. As Nemeth notes, in individualistic cultures, people strive to be sovereign from the community, and even under conditions which present pressure to conform, the ambient individuals keep and maintain their vision in the face of this opposition.[57]

To sum it all up, I have attempted to prove that individualism and collectivism are mutually exclusive terms. Individualism is a Western idea and, in my opinion, is a cultural phenomenon not naturally existing outside of the Western world. Collectivism, in my interpretation, is in vein with Eastern style of life. Throughout all of its histories, the Eastern people have lived in communities. Community life is an essential part of their tradition and religion. It is important to note that in Tajikistan, individualism is a new phenomenon and it is not totally accepted by Tajik society. From the beginning of history, the Tajiks lived together in their communities. Traditional institutions played and are still playing, an important role in Tajik society. The Tajiks cannot imagine life without living together. It is their way of life.

According to Tajik tradition, to be a human, or to have the status of "humanity[58]" (Odamiyat), a person has to work for his society: to prove the membership of his community, to follow religious rituals, common traditions, and accepted morality. Tajiks have such a saying from Tajik Persian classical literature:

Odami Odam nabinad, az kujo odam shawad?
Sham' agar otash nabinad, az kujo rawshan shawad?

(If man does not see a man, how does he become a real man?)
(If candle does not see fire, how does it give light?[59])

These lines clearly simplify and illustrate the significance of collectivistic life for the individual. To be a man in Tajik society, a person must learn everything from the other people of his community. He/she learns the moral duties and the important things for humanity in relation with them. The person has to respect all of the community's laws. From childhood, they teach them to engage in contact with the other members of the community, and through this they discover how much their life is dependent on the assistance of others. Thus, they become accustomed to such a community and they learn to prefer such a way of life. The Tajiks have big families,

57 Nemeth, C. (1985). Dissent, Group processes and Creativity. In E. Lawler (Ed.) *Advances in Group Processes Theory and Research*. Greenwich, CT: JAI Press, pp. 57-75
58 This idea will be later explained throughout the course of my work.
59 Author's translation

and members of these families traditionally live together. However, because of the relation links with their neighbors, relatives, and all other members of the community, they are all like one large family in the community. Therefore, in traditional Tajik society, there is no place for such values of Western culture as individualism, and the prioritization of personal interest is not endemic to Tajik society.

Chapter 2: Mahalla

2.1. Tajikistan

2.1.1. Tajikistan – general Information

Tajikistan is a country located in the south-eastern part of post-Soviet Central Asia. It is positioned within the centre of many enormous mountain ranges: the Kunlun, the Hindu Kush, the Himalayas, the Pamir, and the Tian Shan. Consequently, of the 143.1 thousand square kilometres of Tajikistan's total area, mountains cover 93% of the territory, ranging from a height of 300 to 7,495 meters. Tajikistan has rich water resources, and the country's rivers provide 60% of the water resources of Central Asia[60].

The country borders Uzbekistan in the northwest (910km), Kyrgyzstan in the northeast (630km), China in the east (430km) and Afghanistan in the south (1,030km). According to the CIA The World Fact Book, the population of the country is 7,910,041 million (July 2013 est.)[61]. The majority of Tajikistan's population (79.9%) are Tajiks. Ethnically, the Tajiks belong to the Persian-speaking group, who share a common culture, language, and history with Afghanistan and Islamic Republic of Iran. The Tajik language is also a dialect of the West Persian language. It should be necessary to note that Tajikistan is the only Persian-speaking country in post-Soviet Central Asia. In Tajikistan, there are also people who speak the East Persian language. They live in the Pamir Mountains in the Badakhshan Autonomous Oblast and are known as Pamiris. The religion is Islam, except among the people who are living in Pamir, who are actually Ismaili, a branch of Shii Islam (about 4% of the total population), 95% of the country's population are mainly of composed of the Sunni followers of the Hanafi School of Sunni sect.[62].

According to the Constitution, Tajikistan is a democratic, sovereign, juridical, secular, and unitary country. The head of state is the President, and at the same time he is also the Supreme Commander of the Armed Forces of the Republic of Tajikistan. Parliament consists of two houses: The Majlisi Milli (National Assem-

---

60 Toshmuhammadov, M. (2004). *Civil War in Tajikistan and Post Conflict Rehabilitation.* Hokkaido University Center of Slavic Researches.

61 CIA- The Word Factbook.

62 Ibid.

bly) and the Majlisi Namoyandagon (Assembly of Representatives). Majlisi Milli is the upper house and has 33 representatives while the Majlisi Namoyandagon is the lower house and has 63 representatives[63].

2.1.2 Historical background

The territory of what is now called Tajikistan has been inhabited continuously since 4000 BC. The first recorded descriptions of the population in this territory belong to Herodotus, Ancient Greek historian. This great historian depicts the first states of Bactria and Sogdiana in the fifth century B. C. Many Tajik scholars believe that the ancestors of the Tajiks come from the Indo-Iranian or Aryan population, thus, they differ from other Central Asian people by their race. Unlike their neighbours who were Turkish nomads (Kazakhs, Karakalpaks, Kyrgyz, Turkmens, and Uzbeks) Tajiks were exclusively occupied with agriculture and horticulture, and they built towns in the area of contemporary Central Asia.

The process of the formation of the Tajik people is still a subject of dispute among historians. Most of the modern Tajik scholars claim that the Tajiks have existed as an ethnos since at least from the foundation of empire of Great Kushan, which included the areas of contemporary Afghanistan, Pakistan, and northern India. Until the end of the 8th century, the territory of modern Tajikistan was under the influence of China. This condition has been changed after the conquest of the Arabs. The significant influence has occurred at the end of the eighth century, when the Tajiks have been converted from Zoroastrianism to Islam[64].

It is believed that the first state that the Tajiks built was the state of the Samanids (A.D. 875-999) that existed one hundred years, from the 7th until the 8th century. This period is the most peaceful and fruitful period in the history of the Tajiks. At the court, the poets, writers, and scientists found support and respect. Among them was Abuali ibn Sina, the founder of medicine, who in the Latin world later has become known as Avicenna[65].

Before the conquest of Central Asia by the Russian Empire, Turkestan was being ruled by three khanates: Bukhara Khanate, Khiva Khanate, and Qoqand Khanate. Contemporary Tajikistan has primarily been established in the eastern parts of the Bukhara Khanate. Only the northern part of the modern territory

---

63 Asian Development Bank (2006)

64 Falkingham, I. (2001). *Women and gender relations in Tajikistan. Country Briefing paper.*

65 Masov, R. (1995). Tadzyki: Istoriya s grifom "Sovershenno sekretno" (The Tajiks: history with signature stamp "top secret"). Dushanbe.

has remained under the influence of the Qoqand Khanate. As a result, the developments within Bukhara played a vital role in determining Tajik nationality. Bukhara has been captured on September 2, 1920 by the Bolshevik armies, and its last ruler (Emir), Said Olim Khan, escaped to Eastern Bukhara. The Bukhara Emirate was transformed into the People's Republic of Bukhara immediately after the occupation.

The radical changes began after the consolidation of Bolshevik power in Central Asia. In the whole region the Bolshevik administration has been structured according to the first adopted Soviet federal constitution of 1924[66]. Later on this reform has turned to be crucial in the history of the Tajik nation and has been termed in historiography as *natsionalnoe razmezhevanie* (national delimitation)[67]. As the Kazakh and Kyrgyz territories have been preserved within the Russian Socialist Federated Soviet Republic (RSFSR), Uzbekistan and Turkmenistan have begun a process of formation in the area of the former Bukhara and Khiva Khanates. In 1924, Tajikistan, as the former Eastern Bukhara, acquired status of an autonomous republic within Uzbekistan and has been named the Tajik Autonomous Soviet Socialist Republic (TASSR). In a while, in 1925, the Badakhshan (Pamir region) has achieved formal autonomy as the Gorno-Badakhshan Autonomous *Oblast* (GBAO). As the new Soviet republics have been composing under the one motto: to be "national in form, socialist in content"[68], the new political community "should build socialism with due regard to national differences, but that final aim was to overcome these differences by a merging of all nationalities into a common Soviet and Socialist identity"[69]. Later, in 1929, finally the Tajik Soviet Socialist Republic has appeared. It has been composed from the Tajik Autonomous Socialist Soviet Republic (TASSR) into Tajik Socialist Soviet Republic (TSSR).

As a result of this, Tajikistan was not under the jurisdiction of the Uzbek SSR. With the incorporation of Khujand (the northern part Tajikistan), the region

---

66 Rakowska-Harmstone, T.(1970). *Russia and Nationalism in Central Asia; the Case of Tajikistan.* The Johns Hopkins Press: Baltimore, United States of America, p. 27

67 Masov R. (1995). Tadzyki: Istoriya s grifom "Sovershenno sekretno" (The Tajiks: history with signature stamp "top secret"*).* Dushanbe.

68 Shapoatov, S (2004). The Tajik Civil War: 1992-1997. (A thesis submitted to the Graduate Scholl of Social Sciences of Middle East Technical University.

69 Coppieters, B. (1998). Form and Content in Soviet and Post-Soviet Nationality and Regional Policies. In Waller Michael, Coppieters Bruno & Malashenko, Alexei (Eds.). *Conflicting Loyalties and the State in post-Soviet Russia and Eurasia*, Frank Cass: London, Portland, p. 18

was ready to meet the necessities of being a union republic. At that time, for a nation to be a union republic in accordance to the new Soviet Constitution, three obligatory criterion had to be met:1) having a specific territory, 2) to compose a majority of the total population living in specific area, and lastly,3) having a population of at least one million[70]. After the inclusion of Khujand to the territory of modern Tajikistan, the population of the country reached one million[71].

Till the occupation of Central Asia by the Russian Empire at the end of 19th century, different parts of modern Tajikistan have been dispersed and belonged to other states. The consequences of these circumstances is the existence of the contemporary so-called clans, the very term in ethnography means ancestral or kin group, but in the works related to Central Asia, it is a so-called group of people connected by the special bonds of loyalty born of their residence on separate geographic and historic territory [72].

It is needed to stress that the process of the formation of the new Central Asian republics proceeded with cruel violations of the rights and interests of the native people. Tajik-inhabited lands were divided among the other contiguous Soviet Republics. This monumental decision - made by a group of selfish and narrow-minded politicians-in subsequent years had influenced the lives of millions of people[73].

The process labeled as "clumsy division" means a national delimitation that has changed not only geographical map of Central Asia, but the destinies of the millions people as well. Significantly but the term speaks for itself and in turn mirrors the expansive core of the whole process of formation of new republics not only in Central Asia but in the entire orbit under influence of the Soviets. Officially the date of national demarcation is 1924, but the precondition of it has started many centuries before. It is possible to declare that for Tajikistan both soviet external expansion and internal betrayal has occurred[74].

---

70 Stalin, Joseph. Report to the Eight all-Union congress of the Soviets. In *Marxism and the National Question*, Also In Rakowska-Harmstone, T. (1970). *Russia and Nationalism in Central Asia.* The Johns Hopkins Press, p. 30. Also in Shapoatov, S (2004). The Tajik Civil War: 1992-1997.

71 Shapoatov, S (2004). The Tajik Civil War: 1992-1997.

72 Yusufbekov, B., Babajanov R. & Kuntuvdiy, N (2007). *Civil Society Development in Tajikistan*. Dushanbe.

73 Ibid.

74 Masov, R. (1995). Tadzyki: Istoriya s grifom "Sovershenno sekretno" (The Tajiks: history with signature stamp "top secret"*)*. Irfon: Dushanbe.

The process of formation of Central Asian republics has been initiated directly by the Kremlin. The Kremlin's orders in fact have been altered by the local authorities in their own advantage. As a consequence, the demarcation has presented an opportunity for solving territorial ambitions but not a realization of the set principles imposed by Moscow. Actually for positing a criterion of demarcation two main principles have to be distinguished. The first principle, i.e. the national-political principle, has rested upon the national composition and unity of the lands, while the second principle has accentuated the economic preferences in the laying of the frontiers. In my interpretation, both of the principles exclude so to speak national aspect of the division of the lands, where the frontier lines take into account the nations which inhabit the lands. The commission held for the purpose of setting the frontier lines of the new republics rested on the both abovementioned principles ignoring the interests of the inhabited people. As a result after such an unfair and narrow-minded juridical demarcation for Tajikistan there has been left only one -third of its age-old territory: the Eastern Bukhara and the regions of Mountain Badakhshan and Eastern Pamir were included within the frontiers of composed soviet Tajik republic[75]. Samarqand was only 70 km from the Tajik frontier, but it was not included into the area of Tajikistan. However, Kyrgyzstan had been allotted Osh, which was far miles from Frunze (Bishkek) capital of Kyrgyzstan. Interestingly enough, that according to Bergne, Tamerlane in his memoir, held in London, had described Samarqand as a predominantly Tajik city[76]

2.1.3. Contemporary Tajikistan

The Tajik Parliament has passed a resolution of sovereignty in December 1990. In September 1991, the Republic of Tajikistan became an independent country. Likewise other Soviet Republics, Tajikistan faced severe economic, political, and social problems after independence. Following independence in 1991, the country experienced five years of brutal civil war (1992-1997), which led to the destruction that resulted from the extended period of conflict. The civil war has officially ended with the signing of the "General Agreement on Establishment

---

75 Masov R. (1991). *Istoriya Topornogo Razdeleniya*. (History of Clumsy division). Irfon: Dushanbe.

76 Bergne, P. (2007). *The Birth of Tajikistan: National Identity and the Origins of the Republic*. London and New York: I. B. Tauris.

of Peace and National Reconciliation in Tajikistan" on the 27th of June, 1997, in Moscow[77].

After the Civil War, the economy of Tajikistan sank into a deep crisis. The war brought dramatic consequences - about 50 thousand people were killed (according to some sources, even one hundred thousand). A lot of women were denied the opportunity to get married. Many young people found themselves without jobs and left the country mainly for seasonal employment. The stabilization of the situation in the country has created positive conditions for post-conflict re-establishment and the second stage of the development of the national economy's development only since 2000, when the deepening of economic reforms have caused the casing of new spheres of the economy, which in turn have guaranteed high rates of economic development between the period of 2000-2005. As a result of stability and the high rates of economic development, poverty was reduced from 81% to 64% of the population by 2003. In spite of the fact that many problems of the transitional period have been overcome, economically speaking, there still exist a number of significant challenges to face with connected with the market transformation of the country[78].

2.1.4 Structure of the society

Family

The joint family, as it is scientifically called, is still the predominant family model in Tajik society. This model is common in the countryside, where sons with their own families still reside under their parents' roof. Even in the cases where the son lives separate from his parents, his wife and children will spend the majority of the day at his parent's house helping his grandparents and participating in various household chores. If the son leaves the family home and moves to another part of the country, he is still obliged to return to his parent's household during special occasions and ceremonies, for instance, during the Ramadan period. Living away from his parents does not relieve him from his responsibility towards them. As Kim has noted:

> "Living apart does not necessarily mean autonomy and the independence of a married son and his family from his parents. He and his wife still feel responsible for the parents' well-being, and provide emotional and material support for them...The ideal autonomy

77 Shapoatov Sayfiddin (2004). The Tajik Civil War:1992-1997. (A thesis submitted to the Graduate Scholl of Social Sciences of Middle East Technical University.

78 Yusufbekov, Y. Babajanov R., & Kuntuvdiy N. (2007). *Civil Society Development in Tajikistan*. Dushanbe. AKDN.

of an independent nuclear family is constantly being contrasted with the realities of extended kin networks, in which resources must be shared and faces saved[79]".

The father is regarded to be a head of the family, and his oldest son always helps him. In the situation of the father's death, the elder son acquires the responsibility to take care of the family. The older son is responsible in doing physical works in the family, in providing financial support, and in defending his family's honor. He is answerable for his family and especially for all matters connected with the life of his sisters. He takes care of them where the needs appear. Joint families are rarely found in the city. I have not come across any statistic concerning family structures in the cities. In the basis of my own observation, I think that this family model is leading even in the cities.

In Tajik society, like in other Asian societies, people are differentiated on an age-based hierarchy. As I have mentioned earlier in my work, mahalla maintains respect for old men, who represent the family to the community and strengthen their position at home. The neglect and display of bad attitudes towards old people is an unknown phenomenon in the mahalla. The mahalla also intervenes in family conflicts caused by drunkenness and in general highly prohibits public drinking. This is done efficiently in order to maintain the traditional values.

There is also an age-based hierarchy of authority present within families. This implies a respect toward age and the unquestioning submission to parents, older brothers, sisters, and toward other older people in the mahalla. During the upbringing of children, a strong emphasis is placed on their responsibilities towards the other members of the family.

Parents teach their children to respect their elders and to ask them for advice before doing something. People believe that children are holy, and according to Islam, children are considered to be holy creatures free from sin. In the case of boys, they are seen as a child until they reach the age of twelve years old; for girls - nine years old. Children learn how to behave by observing and unconsciously copying the family relationships in which they live.

In visible contrast to the Western family, in a Tajik family, as an example of an Eastern family, the child is not a witness of the rivalry that could be exhibited between parents. Their siblings and relatives monitor the child's respect for elders and the fulfillment of the age-based responsibilities. Children's behavior is also supervised by all of the neighbors within the mahalla.

---

79 Elliott & Gray (2000). *Family Structures.* (A Report for the New Zealand Immigration Service). Immigration Research Programme.

In Tajik society, where individual's behavior is regulated by the ideal of honor and fear of exposure to shame, one must always consider what the community will say about their behavior. If individuals openly misbehave and violate social norms, particularly if they provoke and challenge the established gender roles, there will be a determined effort on the part of the neighborhood members to press the issue, to ferret out bad behavior, and to disclose it whenever its admission can have the most corrective power. Therefore, family dramas are hidden from the communal observation, and every member of the family is aware that they are responsible for upholding the honor and status of their family within the community.

According to Tajiks' common sense, it is believed that parents are responsible for the behavior of their children. As a method of sustaining their family honor, they react to any neighbor's feedback about their children's behavior. They will try to solve the problem within the family, but if conflict arises between family members, the duty of solving the conflict is subjected to the avlod. The reaction of the neighbors depends on the respect that a family has before the eyes of the community. Whether or not they will disclose the knowledge of a child's transgressions partially depends on the respect that the family has, but particularly, on whether the family is trying to remedy the situation. It is understandable that they are trying their best to continue the gender and age norms of the community, and if the shamed accept their punishment, the neighborhood may then leave them in peace.

In distinction to neighboring Afghanistan (apropos, where a large number of native Tajiks live), murder is not a punishment for sex-related offenses in Tajik society. Female values are fundamental to Tajik morality. The loss of virginity by a daughter or sister dishonors not only the head of the family, but it provokes a destructive effect on every family member's reputation. This family is deprived of their honor, and in the future, it will be very difficult for their female members to find a husband within the community. This is because the family has lost its positive image within the community. The aforementioned social sanctions towards the dishonored members of the family are permitted by Islamic ethics.

2.1.5. Mahalla throughout history

2.1.6. Early period

Mahalla is from the Arabic word المحلة, which, like mahall and the plural form محلات (from the same root, حل), originally means a place where one makes a halt. Mahalla, therefore, came to have the special meaning of a quarter of a town, a meaning which has also passed into the Persian, Turkish and Hindustani languages (where the popular pronunciation is muhalla). The term formerly applied to a quarter of a town. For example, in Egypt, the word of mahalla is regularly found as the first element in the names of towns and villages.[80]

In the case of Central Asian countries, especially in Tajikistan, mahalla is a council or community of people in which all local problems are discussed and resolved. Literally, in the English language, mahalla means "neighborhood". According to Moryakova [81], the concept of the mahalla has begun to circulated in language in the 10th century. The first mentioning about mahalla is found in Narshakhi's book "History of Bukhara" which has been written in Arabic in the 10th century, and afterward translated into Persian in the 12th century[82].

It is worth noticing that very little research has been conducted on mahalla. The historical books include information on mahalla (the book authored by Sukhareva, Semyonov, Khanikov, Bartold, and Ayni,). In most cases in the cases of mahalla it has been associated with the city of Bukhara. Still, the situation has been similar in the territory of modern Tajikistan and Uzbekistan. The first scholar who has studied Central Asian cities and noticed this unusual example of social life in quarters in the early 19th century has been Khanikov N.[83]

According to Sukhareva, on the basis of historical sources, the history of mahalla (quarters) can be divided into five periods. The first period lasts from the 8th century until the 12th century; the second period is from the first half of the 13th century to the 16th century; the third period is from the second half of the 16th century to the 17th century; the fourth was from the 18th century until the first half of the 19th century; and the fifth period is from the second half of the 19th century until the beginning of the 20th century.[84]

Indeed, the division of these phases reflects the stages of the history of the city itself, the changes that have taken place in its life under the influence of the historical process have determined the historical fate of the entire society as a whole. The first phase of the history (8-12 centuries) of quarters as distinguished by Sukhareva is also highlighted in Muhammad Narshakhi's *History of Bukhara*.

---

80 Brill's E.J.(1913-1936). *The First Encyclopedia of Islam*. Netherlands.

81 Moryakova, E. (1998). Mahalla: The Traditional Muslim Neighborhood Community in the Development of Uzbek Civil Society. In Dornisch, D., Elvin, P., In *Post-Communist Transformations*. IFiS Publishers: Warsaw.

82 Narshakhi, M. (1979). *Tarikhi Bukhoro* (History of Bukhara) Dushanbe, Donish.

83 Sukhareva O.A. (1976). *Квартальная община позднефеодального города Бухары* (Quarterly community of late feudal city Bukhara). Moscow. Nauka.

84 Ibid.

In the 8th century, the feudal Bukhara had just been formed, and in period of the 10-12 centuries, it has already fully flourished in terms of crafts and trade.

It is worth noticing that little is known about the quarters in Bukhara at the beginning of the 8th century. Narshakhi writes that at that time the city have been divided into four parts (quarters). If to coincide the term of mahalla with Narshakhi's "ku", then, this source mentions 12 names of quarters (*Kuyi Rindon, Kuyi Vazir, Kuyi A'lo, Kuyi Bu- lyas, Kuyi Mughon, Kuyi Dehkon, mahalla Gardunkashon, mahalla VorotMansura, mahalla Vorot Samarqanda, mahalla Darvozacha and mahalla Fagsodara*[85])

According to information given by the Arab authors from 10th century, Bukhara by this time has acquired a purely urban image, and entire urban development or urbanization have become very tight. Narshakhi mentions overpopulation of the city and a significant development in its craft industry and trade as typically urban occupations[86].

The second phase in the history of Bukhara's quarters touches upon 13-16 centuries. It is very rare to find written sources about this historical period. In these centuries, the destruction of Bukhara by Genghis Khan's troops has occurred, followed by a subsequent slow and incomplete restoration. Even in the period of Timur and the first Timurids- the very period remained as the brilliant one in historiography - the city has failed to return to its former dimensions, and still has maintained the boundaries defined the city walls that in and of itself has probably been built after the restoration of the city originally destroyed by the Mongols. Concerning this period, information about the quarters in Bukhara is very scanty: for instance, according to the sources of the 15 century, the names of 5 quarters are known, but all of them can surely be localized in the territory of the city (apropos, three of them has preserved their genuine names until the beginning of the 20th century).

The third phase of the history of Bukhara's quarters fails on the second half of the 16-18 centuries. This period begins with the construction of new walls, carried out in the eastern part during the reign of Abdul-Aziz Khan[87]. As the result of it, the area of the city had expanded significantly by including within its limits the suburban villages, which were gradually transformed in a while into quarters. At the same time, in some villages the line of the wall had been cut into two parts, one of which was inside and the others outside of the city.

85 Ibid.

86 Narshakhi, M. (1979). *Tarikhi Bukhoro* (History of Bukhara). Donish: Dushanbe.

87 Abdul-Aziz Khan (1614-1683), the fifth Khan of Bukhara Khanate dynasty Ashtarkhanids.

In the acts of the second half of 16 century, the names of 34 quarters have been published and stored in the archives (nine of them have preserved their name until the beginning of the 19th century).

In the fourth stage of Sukhareva's periodization, relative prosperity changes have occurred due to devastation and desolation. According to the sources of the 18th century, this is highlighted by the fact that only two quarters had remained inhabited in all of Bukhara. Many historians believe that such reports generally correctly underscore the situation of that period. Only Bartold, one of the greatest explorers of Central Asia, has expressed the view that the crisis of the 18th century of the Bukhara Khanate impacts urban life to a lesser extent than in Khiva and that hopefully to Bukhara it has suffered less than Samarkand. Samarkand, in its turn, has counted by the 18th century not more than 1000 families, of whom most of them have been settled around the citadel[88].

The second half of this phase is composed of gradually overcoming the consequences of the devastation. The city and its inhabited quarters, or mahallas, step by step have been restored. This phase has been lasting until Central Asia have not become a part of the Russian Empire, and consequently, Bukhara - a vassal state. The main source for studying mahallas and its history in this phase are official acts. In the sources concerning this period of history of mahalla, the names of 113 mahallas are mentioned.

Sukhareva has mentioned five periods, but in my work, but I have used sources exclusively from the last period (19th century until the beginning of the 20th century). The mahalla of contemporary Tajikistan has retained its current functions from this chosen period of time. From cultural perspective, mahalla has been a feature of Central Asian and has been developed as a form of social organization from the extended family structure common to the regions' indigenous ethnic group. Islam has historically provided the religious and spiritual basis for the mahalla, and during the era of Soviet hegemony it has been the mahalla that has played a vital role in the survival of Muslim tradition and faith[89].

It is historically determined that every mahalla possesses own name. In the 18-19 centuries, in terms of construction every mahalla has been separated from each other by the walls with own gate for every mahalla, whose entrances have reminded the castle-like. This is explained for the security reasons related

88 Bartold, V.(1920) A Short History of Turkestan. In *Four Studies on the History of Central Asia* (Leiden: E.J. Brill) 1956 (Trans. V. & T. Minorsky).

89 Ruffin& Waugh, (1999). *Civil Society in Central Asia.* University of Washington Press: Seattle. p. 167.

to the mahalla that the gates – called *Darvozai kalon*", or big gate - have generally been closed at night (apropos in Bukhara, such kind of gates have been remained until the beginning of the 20th century). According to Bartold's comparison, gates similar to those in Central Asian cities have also located in the mahallas of Hamadan in Iran.[90]

From professional perspective, the residents of mahalla have varied depending on the responsibilities which each of them should carry out for the community. The residents of every household besides the duties to keep cleanness have been responsible for the order the in front of the house. Such duties have been part of *hashar* or community work. However, if the mahalla was large, then the members of the mahalla paid a salary from the community's deposit to hire a special person for cleaning the streets. The people of the community called "*farosh*", that in Tajik means "cleaner". The *farosh* has been responsible for cleaning inside the mahalla. His daily duty included the keeping order all over territory of the mahalla in the early morning. The number of cleaners have depended on the territory of the mahalla.[91]

I should note that such kind of community work exists in Tajikistan till now. Mahalla committees can nominate one person from every house for such *hashar*, which includes, but is not limited to, cleaning of irrigation ditches, garbage collection, and the reconstruction of the schools, mosques, and the houses of widows and the elderly. The *hashar* institution still plays a significant role in the entire life of the Tajiks. Mahalla residents renovate schools, repair roads in the streets, and build houses free of charge for each other. According to Islam, the responsibilities of *hashar* mandate that one should do good deed (*sawob*[92]). As the religion declares, it is one of the duties of Muslims to help their community members, seeing as how they refer to one another as brothers. Not participating in community works is an offense against the dictates of religion, and at the same time, this act is regarded as a lack of respect to other members of the community. Therefore, the mahalla residents work to help each other.

---

90 Bartold, V.(1920). A Short History of Turkestan. In Leiden: E.J., Brill (Eds.). (1956). *Four Studies on the History of Central Asia* ((Trans. V. & T. Minorsky).

91 Ibid.

92 The word *sawob* is from the Arabic (ثواب). *Sawab* is generally used in the language of the Middle East, Central Asia and the Indian subcontinent as an exhortation to do good, however, its pronunciation differs by region. In Tajikistan, for example, it pronounced as "savob", but in Arab countries it is "*thawab*", and in India, Iran, and Pakistan as" *sawab*" or "*savab*".

One of the most problematic issues for Bukhara in the 19th century has been the issue with water supply. In the hierarchical structure of power in Central Asia, the network of irrigation channels has been managed by the state ruler (the title of Khan or Emir in Bukhara) and has been at the forefront of the water delivery hierarchy. Each administrative province has been ruled by *hokim* or *bek* (local rulers): each bek has appointed one person – *aryk boshi* – to the main irrigation canal and another person – *mirob* or water boss- responsible for water allocation and the operation of irrigation ditches[93]. This duty has required a proper experience and special organizational skills. Therefore, *mirob* had the right to organize *hashar* for the cleaning and construction of the irrigation canals. The members of the mahallas have participated in all of these works and channeled water supplied by existing irrigation networks to their communities. *Hashar* for irrigation canals was obligatory for all water users in the mahallas. Upstream mahallas that received cleaner and larger quantities of water were expected to supply labor forces[94]. *Mirob* had the right to punish those who object the *hashar* obligation by reducing or depriving their water supply. As practice have showed, such punitive actions did not happen.

Every mahalla has been ruled by a leader called *raisi mahalla*. Traditionally, he has been originated from the community and elected by the community members. Habitually, the members of the community have selected the particular person who has enjoyed the highest respect in that community. Until now, it remains to be a person who has been living long enough in the mahalla and enjoying the reputation of respectful person in all of the communal laws, traditions, and *odat*, customs. According to long-aged tradition, rais has possessed the power to solve the problematic situations in the life of the mahalla, to resolve conflicts, and to manage the organization of weddings, funerals, and circumcisions; additionally, he has been supervised in the selling of property throughout the territory of the mahalla. According to practice, the neighbors had the right to pre-empt the selling of a nearby house. For instance, if one of the inhabitants had intended to sell his house, he would have had to come to the *rais* and to ask him and the neighbors for their permission. At that time the neighbors' rights have

93 Rakhmatullaev, S. A., Bazarov, D. R., & Kazbekov, J. S. (2003). Historical Irrigation Development in Uzbekistan from Ancient to Present: Past Lessons and Future Perspectives for Sustainable Development. In *Proceedings of the Third International Conference of International Water History Association*. Alexandria: Egypt, pp. 79-80.

94 O'Hara, S. L. (2000). Lessons from the Past: Water Management in Central Asia. In *Water Policy*. 2, pp. 365-384

been of importance since their meaning have been taken into consideration [95]. The basis of the neighboring rights in the mahalla was Shariat Law. Shariat Law is Islamic Law derived from the Al- Qur'an, the Holy book for the Muslims, and the hadith, the teachings and sayings of the Prophet Muhammad (BPUH). According to the understanding of Shariat laws, Tajiks are trying to sell their house, after receiving permission from the rais of the community and his neighbors, had to go to all of the inhabitants and inform them that he is going to sell. The mahalla members usually do not agree with the selling of houses to strangers outside of the community.

In the 18-19 centuries in Bukhara, the current role of the *rais* has been played by *aksakal* (An Uzbek term that signifies a man who has a white beard; in certain regions of Tajikistan the Tajik term *muysafed* is used instead). *Aksakal* has been also a chairman of the community with helper – in Tajik *poikor* – literally a man who goes by foot, because his activities have required much walking. *Aksakal* has taken the honorable seat of the leader of the social life of the quarter and has been considered to be – like others representatives of the quarter self-government – a servant to society. It was common belief he was in the service of the community *khizmat*. *Aksakal* as an official representative of the quarter in the affairs with the local authorities, and for this reason, and in the eyes of the community's members, has enjoyed the status of one of the most important dignitaries.

After the election, some representatives of the community have gone to the *Kozikalon* and have informed him about their decision. *Kozikalon* as a Court has been adjudicated according to Shariah – Islamic law, the *kozikalon* has issued the *aksakal* a special document confirming him as the head of the community. The representative of the local governmental administration has also been notified about the election of the *aksakal*. The authority of *aksakal* have allowed him to represent parties in the case of legal conflicts. Albeit, he had also experienced the limited powers to judge. Before bringing the internal conflicts of the mahalla before the attention of the administrative courts, the older people of the community tried to resolve the conflicts amongst themselves. *Aksakals* had greater authority than the remaining members of the community, which is further supported by Sukhareva, who in her book put that they have been as the "slaves of their community" doing all their best for the good of community.[96]

In addition, *aksakal* has played an important role during the redistribution of deceased mahalla members' property. He has divided the property of that per-

95 Ayni, S. (1956). *Dokhunda*. Moscow.

96 Sukhareva O.A. (1976). *Квартальная община позднефеодального города Бухары* (Quarterly community of late feudal city Bukhara). Nauka: Moscow.

son equally among his children as a foster parent of the orphaned children. For lonely people without relatives, and also for widows *aksakal* has served as the assistant and advisor. He has taken care of this heritage for orphan children waiting to their maturity to return it. If *aksakal* was holding onto money for them, he would lend it to traders or market stall owners, thereby ensuring that the child would receive interest on the money that he was managing. In sum, *aksakal* has served as the main advisor for all families in many situations in life.

Every street - *guzar* -had the head - *khodim*. The heads of *guzars* have been elected by *aksakal* with agreement of the inhabitants of the street. They solved daily problems on their streets and have served as *raises* in mahalla but in lower level. They took care of poor people, the elderly, and orphans. They have helped sick people, and in the case of need, they would even sleep in their house to watch them throughout the night.[97]

The structure of mahalla has been preserved in Tajikistan up until the current day. Nowadays every mahalla has its leader – *rais* of mahalla - chosen by the members of that community. Every street has its heads of streets, and they are subordinated to the chairman of the community. The meeting of *rais* and the council of elders usually has an informal character. Their meetings are held in social places (in gaps) or mosques, in tea-houses (*choikhona*), or other places where mature males meet and discuss their concerns about society.[98]

Every mahalla has some financial rites coming from the charitable contribution of the members of the community. The members of the mahalla often gather for mahalla meetings to discuss and solve the problems of the community. For example, they also have the power to decide using the funds if it is necessary to construct public buildings, hospitals, schools, mosques, teahouses, homes for widows, housing for elderly people, and other buildings. In the vast majority of cases, the source of this finance is charity contributions.[99]

The role of the mosque in Tajik society has been and is of great significance, and not only in maintaining the religious spirit of the members of the community. In every mahalla, the primary religious schools (madrasa) in which oth-

---

97 Ibid.

98 Geiss, P. G. (2001). Mahalla and Kinship Relations. A Study on Residential Communal Commitment. Structures in Central Asia of the 19th Century. In *Central Asian Survey.*

99 Sievers, E.W.(2002). *Uzbekistan's Mahalla: From Soviet to Absolutist Residential Community Associations.* The Journal of International and Comparative Law at Chicago-Kent: Vol. 2 Retrived 20, April, 2009, from http://www.kentlaw.edu/jicl/articles/spring2002/JICL%20Sievers%20Mahalla%20final%20for%20publication.pdf

er educational activities have been existed. Sukhareva, in analyzing the life of Bukhara's quarters in the 17-19 centuries, pays attention to the conjunction of the different functions of the mosque which has been mentioned above. That was a typical practice for Bukhara, and she underlines that in the morning, the rais has checked the attendance of the men in the first prayer – *namaz al- fajr* or *namozi bomdod* [100]- and punish the ones who have been absent. The mosque was an important center of public life. The leader of mahalla has noticed the presence of its members in first namaz (the first pray of Muslims) because it is mandatory for everyone to pray in the morning. However, during the other daily prayers, they have been working in different fields outside of the territory of mahalla: for example, some have been working as traders in the marketplace; in general, namaz has been practiced in the mosques nearest to the place of working. In the evening, before the last namaz, when the majority of the members had returned to the mahalla, men would meet and discuss actual issues.[101]

It is necessary to notice the presence of mosque in every mahalla, or at the very least, the members have visited the mosque nearby. It might happen that some rich mahallas include several mosques. Traditionally, the mosque has been built from the revenue of the mahalla. A presence of the mosque is significant for two important reasons; according to the Islamic religion, the sawob, or good deed, will be increased if prayer is to be practiced in the community (namozi Jamoat); and the second reason is that mosque has been the place where people tend to gather and to discuss the main problems and urgent issues of their community. In Tajikistan, as in other Central Asian regions, such meetings to discuss communal life have also been held in *chaykhana* (teahouse). Some old men of the council of elders are so accustomed in such degree that they usually come here at 6 a.m. to *chaykhana*. The council of elders would drink tea and eat common meals that were prepared from products brought from home or purchased with the money donated by contribution feasters. The meals were either prepared by the council or by the *choykhonachi*[102]. According to Sukhareva, *chaykhanas* in Tajik culture is a relatively new institution; this is why the most important place to gather in the life of people remains to be the mosque. Additionally, govern-

100 *Namoz* or *namaz* means prayer in Persian equivalent to the Arabic term of *salah* (صلاة), which is the performance of formal prayer in Islam. For Muslims, salah is obligatory and arranged five times per day, which are measured according to the movement of the sun.

101 Sukhareva O.A. (1976). *Квартальная община позднефеодального города Бухары* (Quarterly community of late feudal city Bukhara). Nauka: Moscow.

102 *Choykhonachi* is the person who is working in the tea house and serving the clients.

ment representatives come to the mosques to have meetings with the people. In this case, it has been easy to gather everybody into the mosque, seeing as how it was either near the mahalla or directly inside of it.

The common ceremonies have played a special role in uniting all the members of the quarter. It has been the custom to celebrate the most important events of human life with the fellow inhabitants of the entire mahalla. It has been considered a duty for all mahalla members to participate in the feasts that have been organized by another family, and failure to do so has been seen as an egregious act of disrespect to the master of the house. In accordance with custom, the common ceremonies have been financed from the communal budget or, for example, by some other mahalla member who felt it to be his religious responsibility to provide assistance. During these ceremonies, men have been preparing a special dish called *halisa* - a boiled cereal made from wheat and mea -, while women have been preparing meal called "*sumallak*[103]". The ingredients for the meals have been gathering from every household, in addition, each participant has been able to take leftovers back to own home. The guests also have not leave empty-handed. Every person who has brought a gift in turn has received a present from the host family. The presentation and acceptance of mutual gift-giving has displayed the attention and feelings of community. In such ceremonies, the mahalla has been looked like a large extended family. The youth and most of the men from the community have done all of the physical labor associated with the events: supply of water, peeling and cutting vegetables for preparing a traditional dish - the meal of plow (*oshi palaw*), without that every ceremony cannot be organized (which is a traditional meal for the Tajiks and Uzbeks)[104]. The owner of the house has been free from the abovementioned works. He as an inviting master of the house has been staying near the gate to meet and welcome the guests[105].

I should emphasize once more time that these events have not been a matter of the private affairs, and their organization has not been a task of one person or family. All of the members of the community have assisted the family who hosted the ceremony or feast. Perhaps in traditional terms the wedding events have been among the most important types of ceremonies. The ritual of marriage is celebrated both in the family of the groom and the bride. In the fiancé's family, mahalla members have gathered from the morning until the evening, and

---

103 *Sumalak* (сумалак) is a sweet paste made prepared for Nawruz (New Year) It is made from germinate wheat, which cooks in a large pot (in Tajik deg).

104 Ibid.

105 Sukhareva O.A. (1976). *Квартальная община позднефеодального города Бухары* (Quarterly community of late feudal city Bukhara). Nauka.: Moscow.

in similar manner later in fiancée's household. Finally, the wedding ceremonies could last anywhere from one day up one week[106].

Such kind of the prolonged rituals have also been held on the occasion of the circumcision, usually lasting for several days. In some rich families, this ceremony has been celebrated about a month. Participants from other mahallas, cities, and even sometimes other countries are welcome invited to attend. Another prolonged ceremony is the burial ritual, and as with other events, it was necessary for behalf of the neighbors to help the family in organization of it. The rituals accompanying funeral feasts have been the most expensive. Exactly expensive in such a way that some families have had no choice but to borrow money to pay for it. Paying off this debt could shake the family budget to its core. Most stories about family bankruptcy have their genesis in the death of one of another member.[107]

When somebody dies, men and women of that mahalla have come to the mourning family's home. They have been praying for the deceased, reading the Al- Qur'an, and helping in performing the burial ritual. They have also been helping in sharing the payment of funeral expenses. According to tradition, the family of the deceased did not prepare meals in their house for three days after the death of one of their kin. The neighbors have been preparing dishes during this time, while also offering their condolences to the family. Women from the community have been wearing special clothes for the funeral, just as the members of the mourning family do. All women have such outfits for this event. They also have been crying for the deceased, just as the immediate family does. In accordance with religious requirements, funeral ceremonies take place after the third, seventh, twentieth, and fortieth day after death. The series of funeral rituals comes to an end after a year, in which all members of the mahalla participate in one last feast.

The neighbors also take upon themselves other ritual duties for their members, such as preparing wedding clothes for a bride, helping with childbirth, and being the first to place the newborn child into the cradle. It has also been customary for neighbors to fulfill their obligation to provide hospitality for the respected strangers arrived to partake in such ceremonies. They have also performed the role of an honor guard by meeting outside guests at the gates of the mahalla. These guests have been greeted by the neighbors holing the cans of

---

106 Ibid.

107 Ayni, S. (1956). *Dokhunda.* Moscow.

water and towel. This traditional custom allows for the guest to wash their hands before entering the ceremony.

The rather unchanged rules of the mahalla have been determined by a common law formed centuries ago that has been transmitted through generations to generations. The life of the mahalla fosters an environment of face-to-face accountability, thereby ensuring the communal control of the common law. Members meet each other on a very regular basis, and they know almost everything about the life and problems of every mahalla member. Because of this, all members of the mahalla know each other intimately and are like one big family. As one of my respondents has stated:

> *The ties between me and others mahalla members are like the ties between family. Mahalla is like an extended family. We know each other well, and in everyday life we are together. All mahalla members are our brothers and sisters. We cannot live without each other separately. Throughout history, we preserved our tradition together. We help each other in difficulties and share our happiness together. It's a part of our life. I cannot imagine my life without it.(male, 58 years old, teacher of history. July 2010).*

Everyone is under the parent-like supervision by the mahalla members; everyone accepts this code of behavior understanding that in any difficult life situation it is possible to rely on fellowmen from mahalla. The mahalla immediately recognizes whenever a stranger arrives within their midst, however, the concept of 'alienness' and the psychological attitudes towards foreigners contrast to each other. At first, the members of mahalla are very careful in observation the individual from outside and are not hurry in judging: if that person is respectful towards the rules and traditions of the mahalla, then consequently, the members will be very open and loyal toward the stranger. If he does not respect the aforementioned, then he is still treated like a guest, although he will not be trusted anymore. In a way such watchful behavior is easily explained as the sense of self-preservation familiar to every member of mahalla and to mahalla as community. As I will explain later, trust is an important and highly appreciated value in the rural areas. The Tajiks usually treat guests in a hospitable fashion, especially if he is the guest from another mahalla. However, their attitude can be changed if he does something taboo regarding mahalla's rules of behavior. The mahalla's openness towards strangers is demonstrated by the fact that the mahalla members are not to be refused trust solely on the grounds of their religion or nationality. In this respect, the Tajiks are very tolerant in their relations to people from other countries and religions. [108]

2.1.7. The Soviet period of Mahalla

In 1924, Tajikistan has been created as an autonomous Soviet socialist republic within Uzbekistan, and later in 1929, Tajikistan has been proclaimed as a separate Soviet Socialist Republic. The politics of Sovietization has began in Central Asia during this early period of republic formation and one of the first steps of Sovietization has been an alteration the alphabet of the native peoples. In such method - fast and brutal in its core - the cutting off with the cultural and ethnicl links has been intended. It is known that for long-centuries long the area of Central Asia has been an Islamic area and that its native inhabitants have been overwhelmingly Muslims. The Tajiks have been using the Persian-Arabic alphabet and speaking Persian before becoming a constituent republic of the USSR. I should note that Tajikistan is the only Persian-speaking country in post-Soviet Central Asia. At first, the Tajik alphabet has been changed to Latin in 1928. It is generally believed that the aim of this change was to separate the Tajiks from their Islamic traditions. Only during the later period of the *russification*- imposing of the Russian as the main language - the Tajik alphabet has again been changed but now into Cyrillic. It has caused a tremendous culture shock for the society: the textbooks in the schools, the books in the libraries and educational centers, the newspapers and journals (even all Tajik-Persian classical works have been translated into this alphabet) have created a vision that old Persian alphabet has not existed at all. Until now, the Cyrillic alphabet is still in use Therefore, young post-soviet generation is growing up being unaware of the rich cultural heritage the ancestors once have possessed.

The Tajik Soviet Socialist Republic has pursued the soviet model of development, coping it like others republics. It has been characterized by the following: rapid urbanization and industrialization, collectivization of agriculture, construction of a secular state by repressive measures, and atrocious eradication of high Islam (i.e. the liquidation of religious schools, libraries, and the persecution of religious scholars and imams). During the soviet times, the traditional institutions such as mahalla have become the guardians of tradition and religion as well, owing to the fact that as informal institutions they could safeguard and

108 Gunda, W. (2009). *Socio-Political Change in Tajikistan The Development Process, its Challenges Since the Civil War and the Silence Before the New Storm?* University of Hamburg Faculty of Social Sciences Institute for Political Science.

protect religious practices from the persecution of local authorities. In the rural area it has been easier to hide from the control from the side of authorities. So mahalla as traditionally and in time of imposed secularism has played a decisive role in the education of youth and the spreading and sustaining of religious knowledge.

As a result it is possible to conclude that the culture of Islam, Tajik traditions and – to say more – the entire corpus of Tajik culture has been preserved in the mahallas. Although Islamic traditions and habits have been prohibited in the sphere of public life, nevertheless they have loyally been practiced in the sphere of public life. Albeit there have not been any de-jure Islamic schools, the Mullahs and specialists in the Al- Q'uran - called *Qori* or *Hofizi Qur'on* – still have been teaching religion in the rural areas. They have taught children about the basis of Islam and traditional Tajik customs, called Adab. As long centurie ago anad in the period of Sovietization the knowledge of Islam has been transmitted through generations from grandfather to father, from father to son. It has turned to be that mahalla has become as the only one institution to sustain and pass on its Islamic heritage: "after the widespread closing of madrassas in Central Asia during the 1920s and 1930s, the role of mahalla in the preservation of Islamic custom and tradition became paramount".[109] According to official statistics, the number of operating mosques has been a few, however, the actual number has likely been several times larger. People who have been practicing Islam have gathered every day in different houses, tea houses, or Soviet clubs in concealed manner. As a illustrative example shows that the Tajiks not remembering the faith have been praying in the places of work, where – according to widespread imposed rule - a portrait of Lenin has been hung.[110]

As I have mentioned above, I have conducted interviews with members of different mahallas in different cities: Hisor, Shahrinav, and Fayzobod. Hisor region - where I am from - is situated in the western part of Tajikistan. It is about 20-25 kilometers from Dushanbe, the capital of the country. Shahrinav is also situated in the western part, and it is located 50 km from Dushanbe. Fayzobod is a region about 60 km east of Dushanbe. According to elderly inhabitants of these mahallas, it has been very complicated to practice Islam in soviet period. For instance, according to information obtained from the interviews, the fasting

---

109 Ruffin& Waugh, (1999). *Civil Society in Central Asia*. University of Washington Press: Seattle. p. 167

110 Niyazi, A. (1999). Islam and Tajikistan's Human and Ecological Crisis. In *Civil Society in Central Asia*. Ruffin, M. H. & Waugh, D. (Eds). (pp. 180-198). University of Washington Press: Seattle.

children have been forced to eat and drink in the schools. However, in spite of the great number of difficulties, nevertheless, people have preserved religion and tradition. Raisi of mahalla, a head of mahalla, has been compelled to be a member of the Communist Party, but, in fact, he has openly practiced religion with the people of the community. The fidelity to religion has happened to be an issue of the secret practice, under silence and calm and in highly intimate manner.

The religious practices have mostly taken places in off-limits to strangers from outside the mahalla, and in terms o security the secret place of prayer has been changed every time. In the Holy month of Ramazan and in *idi Qurbon* (*Eid al-Adha* – festival of the sacrifice after Ramadan), believers from the mahalla have practiced the meetings in the mountains in such a way far from the urban settlements, noise, and possible spies, they have been able to practice the religion freely during their holy days without fear of being discovered and revealed by the authorities. In their turn the anti-religious propaganda has gained its speed: the authorities would check every house during these religious periods and search for people performing religious activities. Traditionally, the Muslims are fasting during the month of Ramadan – they are obliged not to eat and drink from the morning until the evening, the very act is a bit complex to hide from the outsiders' eyes. They members of Sufism in their turn have practiced the rituals in clandestine manner: gathering to partake in these rituals in secret time and place. In accordance with religious tradition, people who have learned Al-Quran by heart have to stay at special place for 40 days in order to pray, read, and repeat Al-Quran. Again in means of secrecy *khonagoh* or *chilakhona* temporarily have served as such places[111].

It is generally considered that during the Soviet time, Tajiks have been compelled to have two distinct identities: the communist identity and the Muslim identity. Under the pressure of social requirements, Tajiks have presented themselves as communist in the workplace but have been conducting as Muslims in their community. It has also been common for the students be teach imposed rules of the communist ideology in the places of studying, but to live according to religious customs inside the community. Sometimes the religious Tajiks under such pressure have decided not to let children to attend Soviet schools, as a means to keeping them away from 'negative' influence. Instead the parents have preferred to send their children to unofficial schools. Since the secondary education in the soviet republics has been compulsory, the parent have intended to stop the educational process at this level, and not to prepare for entering col-

111 Chilakhona is the place where the person who learned Al-Quraan (Qori) by heart stays for 40 days to repeat Al-Quran. Sufi Brotherhoods also use khonagoh or chilakhona for their common zikr.

leges or Universities. For example, for the girls the solution has included the early marriage. As one of my respondents says:

> *During Soviet times, it was difficult to perform religious rituals. However, in spite of all the hindrances, the Tajiks could not eradicate the practicing of Islamic rituals in Tajikistan. Their anti-religious politics could be conducted only in the official places. At schools, students were taught principles of communism, but at home they behaved according to the principles of their own religious customs. The supporters of communism were alienated in rural areas by their communities. The majority of the population of Tajikistan was rural, therefore members of the Communist party had no other choice but to obey the local customs. For example, rais of our mahalla was an active member of the Communist party in his work, however, within the community he was performing rituals with us. Even during Ramazan and Kurban prayers, he was helping us to perform prayers. With his advice, we were changing the place of prayer every time. People who did not respect religious customs were threatened not to be buried according to Islamic rituals (Male, 74 years old. August, 2012).*

After the collapse of the *Basmachi* uprising in 1920's -a movement in defense of Tajik tradition and culture-, there had not been remained any collective anti-Soviet opposition. However, Soviet ideology has met resistance in the hidden way: in the continuation of tradition and culture within the mahallas. It is also worth noting that in the sphere of social reconstructions, the Soviet period has been characterized by the mainstream purpose of destroying the foundation of the indigenous cultures of each Central Asian republic. In addition, anti-religious propaganda has resulted in the destruction of completely of all mosques. It has been a merit of the traditional institutions to utilize and to minimize the speed of a mechanism of spreading Soviet ideology. This form of resistance has been of informal, inner, clandestine character.[112]

2.1.8. Post-Soviet period of Mahalla

As to the current state of civil society in Tajikistan and the other former Central Asian Soviet Republics, different events inherited from the Soviet systemic transformation have influenced in a decisive way. The Soviet regime has banned any organization independent from the state, and such organizations have been dispelled out or put underground as decadent ones. The development of civil society has been possible due to the political and public openings that has appeared in the 1980s during Gorbachev's politics, so-called policy of "*perestroika*". A specific defining moment has symbolized the adaptation of the law "On

112 Moryakova, E. (1998). Mahalla: The Traditional Muslim Neighborhood Community in the Development of Uzbek Civil Society. In Dornisch, D., Elvin, P. In *Post-Communist Transformations*. IFiS Publishers: Warsaw.

the State Language" by the Supreme Soviet of the Tajik SSR in 1989. This crucial event has opened up a possibility for a large public debate. In different places and universities, various spontaneous meetings have begun to be held where professors and students heatedly have been discussing the qualities and faults of the draft legislation. This has rapidly developed into a debate on national identity, and these problems have turned to a critical turning point for the development of civil society.

Numerous debates have been organized in 1989 by the Tajik intellectuals. For instance, the *Rastokhez* movement has been launched aiming a rebirth of Tajik culture. However, this cultural initiative has failed to become a real national movement in comparison with the analogous movements in Central Europe (for example Solidarity in Poland). The serious regional division typical for Tajikistan has led to the failure of it and other similar projects. Notwithstanding many public associations and civic movements – albeit of regional, local character- have appeared throughout the country: for instance, the ideological movements like *Lali Badakhson*, *Ekhyoi Khujand* ("The Revival of Khujand") *Oshkoro* "Glastnost"), and *Vakhdat* ("Unity").

A significant number of unofficial associations have also been launched during the period of *perestroika*; it has been estimated that around 60 and 120 thousand people counted as the members of these associations. As a result, he government have had to answer to the new challenges and to revise the legislation inherited from USSR, which excluded non-governmental organizations, though 90% of those associations have been based on voluntary work. They have promoted the free type of participation among their members for the sake of national identity. However, this spontaneous movement at the beginning yet later has become a major politic3al opponent to the state authority in the issues of promotion the development of civil society.

It has happened that most of the rapidly increasing number of civic institutions have not been of the political orientation: only as cultural and religious associations, for example, the diverse minority groups such as Koreans, Jews, and Armenians have formed their own civic institutions to arrange cultural and ethnic harmonious relations with the other ethnic groups. In general, the search for Tajik national identity has been stimulated by the rapid rebirth of Islam. Religion has begun to have an influence on politics. The Islamic religion, as I have pointed out above, has always played a vital role in traditional Tajik society. Thus, the religious rhetoric has become the rhetoric of the mobilization of political society. In almost every mahalla, new mosques have begun to be constructed and reconstructed, partly due to the strong public financial support, collective work efforts, and the participation of traditional craftsmanship. The mosques in the rural areas have become to displace the traditional tea houses (*choykhona*), in a way symbolically turning the time again: the anti-religious soviet propaganda has built on the places of ruined mosques the civic places for meetings and leisure – teahouse, and now after collapse of soviet rule the mosques are rebuilt on the places of ruined teahouses.

It should be noted that except among those who has adhered the communist ideology, the influence of Islam still has held the very strong influence among the population. The Tajiks have been continuing to follow the principles of Islam either in Soviet period or after it. Despite numerous anti religious campaigns, data speaks for itself: in 1999, 97% of Tajikistan population have declared themselves as the believers[113].

Likewise others Soviet Republics, the collapse of the Soviet system, has caused the severe economic, political, and social transformations in Tajikistan. Firstly, the most visible and material consequences of the collapse have mostly been of economic character. A serious economic crisis appeared shortly after the collapse. The crisis motivated by the swift need of transition from planned –based economy to market-based one, for the very economic leap the preconditions have turned to be absent. As in others republic there has been a monopoly on certain products. For example, the only plant producing electricity meters have been produced in the Baltic countries; rye and wheat from Ukraine, fruits and grapes from Moldova, cotton and aluminum from Tajikistan consequently. Moreover, the Moscow supplies have intended to counterbalance deficits in each of republics. Secondly, the economic condition of Tajikistan has quickly been deteriorated because of the country's exit from the ruble zone and the introduction of a new currency. Thirdly, Tajikistan was the poorest country of the former Soviet Union dependent on subsidies coming from Moscow could not in the shortest terms recover and make step in the field of new economic relations. As a direct result of the dissolution of the USSR, the subsidies have significantly been cut off, and the republic was unable to cope with the challenge of improving the standard of life in its poorest areas, among which Badakhshan was prominent one. The worst period following independence after 1991, is connected with the five years of brutal civil war that caused enormous humanitarian, social and economic damage to the country.

Tajikistan has been the one post-soviet republic to experience the break and bloody-lasting of the civil war. In early 90's the wave of separatist conflicts based

---

113 Olimova, Saodat. (1999). 'Politicheskiy Islam i Konflikt v Tajikistane (Political Islam and Conflict in Tajikistan). In *Central Asia and the Caucasus*, № 5, Sweden. Retrieved from: http://www.cac.org/journal/cac-05-1999/contcac_5_99.shtml

on the ethnic criteria has come across former Soviet countries: Turkmens against Armenians, Uzbeks against Kyrgyz, Transnistria conflict in Moldova, Nagorno Karabakh in Azerbaijan, Georgian-Ossetian conflict. The brother-killing Tajik civil war has pitted Tajiks against one another. In Tajik history, this war is remained as "*Jangi Barodarkush*", meaning that it was compelled brothers to kill each other. Regarding the causes of the civil war the scholars studying this topic consider regionalism as a key factor. The clan-based partition among Tajiks generally has occurred in the regions or oblast –adopting the word from Russian -; Khujand (formerly Leninobad), the northern oblast, associated itself with the Leninobod clan; the two central oblasts, Kulob and Kurghon-Teppa, which in spite of their mutual hostility had recently been merged together as the "Khatlon Oblast"; and Gorno-Badakhstan, which has mainly identified itself with the Garm clan, but also with the Pamir (*Badakhshani*) ethnic group.

The Tajik civil war has attracted the attention of several international scholars such as Aziz Niyazi, Bernett B. Rubbin, Oliver Roy, Iver B, Lena Johnson, D.V. Mikulskiy, Saodat Olimova, Muzaffar Olimov, Bushkov and others. These abovementioned scholars indicate rather diverse reasons as to the causes of the war, however, all of them believe that the regionalism played a pivotal role. Oliver Roy states that one of the principal causes of the conflict is "regionalism". The issue of Tajik national identity in period of transition from soviet past to democratically-based future has turned to be weak, unprotected, and fragile, and as solution the membership in regional "clans" for people has substituted the disputable question of self-identity process. The Gharmis (a term that includes natives of the areas of Qarategin, Wakhiha, and Darwoz) and Pamiris (natives of Gorno-Badakhshan) have supported the opposition. The Sughdi (Leninabadi) clan which has been dominating in the communist nomenclature has led the government, while the Kulobi and Hisori clans have provided the armed forces that will lead to victory[114].

Some scholars alternatively believe that ideological rivalries lead up to the Tajik Civil War. The ideological rivalry between communism and Islam did play a significant role throughout Tajik civil war, and possibly could be a reason to break it up. The cause of ideological rivalry has been analyzed in the general factor of regionalism. For instance, concerning this issue, Aziz Niyazi mentions the following:

---

114 Roy, O. Civil war in Tajikistan. Cited In Rubin, Bernett. (1995). *Causes and Consequences of the Civil War in Tajikistan*. Columbia University: USA., p. 50

> Regional rivalries are the main factor in the conflict. This factor has been shaping the process in Tajikistan. As a result talking about the role of ideology in Tajik politics is not accurate. All political allies and parties, except Communist Party, were established for the maximization of interests of certain regions[115].

It is necessary to note the complexity of the location of the regions in Tajikistan in order to understand this issue better. From the geographical perspective, the area of Tajikistan is divided into four regions, each of that may be observed as a specifically unique place. Thus, the diversity and differentiation between the regions have resulted in not only geographic contrasts, but also in causing the political and economic conflicts. The four regions or oblasts are: 1) Capital City Dushanbe and its surroundings, 2) Badakhshan Autonomous Region (BAR), 3) the Sughd Region (until recently called as Leninabad, and 4) new region Khatlon Region (created in 1993 by uniting the Qurghon Tepa and Kulob Regions).

The capital city of Dushanbe region is located in the western part of Tajikistan, its population accounts for more than 700,000[116]. It is interesting to note that Dushanbe has a relatively young history. The proclamation of the status of capital dates back only to the 1920s. Particularly this area has been chosen for new capital because of its convenient location for the construction of a railway. The city has originally been called Stalinobod, but during Khrushchev's *ottepeli* (course on de-Stalinization or dispelling the cult of Stalin) during the 1960s, it was renamed as Dushanbe. This name has likely been chosen for two reasons: the bazaar, a place known for ages as the center of trade, typically takes place on Monday (Dushanbe means Monday in Tajik), and the small river running within the city is called Dushanbinka.

All over the Soviet period, Dushanbe has mostly been populated with emigrants from the other soviet republics. Most of them had been of Slavic origin: Russians, Ukrainians, and Belarusians. It had been a result of the principles of the policies called *korenizatsiya* – a policy artificially aiming to mix the native population with the arrived population. For instance, population of Dushanbe in 1959 had counted only 13% Tajik. 30 years later in 1989, the situation had not been significantly changed: Tajiks constituted only but 39.1% of the capital's population. Only the social cataclysm of the Tajik civil war compelled the Rus-

---

115 Niyazi Aziz. (1997). 'Tadjikistan. Ot Sistemnogo Krizisa k Ustoychivomu Razvitiyu (From Systematic Crisis to Stabilized Development) In *Central Asia and the Caucasus* № 9, Sweden, p. 10. Retrieved from: http://www.ca-c.org/journal/09-1997/st_10_nijazi.shtml

116 King J., Noble J. and Humphreys, A. (1996). *Central Asia, A Lonely Planet Travel Survival Kit*. Lonely Planet Publications: Oakland, p. 428

sian-speaking population swiftly to leave country. Present-day statistics provides data explicitly illustrating the national changes in society: in 2003, the percentage of the Russian-speaking population constituted only 1% of the total population of the capital[117].

Next region for discussion is distinguished by its geographical location. This is the Badakhshan Autonomous Region (BAR). It is situated in the eastern part of Tajikistan. The population of this region enjoys life in one of the highest mountain ranges in the world, the Pomir (Pamir in Russian transliteration), that in Tajik is poetically called the roof of the world (*bomi jahon*). The highest peak of the Pomir mountains is called Ismoil Somoni (7495 meters), that in the Soviet period has ideologically been named the Peak of Communism. The population density is very sparse owing to the difficult conditions for living, the inaccessibility to other Tajik regions, the specific climate, and the potential for environmental disasters. Although it constitutes nearly 45% of Tajikistan's territory, its population accounts for only 3% of the country's actual total population[118]. The isolation of the region also results in the isolation of its population from the influence of most events throughout the country. In cultural terms, unlike the Tajik, the Pomir people speak an eastern dialect of Persian.

The third region is Khatlon Region, and it is located in the south of Tajikistan. It is the youngest region, having been formed by the unification of two previous regions, Kulob and Qurghon Tepa. The improvement of the economic situation and the acceleration of solutions towards social problems have been the primary reasons for unification. This area is bestowed with a rich agricultural sector. Cotton production has been the leading export priority for the region, supplying the lion's share of the budget, and has necessitated a massive labor force to uphold itself. Therefore, during the Soviet period, there had been an emphasis on increasing population settlement to this region. As a result, the region has become largely populated, especially by formerly nomadic tribesmen. The focus is more on agriculture and less on industry. The region is considered as a 'winner' of the civil war, in that Khatlon enjoys a privileged position in terms of governmental administration. As a case in point, almost a majority of Tajikistan's bureaucrats come from this area[119].

---

117 Tukmakov, D., Aleksandrov, V. (2003). *Tisyacha Vtoraya Noch. Jizn Posli Skazki* (One Thousond and Second Evening. Life After Fairy Tale). Zaftra 10(485), Russian Federation. Retrieved from: http://zavtra.ru/cgi/veil/data/zavtra/03/485/451.html

118 King J., Noble J. and Humphreys, A. (1996). *Central Asia, A Lonely Planet Travel Survival Kit.* Lonely Planet Publications, Oakland p. 429

119 Shapoatov, S. (2004). The Tajik Civil War: 1992-1997, p. 64.

The fourth region is Sughd. This region is situated in the northern part of Tajikistan. It is an interesting fact that the name of this region has been changed three times: in the pre-Soviet time it had been known as Khujand, during the Soviet era its name had been changed to Leninabad, and in the post-independence period in 2000, Leninabad had been renamed as Sughd. The capital is Khujand[120]. It is one of the oldest Tajik cities – according to some legends it has been founded by Alexander the Great - and the second largest city of the country. The geographical location of Khujand is in the famous Fergana Valley that is shared between Uzbekistan, Tajikistan, and Kyrgyzstan.

This region is regarded as the most sovitiezed. The Bolsheviks had appeared first in Sughd, and the majority of the Tajik Communist Party members came from here. It is the most economically and socially developed region of Tajikistan because of its connections with European achievements. According to data, Sughd's urbanization level in 1926 equaled that of Tajikistan as a whole in 1989[121]. During the Soviet period, it has been regarded as a region larger than Dushanbe because of the inclusion of some of the four biggest cities of the country: Khujand, Uro Tepa, Konibodom and Isfara[122].

Due to its geographical position, it is isolated from the other regions and is closer to Uzbekistan than to others parts of Tajikistan. It is also the most industrialized region. Sughd have been enjoying a kind of administrative privileges due to all the First Secretaries of the Party having originated from here since 1946 onward. As one of the potential guiltier parties in the run-up to the Tajik civil war – if one is to consider regionalism, namely, the conflict between the two major regions of Sughd and Khatlon, as the primary cause – Sughd region in the post-independence period could not be permitted to maintain its former position of power.

According to Sayfiddin Shapoatov, an author of the MA thesis titled *The Tajik Civil War: 1992-1997*, regionalism is one of the plausible reasons as to the origins of the civil war. The fact is there is no single region in Tajikistan, and in geographic terms, Tajikistan is not homogeneous, but rather is split into four separate regions or *oblasts*. The word *oblast* had been adopted from the Russian language since Soviet period and means the region, and is a standard administrative term.

---

120 Ilolov, Mamadsho & Khudoiev, Mirodasan. '*Local Government in Tajikistan, Developing New Races in the Old Environment*', p. 610

121 Rubin, Bernett. *Causes and Consequences of the Civil War in Tajikistan*, p. 21

122 Ibid.

Historically and geographically, each of regions – Dushanbe region, Badakhshan Autonomous Region (BAR), Khatlon region, and Sughd region – is distinguished by differing demographic, economic, and political criteria. The disproportional development of each of Tajikistan's region presupposes the seeding of discord within the country. The geographical isolation, for instance, of BAR region, has decreased the opportunities of its inhabitants to take an active part in socio-political life. In its turn, the inhabitants from Sughd traditionally controlled and managed the administration of high political power in the country. The nomenclature members come from this region as well. The leading position of Sughd's elites is a direct result of the local encouragement of educational opportunities that are extremely lacking in the other regions. The rapid boom in political-economic development of one region inevitably fires up the process of competition. As a consequence, the north and south have begun rivalries with each other for the placement in the ruling party.

It is interesting enough that Sughd representatives have ruled the country without sharing political power with the other regions. In a way, this has been a kind of monopoly in politics, or an explicit example of a one-party system. This continued until the 1970s when the Kulobis started to enjoy significant political power in the local administration of the south. However, the methods they had employed were far from decent and lawful standards, and they abused their posts to advance private interests. This did not hamper them from becoming a powerful political group during the period of perestroika, however as their rhetoric had been mostly colored in an anti-communist critique, namely anti-Sudhds, as they accused their northern brethren of being servants of the Kremlin.

The opportunity for a new political power – the Gharmis – to show up occurred during perestroika. The orientation to socio-political changes, the opportunity to discuss previously forbidden themes, and *glastnost* all together paved the way for a new party to come into being. Significantly, as a geographical reconciliation of the two opposite regions and political powers – Sughd and Kulobi (the Gharmis originate from both regions) – the new political force stood against the leading powers with the pretense of occupying their position.

Shapoatov argues:

> Their places of origin were divided into small regions and were under the control of the Sughdis. Those Gharmis living in Qurghon Tepa was under the control of Kulobi dominated administrations. Thus, they had little chance to climb upward. Majority of them established their way in Academic of Sciences and the newly emerging market economy. Perestroika gave the Gharmis the opportunity to form their own political parties. They gathered around the Democratic Party of Tajikistan (DPT) and the Islamic Renaissance

> Party. By joining these parties, they could stand up against the Sughdis and Kulobis (Shapoatov, p. 71)[123].

The issue of clan relations, so to speak, are generally ascribed to Central Asian political systems and as a issue must not be neglected here. In the definition of many researchers – Zviagelskaya Irina in *The Tajik Conflict* and Rubin Bernett in *Causes and Consequences of the Civil War in Tajikistan* as the prominent examples – clan relations, rather than mafia-like relations, have influenced on the way of life in Soviet Tajikistan. The patronage and mobilization are the key components of clan relations that explain the popularity of this type of administrative governance. Territorial identity as a process has been forging through the agricultural economy, the strong dependence on Moscow's subsidies and the spreading of the kolkhoz and sovkhozs with a particular leader or patron. In the situation of the fierce competition for resources precisely the clan relations had helped to mobilize people's forces and to go through the soviet standards and norms of living. This has resulted wide spreading of the clans or enlarged families as an essential phenomenon within the unstable character of the agricultural economy.

In my view, the prominence of family values might provide a kind of psychological explanation as to the validity and 'rootedness' of clan relations as a form of governance. Traditionally, the Tajiks perceive and accept forms associated with family relations because the institution of the family has been the prism through which all Tajiks view life and the world around them.

The economic development of the regions have also varied significantly. The Sughdis have become dependent on central subsidies, and when this amount has dwindled to nothing, their political power simultaneously has shackled. The Kulobis, on the other hand, relied on their own forces and managed to control their local economy and politics. The competition between these two regions is a source of rivalry even after the civil war has ended.

Generally, outbreak of the Soviet-Afghan War has affected all four regions, and in my interpretation, has united them under an ideological basis. Henceforth, the war was seen as an ideological battle between Soviet atheism and Islam. The Muslim Tajiks had experienced a religious vacuum for 70 years, and they finally found a chance to openly practice their religion by supporting Islam. The young generation had especially inclined to support the rebirth of Islam, seeing it as a dynamic and vital foil to conservative and imposed Marxism. In comparison

123 Shapoatov, S. (2004). *The Tajik Civil War: 1992-1997*, The Graduate School of Social Of Middle East Technical University Sciences p. 71

with the out- of -date ideology of Marxism the spreading of Islam had a powerful unifying factor. In this context, the Sughdis had been perceived as nothing more than local communists, and their influence subsequently vanished. The authorities had become sidestepped, and community members increasingly began to confide in unofficial Muslim representatives, such as those who personally made the decisions in the unofficial buildings of mosques and madrasas.

I partly agree with Shapoatov's opinion concerning the causes of the Tajik civil war. In his opinion, Islam, regionalism, and external factors led to the civil war, although he adds that these factors are not the single contributors to begin the civil war. His argument is that all of the three factors played an active and equal role in the conflict. In the case of the absence of *any of* these factors, such a brutal as the civil war would not have taken place.

Both sides, soon after the end of the civil war, came to understand its causes and consequences, as well as the unpredictability of resolving conflicts by force in the future. The important role in establishing negotiation and communication links was played by the international community, specifically Russia, Iran, and the United Nations have been engaged in a peace-making settlement.

In the process of political negotiations, Emomali Rahmon represented the government of the Republic of Tajikistan (RT) and Said Abdulloi Nuri represented the United Tajik Opposition (UTO). These mentioned negotiations under UN patronage, and with the participation of the abovementioned countries, lasted four years[124].

- 1 round (5-15 April in Moscow)
- 2 round (18 – 25 June 1994 in Tehran- Islamic Republic of Iran)
- 3 round (20 October – 1 November 1994 in Islamabad - Pakistan)
- 4 round (22 May –1 June 1995 in Almaty- Kazakhstan)
- 5 round (3-24 November 1995, 26 January - 18 February, 8 - 21 July 1996 in Ashkhabad- Turkmenistan)
- 6 round (5 January –19 February 1997 in Mashhad and Tehran - Islamic Republic of Iran)
- 7 round (26 February - 9 March 1997 in Moscow- Russian Federation)
- 8 round (9 April - 28 May in Tehran- Islamic Republic of Iran)

On 27 June 1997, both sides have signed the "General Agreement on Establishment of Peace and National Reconciliation in Tajikistan" in Moscow, which is commonly known as the General Agreement. The main instrument of the

124 Shapoatov S. (2004). *The Tajik Civil War:1992-1997.*

achievement of the General Agreement has been embodied in the creating of the National Reconciliation Committee (NRC), including 26 members – 13 members from Government of the RT and 13 from UTO. The Chairman of NRC has been appointed the UTO leader Sayeed Abullo Nuri and his deputy chairman Abdulmajid Dostiev, the Deputy speaker of the Tajik Parliament (Majlisi Oli).

The abovementioned commission (NRC) consisted of four sub-committees that focused on military, political, juridical, and refugee issues. In every sub-committee, three representatives from both the government and the UTO were present. It has been on behalf of NRC's productive relations, that all war prisoners had been freed in line with the Act on Mutual Forgiveness and the Amnesty Law.

The temporary government has been divided between the Tajik Government and the UTO. According to the General Agreement on Peace, 30% of the government ministries would be represented by members of the UTO[125].

According to the analytics, during the civil war, by 1997, about 100,000 were killed and thousands had become handicapped. However, unofficially, according to the opposition, the number of people killed was as high as 300,000, which is more than 5% of the country's total population[126]. About one million people became refugees, and even more people were displaced[127]. The socio-economic situation has improved since then, however, 60% of the total population continues to live below the poverty line. About 50,000 homes were damaged. The costs of the war are valued at about US$ 7 billion.[128] As it has been reported:

> After declining an estimated 40% between 1990 and 1993, industrial production dropped another 31% in 1994. Declines in the Dushanbe and Sughd regions exceeded that figure. The most serious declines were in chemicals, engineering, metal processing, building materials, light industry, and food processing. According to government reports, production declines generally were greater in privately owned industries than in state enterprises[129].

---

125 Ibid.

126 Bushkov, V.I. & Mikulsky D.V. (1993). *Anatomiya Grajdanskoy Voyni v Tadjikistane* (Anatomy of Tajik Civil War). Institute of Ethnology and Anthropology of the Russian Academy of Sciences: Moscow, p. 87

127 Kuzmin, A.I. (2001). The Causes and Lessons of the Civil War. In Alexei Vassiliev (Ed.), *Central Asia: political and economic challenges in the post-Soviet era*, Saqi Books: London, p. 175.

128 Toshmuhammadov, M. (2004). *Civil War in Tajikistan and Post-Conflict Rehabilitation*. Hokkaido University Center of Slavic Researches.

129 Zickel, R.(1996). *Kazakstan, Kyrgyzstan, Tajikistan, Turkmenistan, Uzbekistan*, U.S. Library of Congress, USA. Retrieved from: http://countrystudies.us/tajikistan/

The oscillation of the war situation with no one absolute winner has fired up the total instability and crisis: in one day the building of the Government has happened to be in the hands of the opposition, and another day - in the hands of the Ex-communists. The economic costs have included the unsteadiness in paying budget salaries and total weakness of government functions and responsibilities. One can say that the government has ceased to exist because of the intense state of the civil war. Those who have hopefully survived owe a great deal to the traditional institutions rather when to any kind of governmental support. In mahallas, people have been helping each other by sharing food and other necessary products. In this case, avlod, the traditional Tajik kin, has played an exceptionally important role. Migration within the country has become a typical phenomenon, as people have been fleeing from the war-torn areas to resettle in more stable ones, where they could live in the houses of their avlod members (there have even been cases of more than 100 people living under a single roof!). The avlod has provided the refugees with necessary products, shelter and moral support.

The achievement of independence has initiated a significant political change. On the 6th of November, 1994, a new constitution has been adopted. According to it, the Republic of Tajikistan is a sovereign, democratic, law-abiding, secular, and united state[130]. The constitution is saturated with an expression of the aspirations to transform the political system and replace the Soviet state institutions with democratic ones. Interestingly enough, almost all Tajiks continue to be devoted Muslims, while Tajikistan in official level has been proclaimed as a secular state where religion by definition must be separated from the state.[131]

As I have mentioned before, Tajik culture's ideal is to shape all human relationships on the model of the close ties exhibited between family members. In mahalla, everybody is treated as a member of the family. This has a particular importance in the case of women. One of the most dramatic consequences of the civil war has been an uncertain fate of young girls – almost deprived to get married - and increased number of widows. After the civil war, many young people have found themselves without job's opportunities that as a push factor has stimulated the seasonal labour migration. Many educated professionals have left for Russia and other neighboring countries, and as a result, significant numbers of children have been left without their parent's supervision. The scale of these prob-

130 *Constitution of the Republic of Tajikistan* (1994). Retrieved from: http://unpan1.un.org/intradoc/groups/public/documents/untc/unpan003670.htm

131 Milikbekova, M.(2005). *Irregular Migration and Human Rights: Tajik Irregular Migrant Workers in Russia*. Lund: Sweden.

lems is demonstrated by the fact that, according to the estimate prepared under the auspices of the Dushanbe office of the International Organization of Migration (IOM), up to 500,000 Tajiks leave the country each year in search of seasonal work. Unofficial statistics claims that upwards of one million Tajik migrants is working in the Russian Federation.[132] Certainly, Russia is the main country of destination for migrants looking for seasonal jobs, but it is not the only one. In less amount, the Tajiks are also migrating to Europe and other Asian countries.

Mahalla has still preserved its character and existing institution under the auspices of Islam. As it has been mentioned above, almost all of the inhabitants of Central Asia are Sunni Muslims belonging to the Hanafi school, the most tolerate sect of Islam[133]. Islam regulates nearly all aspects of the life of a devoted follower. It regulates the behavior of believers according to the al-Qur'an and the sayings of the Prophet (PBUH)- hadiths. Imitating the Prophet is praised in Islam, and pious Muslims try to replicate Prophet's actions in a detailed way. Because of this reason, Islam has deep roots in the social life of Central Asia, particularly among the Tajiks and Uzbeks. Religion has a significant influence among these two nations because of their systematic way of life and sophisticated educational institutions.. However, it is important to mention that after collapse of Soviet Union, people are also becoming more religious in Kazakhstan and Kyrgyzstan.

In spite of seventy years of anti-religious campaigns, most of Central Asia's people are continuing to identify themselves as Muslims[134]. This was in spite of that fact that some of them did not actively practice religion (the five pillars of Islam). It is very interesting that even active members of the Communist Party identified themselves as believers. For instance, according to a statistic conducted by the International Foundation for Election Systems (IFES), in 1996, 97% of the inhabitants of Tajikistan stated that they believed in God, with 90% of adults (18 years and older) identified themselves as Muslims[135].

---

132 Ibid.

133 Muminov, A. K. (1999). Traditsionnie i Sovremennie Religiozno-Teologicheskie Shkoli v Tsentralnoy Azii (Traditional and Modern Religio-Theological Schools in Central Asia. In *Central Asia and the Caucasus* № 5, Sweden. Retrieved from: http://www.ca-c.org/journal/cac-05- 1999/st_13_muminov.shtml

134 Abdullaev, E. (1997). 'Islam i Islamskiy Faktor v Sovremennom Uzbekistane (Islam and Islamic Factor in Modern Uzbekistan)', In *Central Asia and the Caucasus* № 6, Sweden, Retrieved from: http://www.ca-c.org/journal/cac-05-1999

135 Olimova, Saodat (1999). Political Islam and Conflict in Tajikistan', In Lena Jonson and Murad Esenov *Political Islam and Conflicts in Russia and Central Asia*, Conference Paper no. 24, The Swedish Institute of International Affairs: Stockholm.

As it currently stands in post-Soviet Central Asia, Tajikistan is the only country where an Islamic Party is officially registered. After the civil war, the Islamic Renaissance Party has become an official party in the Tajik Parliament. Following independence, every mahalla has begun to open its mosques. Some of them even have more than one or two. It all depends on the financial welfare of the mahalla. For example, in the western part of Tajikistan where I have conducted a major part of the interviews for my research, one mahalla has counted mosques. The number of Islamic schools, madrasas, and mullahs has been also rapidly increasing.

It is necessary to note that every mahalla has good relations with its neighbouring mahallas. They support each other through hashar during the run-up to the celebration of various ceremonies. Also, during weddings and funerals, people from the neighbouring mahallas come to help to organize the event in a proper way. Mahallas cooperate with each other in important issues. In regards to providing the needy with the necessary help the financial support comes from the mahalla's fund.

> *It is not possible to live without cooperation with other mahallas. Neighboring mahallas are like our personal members and relatives. We help them in their problems and they also help us. We support each other in difficulties and share our happiness. If they have hashar, people from our mahalla will go to help them, and if we have hashar, they will come to help us. We are living like this. Every mahalla has a special transport for the council of elders and other members of the mahalla. If there is a funeral in another mahalla, rais, mulla, and council of elders go with this transport to that mahalla and they will do the same to us. Our elders have good relations with neighboring mahallas and try to avoid any conflicts. We marry from neighboring mahallas and they marry from our mahalla. That's why we have very close relations with them (man, 35 years old, economist. June, 2011).*

2.2. Structure of mahalla

2.2.1. Social composition of mahalla

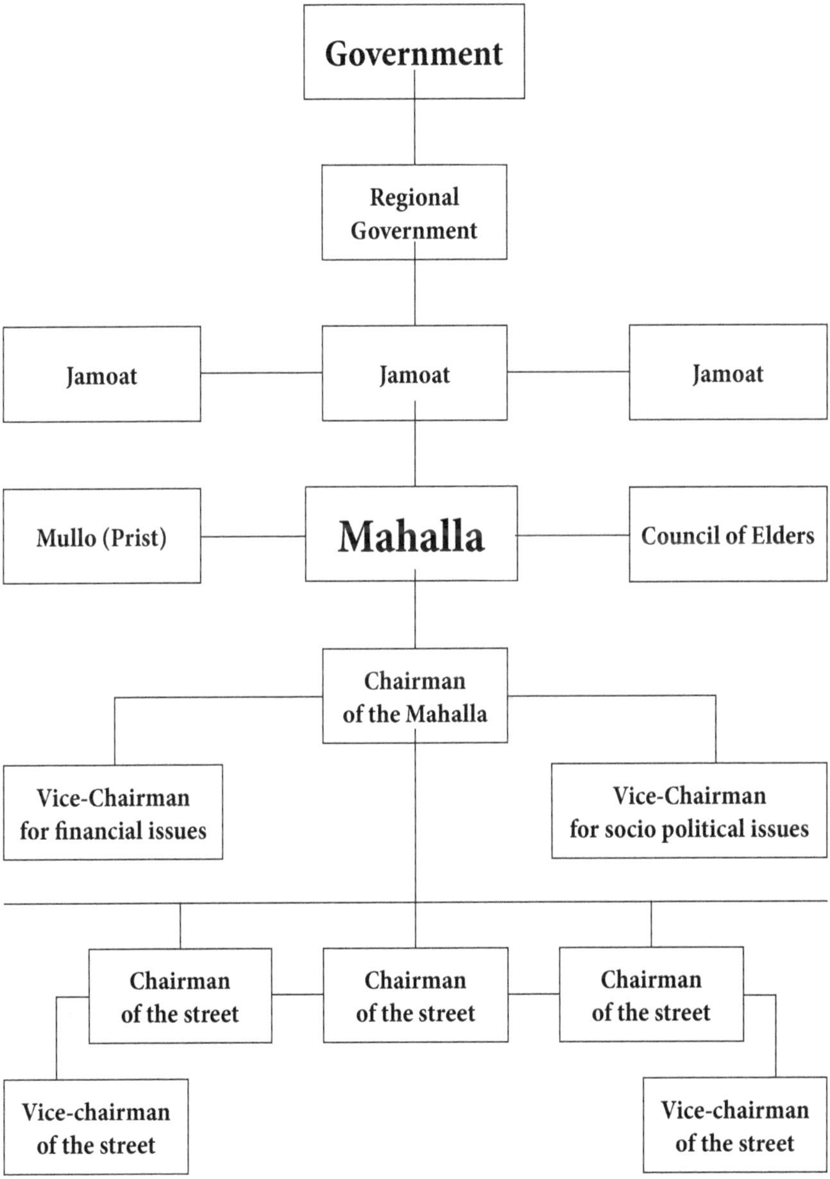

2.2.2. The Head of the Mahalla

From the organizational point of view, every mahalla has its own leader – the chairman of the mahalla (*raisi mahalla*) – that is chosen by the members of that community. *Rais* in the Tajik language means' head' or 'chairman'. Traditionally, as we have noticed in the first chapter, concerning the position of *raisi mahalla*, predominantly elders have been chosen in most cases. However, in present day reality the candidates of young or average age are also present. For becoming a *raisi mahalla* or being a candidate for this position, first and foremost it is necessary to enjoy the respect among the community members. The *rais* must be educated, active, and gain the trust of members of the community; for the members of the community fell confidence that electing *rais* will entrust them in achieving the betterment for all. The candidates for this position are determined in the meeting of the elders prior to the vote, that are called majlis. The place of such meetings of the council of elders can be the mosques, tea-houses (*choikhona*), or some other special places where mature males meet and debate their interests and concerns for their community.[136] Majlis took place in the mosque, voting took part in the form of rising a hand, or in writing the name of candidates and putting them in a box. The result of the elections is announced at the same day.

As I have mentioned above in my dissertation, I have been conducting interviews in different parts of Tajikistan. Asking them about *raisi mahalla*, almost all of them have expressed a positive view about their head of the mahalla. Only in one mahalla I have met some people criticizing the *rais* in such a way that the question of re-election has been risen. I think it is relevant to exemplify one of the respondents' opinion about what qualities an ideal *rais* must represent.

> Respondent 1:
> *Every person who is chosen for this position (I mean the position of rais) must be an ideal rais. If rais –the head of mahalla- is not ideal and does not care about his community, people do not need him. Mahalla inhabitants will immediately change him. An ideal rais has to be like a caring father. He has to do all his best for his mahalla. He must be present in the happy days and in the bad days, and always be with his people (I mean in the weddings and funerals). Rais has to be aware of the problems of mahalla and try to solve them. The head of mahalla must be equal and helpful in relation with rich people and poor people (with persons with high administration position and simple inhabitants). He has to work for developing of our mahalla. Together with the council of elders, he has to solve the mahalla's problems. We choose him as our rais; it means that he is our representative to the governmental administration. He must support our interests in relation with the government (Male, 58 years old, teacher. July, 2011).*

---

136 Geiss, P. G. (2001). Mahalla and kinship relations: A study of residential communal commitment structures in Central Asia of the nineteenth century. In *Central Asian Survey*, 20 (1) pp. 97-106.

Raisi mahalla has two vice rais (*jonishin* in Tajik language), one is responsible for financial issues and the other - for the social issues of the community. Every street has its heads of streets -*raisi guz*ar - who are chosen by the people of the given streets. *Raisi mahalla* is notified about the results of the selection. Every week on Fridays, *raisi mahalla* has a meeting with the heads of streets in the mosque. Sometimes the meeting takes place twice a week or twice a month. It depends on the needs of the community. Friday is the only mandated day for permanent meetings, and regular meetings are held after the Friday prayers. However, in the case of some urgent problems requiring immediate solutions, the meetings might take place the other days. Such extraordinary meetings are held at the request of the heads of the streets. In the meeting they inform *raisi mahalla* about some important problem of the community and give a report about what they have done during the last week. *Raisi of mahalla* considers the issues and gives them advice on what to do during the next week. The heads of the *guzars* are responsible for the cleanness of the streets. Their other duties include the issue of water, electricity, and the resolution of family conflicts. In the case of conflicts, when their intervention does not bring any reconciliation, the matter will be referred to the head of the mahalla. The rule is that the head of the mahalla tries to find a solution to this conflict without resorting to the assistance of the police or the courts. Such cases rarely go to the police. Even if both sides of the conflicts want to go to police, they must have the permission of the head of mahalla. Such kind of behavior applies to all members of the mahalla regardless of their profit, possessions, and roles outside of the community.

Every member of the mahalla is equal in the community, and for this reason everyone has to respect all the rules. *Raisi mahalla* has an especially important role in organizing weddings. In the wedding ceremonies, he is an important advisor to that family. He will discuss everything with the family members and he will help them. The head of mahalla nominates people in different places for serving guests. It is traditional that Tajiks have many guests at their weddings (in the case of weddings organized by rich people, the number of guests goes up to a few thousand people). The weddings last from three days up to one week. *Raisi mahalla* helps in seating everyone, and he mobilizes the members of mahalla to serve the guests of the mahalla.

The guests take their seats related to their position and prestige in the community. In the terms of hospitability for guests outside of the mahalla the special separate places are always prepared. *Raisi mahalla* along with the head of the family, supervise the ceremony until the last guest leaves. The head of the mahalla observes how his members service the guests. Another important role of *raisi mahalla* includes the organization of funeral ceremonies. He sends special messengers to inform all the about the death of one of fellow residents. It is the duty of every mahalla member to gather at the home of the deceased. They may even help that family financially if it is within their means. Every member of the community gives money as much as capable of giving. From this money, *rais* buys all the necessary things for the ceremony. He also sends special people to the ceremony to prepare the place to lay the deceased. In addition, he also supervises the washing of the body, and in the case of the absence of remaining relatives who can perform this task, he will delegate another mahalla member to do this. The family and home residents of the deceased are free from any obligations on this day. The members of the mahalla do the organizational work. The guests from far areas are invited to quarter with the neighbors of the deceased. They are welcome all night. At least one person from every household must participate in the burial ceremony. It is usual for two or three people to participate from every house. The duration of the mourning period depends on the territory of the mahalla. It is accepted that during this time, people will not organize any wedding ceremonies out of respect to their fellow mahalla mourners. It may last in some cases anywhere from a week to forty days (in the case of the larger mahallas).

Funerals are called *janoza* in Tajik, which is in turn derived from the Arabic *janazah*. According to Islamic tradition, the funeral takes place as soon as possible, usually on the actual day of death. In the case that some relatives or family members need to arrive from abroad, the people will be kept for one or two days. According to religion and *sunnah*[137], the corpse should be washed (*ghusl*, meaning 'bathed') exactly the bathing of the corpse is an important ritual of Islamic Sharia. Therefore, it should take place as soon as possible after death, preferably within a few hours afterwards. The "washers" are normally adult members of the immediate family and of the same gender as the dead. After bathing the dead body, the corpse is usually wrapped in a simple white plain cloth (*kafan*). Later, the members of the community gather to offer their collective prayers for the forgiveness of any transgressions committed by the dead person. This prayer is called *amozi janoza* in Tajik and it means 'funeral prayer'. The corpse is then taken for burial (*dafn*). The grave should be aligned perpendicular to the *Qibla*[138] (in the direction to Mecca,

---

137 *Sunnah* – The word sunnah is derived from the Arabic (سنة), which means "habit" or "usual practice". In Islam, the word sunnah has come to denote the way the Prophet Muhammad (PBUH) has lived his life. It is the second source of Islamic jurisprudence (the first is Al-Quran).

138 Qiblah comes from the Arabic (قبلة) and means direction. It is a direction that should be faced by the Muslims during everyday pray, salah (namaz). Qiblah is set as the direction of the Kaaba in Mecca (Saudi Arabia). There are wall niches in the

the holy city for all Muslims). The body is positioned in the grave without a casket, lying on its right side, and facing the *Qibla*. It should be noted that in Central Asian cultures, women are generally discouraged from participating in the funeral and entering the cemeteries. I have personally heard two opinions. Some people say it is forbidden for women to attend because usually they are very emotional and they will wail loudly in the cemetery. Other people say that this is because women traditionally have not been the members of avlod. Depending on the circle of friends of the deceased the funeral might include from several hundred to thousand guests.

Funeral participation is one of the reciprocal rules of traditional Tajik culture. The Tajiks justify this kind of behavior by acknowledging that if they help their neighbor today, their neighbor will help them tomorrow. Absence from funeral ceremonies violates the rules of living of the community. As a result, a person who has not participated in the funeral ceremony is no longer respected in the community. If the head of one family is sick or has left the region, one of his children should take his place and participate in the ceremony. Raisi or one of his vice-rais checks the community's attendance at the funeral. According to Islam, everyone is a brother to each other. The presence at the funeral is regarded not only as an obligation, but as a manifestation of love for the deceased and his family. The inhabitants of the community express this through the following slogan: we have to be together in all times, as well in a happy time and unhappy time. As I have mentioned in the above chapters concerning the history of the mahalla in accordance to Tajik tradition, the memory of the deceased is celebrated by a feast after seven, twenty, and forty days, and also after the one- year anniversary of their departure. On this occasion, the deceased's family prepares food and invites people from the mahalla as well as from other mahallas. One of my respondents argued:

> *In such a day, we have to support each other. This day is not mourning only for the family of the dead person. It is a mourning day for all of us. Because such a black day (we call it like this) has entered to our community. We believe in God and we believe in the death. Nobody can escape death. Death will enter each house. Today it is in our neighbor's house and tomorrow it will come to our house. That's why we have to be ready and we have to support our brothers in such a situation. In that day, and also till the seven days, all mahalla members help that family. Because in such a situation it is very hard for them. You know how difficult it is to lose someone from your family. Therefore, we organize everything. For example; we buy the necessary things for the ceremony, we prepare our houses for the guests who are coming from other regions, and we send our special people to prepare a grave for*

---

mosques called mehrob which indicates the Qiblah. All Muslims are praying towards the same point, and it is symbolize the unity of all Muslims from all over the world under the Law of God.

the dead person. All these are our duties and it is our obligations. Even I could say that more than obligation and duty. In my opinion, if somebody does not support and help in such situation, he is not a real human and he cannot live among us. One day he also will die. Who will bury him?(man, 53 years old. September, 2010.)

The dishes and other accessories that are needed to organize for such events are purchased from the mahalla's funds, and, therefore, they become the common property of all members. In every mosque there is a special room for the keeping of such things (dishes, carpets, etc.). For weddings, feats, and other kinds of ceremonies, they can borrow these items and return them clean and washed. There are also special cooks in the mahalla who prepare different kinds of traditional meals during ceremonies. The cooks presiding over all ceremonies are always male. There are also some female cooks, but they only prepare some meals for the ceremonies where most of the participants are traditionally women.

As it has previously been emphasized, every mahalla has some finances that are collected through the voluntary contribution of all members of the community. The members of the mahalla often gather in the mahalla meetings to discuss and solve the problems of the community. For example, they also decide if it is necessary to construct new public buildings, hospitals, schools, mosques, teahouses, houses for widowers, housing for the elderly, and other buildings. The source of all these works is a voluntary contribution. Using this source, they also organize weddings and the circumcision ceremonies for orphaned children. To promote good health among young people, the mahalla builds special places for sports activities, especially for the national Tajik sport of *gushtingiri*[139] (wrestling). The mahalla organizes *gushtingiri* competitions once a year. The prizes for the winners are purchased from the fund of the mahalla. Mahalla also organizes *buzkashi* [140](goat game) which is a traditional team sport played on horseback.

---

139 *Gushtingiri* is a Tajik national wrestling kind of sport. According to old-aged rules, the wrestlers have to wear chapans (traditional coats) and to fasten soft belts around their waists. During the Soviet time, traditional coats were replaced by judo jackets and belts. It is a bare fisted fight in which the combatants engage in battle. The purpose is either to knock the rival down and pin his shoulders to the mat, or if not, to incapacitate him, allowing the scoring of points. From: Abdullaev & Akbarzaheh (2010). *Historically Dictionary of Tajikistan*. Second edition.

140 *Buzkashi* is traditional game for Central Asia. Besides Tajikistan it is very popular as a national sport in Afghanistan as well. Mostly, it is compared to polo. Both games are played between players on horseback, both are focused on propelling an object toward a goal, and both get quite rough. The aim of a Buzkashi player (which is called *chowandoz* in Tajik) is to grasp the headless goat and then get it clear of the other players and throw it across a target line.

141

141 Retrieved May 13, 2012, from: CX9dVS5dROU/UDKGd7srjWI/AAAAAAAAAWA/V3LUjIcGnbs/s1600/Novruz.jpg

142

142 Retrieved from: http://www.todaysaccheadlines.com/2011/03/pictures-of-day_23.html

Another important action of mahalla members is keeping the area clean and providing water to the community members. For this purpose, members construct artesian wells and channels to carry water to the fields and gardens. This network of channels requires constant maintenance. From their financial resources, specialists are also paid for regulating the flow of water from the field to field. If necessary, the committee organizes the delivery of water and garbage disposal. Also cooperation includes the modernization of houses by bringing the amenities of water and gas to them. Some mahalla includes live-in neighborhood doctors to perform prophylactic medical examinations for the mahalla members[143].

Mahalla is also financially supporting the arrangement of such ceremonies as weddings and circumcisions for children from poor families. On the base of my observation, in one well-off mahalla in Hisor region, on the celebration of *Navruz* (a New Year celebration generated from pre-Islamic Persian tradition, which is annually celebrated on the 21st of March), 25 weddings and 40 ceremonies of circumcision have been organized on the basis of voluntary financial contributions. In the case that the collected financial resources are not enough to pay for a ceremony, so the members of another mahalla are eager to support economically the event's organization. [144] When I was asking my respondents about how they had managed to solve economic issues of mahalla, one of them answered:

> *For solving mahalla issues, usually rais, council of elders, mulla, and a person with high authority in the mahalla gather for a meeting. They have the special meeting where they discuss the problems and the way of solving them. Every mahalla has its financial funds from voluntary contributions and also some inhabitants of mahalla give their zakat to this fund. If the project is too expensive and the mahalla fund is not enough, we will do meetings with local businessman and everybody helps as much as he can.*
> *Concerning our successes, in autumn 2009, in our mahalla, we have built the biggest mosque in our republic. People built it through hashar. All mahalla members and even people from other mahallas and other regions, came and helped us. Also, we reconstructed one building of our hospital and two buildings of our school. We also built a sports complex and a mini stadium. From voluntary contribution, we have reconstructed houses for the widows of our mahalla. In spring in the day of Navruz, we organized weddings for 25 families and 40 ceremonies of circumcisions. Every year in the Navruz celebration we organize weddings for poor families. These are the main successes, except these every day we are doing something for our mahalla* (male, 38 years old, mahalla member. July, 2011.)

---

143 Jasiewicz, Z. Mahalla w Uzbekistanie. Tradycyjna Społeczność Dzielnic Miejskich w Życiu Współczesnym. (Mahalla In Uzbekistan. Tradition and Urban social districts In modern life)

144 Sievers, (2002). Uzbekistan's Mahalla: From Soviet to Absolutist Residential Community Associations. In The *Journal of International and Comparative Law at Chicago-Kent*: Volume 2.

145

One of the pillars of Islam is giving a *zakat*, a kind of the tax contributed from the wealthy people to the common source of community. It means that every rich person has to give some percentage from his income to poor people. *Zaka*t

145 Navruz celebration in Dushanbe, Tajikistan, 25 of March in 2012. Retrieved from: http://rus.ozodi.org/content/article/24526525.html

(2.5% from the annual rate)is responsibility of Muslims to minimize the economic challenges and to reduce the level of inequality in society. It may be realized in two forms: by giving money or by satisfying other needs of the community. Usually *zakat* is given during Ramazan, the holy month for Muslims. The person who wants to give *zakat* comes to *raisi mahalla,* or *mulla*, or *khatib*[146] of the mosque to discuss *zakat* issues. They choose amount of money and prepare a list of needy people in the mahalla. After preparing this, *raisi mahalla*, mulla and one representative from that person will give *zakat* to the members of the community. Frequently it is in form of money or 100 kg of flour or oil.

Raisi mahalla serves as a mediator between the mahalla and the local government (*hukumat*). *Hukumat* is the authority administration of the region that consists of several jamoats. The heads of *hukumats* are chosen and dismissed by the president, and later on they are presented to their respective administrative councils for approval. If a community has some problems or questions, *raisi mahalla* directly informs the *hukumat* about it. Employees of the state administration, should they intend to find something out about the mahalla, will call *raisi mahalla* and speak with him. Moreover, in the case of land distribution for new families, *rais* serves acts as a member of the governmental commission for being acquainted with the number of the needy families and their legitimacy to require the piece of land.

2.2.3 The role of mullah, the council of elders, and duties of mahalla members.

Each neighborhood community has its council of elders – called *Shuroi muysafedon* in Tajik-, aims to solve local social issues and conflicts among members of the mahalla. Such social institutions act informally and they are not defined by law. The composition of the council of elders consists of men of old age that enjoy the respect among the community members. Traditionally, in the past, *rais* has been elected by elderly people and automatically might occupy a membership in the council of elders. However, nowadays it happens that for the position of *raisi mahalla,* a young candidate is sometimes elected. In such a situation, he is no more eligible for being a member of the council. The members of the council are elected in the meeting of community members which is held in the mosque after Friday prayer. Every member of the community has to accept the decisions of the committee of elders. This is because elders enjoy a great respect among all

146 Khatib is from the Arabic term خطيب (khaṭīb), meaning a person who delivers the sermon (khuṭbah) during the Friday prayer and Eid prayers.

the community members. This council advises the head of mahalla, who in most cases adheres to their advice because of the respect according to them because of their age, experience, and authority among the community members. The council is the first institution to which people appeal in the case of conflicts. Only then, when the council is unable to solve the conflict, the matter will be referred to the competence of the *rais*. The members of council help *rais* in organizing such abovementioned duties as weddings, funerals, and sports competitions. One of their primary obligations is the taking care of orphans, elder people, and others needy fellowmen. They also help to resolve community problems, family conflicts, and generally, their work aims to preserve the peaceful climate in the community. In other words, through *Shuroi muysafedon*, i.e. institution of self-government, the community can fully function harmoniously.

***Imam khatib* with the Council of Elders in Tuda mahalla**

As I have already explained above, one of the customs of Tajiks is *hashar*, social (unpaid) work for the community. *Hashar* work is directed to the cleaning of the streets and the reconstruction of schools, mosques, libraries, and other public places. The heads of the streets select at least one person from every house to do such work. [147]. Street cleaning days are obligatory and mahalla residents gather and clean the areas near their houses. *Hashar* work includes aiding mahalla members in the construction of new homes. It is worth noting that all of these services are provided free of charge. The mahalla is like one big family, and thus, every member is sincerely eager to help. *Hashar* also traditionally includes assistance to one another in organizing the events of the Islamic Holy holidays of Ramazan and Qurban Eid. As a rule, people will organize the cleaning of mosques, cemeteries, and other places throughout the village before the religious holidays commence. The cleaning of cemeteries before these days is like an unwritten rule for all the members of the mahalla. Personally, I have been witnessing the work of one hasher in Hisor region, in the village of Tuda. Apropos, to mention that people of this village with honor have been assisting in the building of the largest mosque in Tajikistan, named after *Imomi A'zam*[148] (Abuhanifa Rahmatullohi Alayh). The grand opening of the mosque took place in October of 2009. In this *hashar*, even people from other regions proposed initiatives to help in building the mosque, the largest in contemporary Tajikistan (such a kind of *hashar* is regarded as being the most honorable of work).

Asking one of my interviewees about the responsible person for decision-making on organization of *hashar*, he has answered the following:

> *Usually the council of elders and rais make the decision about hashar. In hasher, at least one person from every house must participate. However, usually between two and four people participate in hashar. I personally participate in all hashars (of course if I am in our mahalla during the organization of hashar). If not, then my sons will go instead of me. Rais or mulla will announce the date of hashar in the mosque before or after performing prayer. There are hashars which everybody knows the exact dates. For example, before the Ramadan and Qurban holidays, we go and clean cemeteries, streets and other public places. In these hashars, all mahalla members gather without any announcement of hashar, because it has already been a part of their life and religion for centuries.*
>
> *People who by reason of the obligation outside the mahalla (for example working in the government or doing business) cannot participate in hashar, they will send somebody else instead of them. Sometimes they come in the morning to the place to present themselves and tell Rais their obligations, and they then go to their jobs. In some other cases, if such people cannot participate in hashar, they provide food for workers during hashar. (Respondent 3. Head of mahalla, 52 years old. September, 2010).*

147 Dadabaev, T. (2006). *Changing nature of the mahalla: Outcomes of the project*. Tokyo: RICAS

148 Nu'man bin Thabit bin Zuta bin Marzuban (699 — 767 CE / 80 — 148 AH)is better known and is famous as Imām Abū Ḥanīfah or *Al-Imām al-A'zam*, (the Great Imam), he was the founder of the Sunni Hanafi School of fiqh (Islamic jurisprudence).

The mosque named by Imomi A'zam in the village of Tuda, Hisor region, Tajikistan

The residents of mahalla in Hisor region during hashar (community, volunteering work)

149

149 The elders of mahalla are starting work in the building of mosque. It is believed that in hashars and other community works, elders must start the work and after that others may continue working.

[150]

150 The people of Qizil Namuna mahalla took part in a hashar: they are digging a trench for 4-kilometer pipe for providing drinking water for their community. Retrieved from: http://centralasia.usaid.gov/sites/default/files/pdfs/success_story_090915_en_kizil_manuma_taj.pdf

It is necessary to note that every mahalla member in accordance with unwritten rule feels responsibility for their families, community members, and for entire mahalla. They have to participate in certain rituals of mahalla. Even in the case when the son of the family moves to another mahalla and his parents are already dead, he continues to be a member of his father mahalla and has to take part in the rituals of this community. Also, he should take part in the mahalla's events where he came from. Such a custom helps to preserve the roots of families. The member of the mahalla remembers his parents, and the taking part of their son is important and analytical for them. He displays his respect for the community by participating in important events. One of my respondents spoke about his duties as a mahalla member:

> *As a member of mahalla, I have to live according to its rules. I have to participate in hashars, funerals, and weddings, and I have to help and respect all members like they are my own family. I have to respect people older than me. I have to keep the image of my family in my community. I have to be a good person and helpful to people. First of all, I have to take care of my parents because I am living for them. They brought me to this world and they did all the best. My first duty is to help them and to take care of them. I want them to be happy. I do not want anything more than my parent's happiness (Ph.D. student 27years old. June, 2011.).*

One of the important exercising authorities in the life of mahalla is the *Mulla* or *Imam Khatib.* He is the undisputable religious authority of the community. As a *raisi mahalla* he is also elected by community members. It is a rule that the candidates for this position must have a good religious education. Among his duties is the teaching of Al-Qur'an, hadith, Shariat law, and traditional morals (Adab). The members of the mahalla are addressing him in all religious matters. He advises people how to arrange religious ceremonies. It is worthy to note that in most situations, the members of mahalla elect their *mulla* through competition. *Mulla* is responsible for the religious aspect of the weddings. Before certain events such as weddings, trips abroad, or building houses, Tajiks customarily go to mulla asking for a blessing. In addition, mulla must participate in all funeral ceremonies where he will read Al- Qur'an and pray for the deceased. He may also participate in the funerals of other mahallas as a representative of his community together with the council of elders.

Writing about the place of tradition, the role of mahalla in maintaining certain elements of the socio-cultural model with its supreme values should be noted. These values are consistency, a great family, and an integrated local community. Committee members will visit the quarrelling spouses and try to persuade them to avoid divorce. The main arguments in preventing divorce are the miserable future fate of children from broken homes and the scant chances of re-marriage for a divorced man and women.

2.2.4. The role of women in mahalla

Separately, it is necessary to note the role of women in the authorities of mahalla. It is consistent with the tradition that certain functions of mahalla can be realized by women. For example *Bibi khotum* and *Bibimulla* is a female religious teacher. *Bibimulla* assists *Bibi khotum* in performing some functions, and their work in mahalla is also voluntary work. *Bibimulla* or *bibiotin* is a female Muslim personage who supervises the affairs of daily life of the female believers in a particular area. In addition, she is responsible for the religious education of women, for the recitation of prayers during celebrations, both religious and familial, such as birth rituals, marriages, or funerals. There is a clear distinction in the area of social relations between *bibiotin* and the other women who are under her control. Even if these religious women do not always have a formal knowledge of Islam, they none the less have real authority over the female population of the community. In such a way, they realize the same functions as mullahs, and, therefore, they sometimes are referred to as "women mullahs".[151]

Every *bibiotin*, in order to be able to pass on her religious and traditional heritage, is answerable for the education of a certain group of young girls. Aiming to rise the number of educated girls in religious sphere the religious courses in their homes are being organized (usually two or three times a week). The girls are taught correct recitation of the verses from the Al-Quran exclusively in Arabic, and to perform certain ceremonies, like those associated with births and funerals. At home almost all girls might continue repetition of the learnt material from some religious books in the Arabic script, accurately hidden from the Soviet censors by their mothers or grandmothers.

It is necessary to accentuate that the significant role of *bibiotin* is not limited to the teaching of the girls in the community. The role is morally highlighted for *bibiotin* as female spiritual leaders guide all women from birth to adulthood by teaching the moral norms which women will live with. Thus, in this regard they exercise a powerful influence in the sustaining the level of morals in the whole society. They implement in this way a kind of social control in the form of a sta-

151 Habiba Fathi Otines: The unknown women clerics of Central Asian Islam. The Institut National des Langues et Civilizations Orientates, Paris available online: 13 Sep 2007

ble reminder of the obligations to the community, including respect for elders, rejection of mixed marriages, the observation of religious practices, and etc. [152]

Nowadays as well in the past, in all mahallas, *raisi zanon* (a woman who has been elected as a head of all women in mahalla or as a representative of the women in mahalla) is found. She is selected among all women based on criteria such as experience, knowledge, and the ability to represent the interests of mahalla in front of the administrative authorities.

Performing her duties, *raisi zanon* is subjected to the power of the head of mahalla. She informs him about female issues and gives advice on ways to solve these affairs. Acting through her as an intermediary, women can influence the decision of *rais* of mahalla and the council of elders. In the northern region of Tajikistan, where women seem to be more socially and publically active, they may even force a change in the decision of *rais* and the council of elders.

For outside observers, it seems that Tajik women do not have an interest in the affairs of mahalla at all. Their presence in public life may not be noticed and might be interpreted as a small in quantitative terms for an outside observer. Partly it is true, for that women's main activity is mostly concentrated on family issues. The family's obligations are considered to be the most important duties for women.[153] This situation is justified by religion.[154]. However, some women tend to be involved in the public activity: teaching, working in social, medical spheres or administration.

The general attitude to Tajik women generates from the status of women in Islam. In Al-Quran, the Holy Book of Islam, there is a separate surah dedicated to the women[155]. As undisputable orders the ways to treat women as mother, sister, or wife are given to men: "O you, who believe! You are forbidden to inherit women against their will. Nor should you treat them with harshness, that you may take away part of the dowry you have given them-except when they have become guilty of open lewdness. On the contrary, live with them on a footing of kindness and equity. If you take a dislike to them, it may be that you dislike something and Allah will bring about through it a great deal of good[156]".

---

152 Ibid.

153 Cook, D. (2001). Hadith, Authority and the End of the World: Traditions in Modern Muslim Apocalyptic Literature. In *Oriente Moderno*, 21 (n.s.), pp. 1-22.

154 Ibid.

155 The fourth surah called An-Nisa, *Women,* explains how men have to treat women, also the rules on marriage, divorce, childbirth, status in husband's family, amount of inherited will, and so on.

156 Holy Al-Quran (4:19).

The status of women invokes the respect and honor. The men and women enjoy the similar rights as the creations of God. The social duties and capacities are dissimilar: since man is a protector of the family and its members: "Women have the same rights (in relation to their husbands) as are expected in all decency from them, while men stand a step above them[157]".

Traditional family ties remain very strong in the country. Tajikistan had one of the highest proportions of family members living together in comparison with the other countries of the former Soviet Union. According to Tajik tradition, the model of the Tajik family is the model of a big family. Such a model has also been propagated in Soviet period. From the demographical point of view the Soviet laws have widely encouraged childbirth. In the society, motherhood has been honored and awarded with a number of privileges. The highest rank has been named 'Hero Mother' for those women who had given birth to and raised 10 or more children. Women with seven to nine children has achieved the status of 'Mother Glory'. The next status 'Medal of Maternity' has been given to women with five or six children. Also, such women have been awarded with special pensions[158].

It is necessary to note that the attitude toward women is determined by the high value of the role of mother. The attitude toward the mother is illustrated in one of the messages of the Prophet Muhammad (BPUH), and in turn, that is expressed in the form of a duty that must be obeyed as one of the most crucial moral principles. It is beautifully written in Hadith that "the paradise is under the foot of the mothers". In the rural area sometimes mother decides who will be her son's wife. Traditionally, the marriage of the son is the most important life cycle to all Tajiks. This is because the mother of the son and the son's wife are simultaneously bestowed with new duties and obligations. Generally, Tajiks express deep esteem and high admiration to mothers, wives and sisters. Children are bought up to hold mothers, sisters, and grandparents in high esteem. Women's high esteem in society is evidenced by the strong influence they can have on their husband's decisions, and by women supporting their representative (*raisi zanon*) and indirectly influencing the mahalla's decision-making process.

The socio-political changes in Tajik society carried out by the Soviet authority have influenced on the status of women in society. One of the cultural vectors of the process of sovietization has concerned the compulsory elementary education

157 Holy Al-Quran (2:228).

158 Falkingham & Vlachantoni (2010). *Pensions and Social Protection in Central Asia and South Caucasus: Developments in the Post-Soviet Era.* Centre for Research on Ageing, School of Social Science, University of Southampton: UK.

in order to erase the illiteracy, under such auspices the total access to school education has been launched in soviet Tajikistan. For an illustration, in the 1920s, the literacy rate among Tajik men was over 2% and 1% that among women. Such low indicators state that education had been a privilege of the elites in pre-Soviet Tajik society. The situation had been completely changed when primary education became compulsory and free of charge under the Soviet regime. As a consequence, by the independence in 1989, the level of literacy reached 93% of the total population.

To any possible critical statement that the mahalla governance undermines women rights it is possible to object in such a way: first of all (in cultural terms) as it is explained in the work, mahalla, in the eyes of the Tajiks, is treated as an extended family. I remind that in a Tajik family, there is a specific division between men and women, and contrary to any claims of social stratification, this is an old tradition in the basis of the Tajik culture. This gender division extends throughout the whole mahalla, yet it does not exclude women from the activity in the public sphere beyond it. Secondly (using recent data) it is relevant to declare that women occupy important management positions in many international NGOs, and they can be businesswomen or managers in other fields as well. Albeit, the reconciliation of so to say private and public duties still is taking place when woman returns home, she reassumes her important role as the mother of the family. According to data provided by Asian Development Bank (ADB), in February 2005 women have presented 18 percent of all positions in Majlisi Namoyandagon (Assembly of Representatives), while in other elected bodies the proportion is faintly smaller: 12.1% in the Majlisi Milli (National Assembly) and 11.5% in local Majlisis. It is worth noting that it is the higher proportion than in other Commonwealth of Independence States CIS countries, post-soviet countries[159]".

Also in this context it is worth noting that in the case of conflict situation within mahalla women are given word without mistreatment and intolerance. This is predominantly because of respect, admiration and high esteem Tajik woman enjoys in society and this does not put her under brutal treatment by the officer. As one of my informants has said:

> *The majority of Tajik women prefer to stay in their house and take care of their children. For example, I have been working for about 15 years in different positions in a governmental body. At work, I am doing my job as a manager. When coming home, I forget about my position, because, at home, I consider myself as a wife and mother of the family (female, 40 years old, manager. August, 2012).*

---

159 ADB. (2006). Tajikistan. Country Gender Assessment. Association "Women Scientists of Tajikistan". Retrieved from 20 December, 2008 http://www.tajik-gateway.org/index.phtml?lang=en&id=3941.

2.3. Mahalla and traditional informal social institutions in Tajikistan

Traditionally the Tajiks participate in the life of the mahalla they belong to, and in turn are capable of influencing on its issues in the active way through such informal institutions as avlod, qawm, maswarat, jamomad, gashtak or davra, and etc. They are sanctified by centuries-old traditions. Characteristically that despite the imposed and intensive social transformations of the Soviet period - such as industrialization and urbanization - these institutions have survived and have remained to be almost unchanged.

Jamoat

It is an institution of self-government met both in the towns and villages. Moreover, it is possible to claim that according to the history of Tajik society, all elements of civil society stem from the community. The main difference between jamoat and mahalla is that several mahallas might be united in one jamoat that is controlled from above. The head or chairman of the jamoat is elected for a five-year term by the government of the regions.[160]

Jamoat as a self-governing institution was established as a jamoat council in the new Tajik Constitution on November 6, 1994. Jamoats are formed on a territorial basis and have a legal status and an official seal. Community possessions include means of transportation, equipment, and other services, public or social, which these governments have built, purchased, or otherwise transferred to their ownership. Town or village self-government revenue sources include budget allocations from the city or rayon councils, voluntary donations from citizens and working collectives. However, the Law on Local Self-government in Towns and Villages does not address other traditional institutions of local self-governance that are presently active, such as mahalla (community) committees, microrayon councils, housing block committees, or other *kishlak* (village) organizations. The most important duty of the jamoat councils as a local self- governmental organization is to bring together people and solve the problems of their province. Also, one of the essential task of such councils is to control problems like land use, water, wedding ceremonies, and divorce. The

---

160 Abdullaev, K. (n.d). Current Local Government Policy Situation in Tajikistan. In *Tajikistan at the crossroad: The Politics of Decentralization.*

members of jamoat manage the elections in the villages and also organize the administration bodies in tax collections.[161]

2.3.1 Avlod

Avlod in Tajik means a kin. Although blood relations are the principal basis of avlod, however, each of them is not homogeneous and is based on a distinct hierarchical structure. Every avlod has its leader (*kaloni avlod* or *sardori avlod*). Habitually, the heads of avlods are males, but sometimes an old woman might hold this position. The fathers of the families occupy the higher level of the hierarchy, whose prestige are determined by their age. The members of avlod meet regularly on such occasions as weddings, funerals, circumcisions, or iftar (a traditional dinner at the end of the fasting day during Ramazan). The elders of the avlod make the decision on important cases for the entire avlod or the whole mahalla. In the most urgent cases, the members of avlods can gather with their respective heads for a discussion, or to ask for advice about certain situation that calls for the meeting (*maslihatoshi*[162]). It is possible to note that the function of avlod is analogous to that of a small state. The avlod possesses economic, social, spiritual, cultural, ideological, territorial, and juridical tools. Historically, avlod has played a key role in the preservation of the language, culture, and tradition of their communities. In addition, it is the strongest informal traditional institution in the social life of the Tajik people [163].

Avlod respects own history by keeping its traditions of origin, memorial places, and data on the places, where its members lived in the past and where its members came from. According to Matveeva, the most respected and famous avlods came from such Central Asian cultural centers as Bukhara, Samarkand and Khujand, among others. The prestige of a particular avlod depends on the personality of its leader and ancestors. All Tajiks remember their ancestors up until the seventh generation. A special authority is attributed to such families among which the *mullas, beks* (rulers of the area), or teachers are originated. Their memory is circulated within the community, and their achievements performing in the name of the common good are not forgotten. It is estimated on

161 *Civil society and Human Development in Tajikistan.* (2006) Retrieved 24, April, 2009, from: http://cfapp1-docs-public.undp.org/eo/evaldocs1/adr/eo_doc_597030542.pdf

162 From the Tajik word *маслихатоші́* (council for the preparation of the celebration). Usually before weddings or some other special events, the close relatives gather in that house and discuss the issues pertaining to the preparation of the celebration.

163 Abdullaev, K. (2006). Current Local Government Policy Situation in Tajikistan. In *Tajikistan at a crossroad: The Politics of Decentralization.*

the basis of the sociological research of the Sharq Center in Dushanbe that 68.3% of Tajiks belongs to an avlod institution, which includes 82.2% of the population in the Kulyab region, 78% of Kurgan-Teppa and Gornyi Badakhshan, and 75% of the Rasht Valley.[164]

The heads of avlods control their member's behavior and implement traditional marital norms. In the case of marriages, the elders of the avlods gather together and debate whether to accept the mother's choice for his son's wife or not. Before such a meeting, they usually gather information on where the candidate for a wife comes from. The *obru* or *oburu* (reputation- meaning in Tajik) of another avlod is very important for them. Literally, the translation of *oburu* to English is 'water of face'. This concept is well known in different cultures of Asia, for instance, in China, the equivalent to the Tajik *obru* is mian- zi. The possession of *obru* is very important for Tajiks. The level of oburu depends on the respect the Tajik enjoys in their community. *Obru* that is acquired by belonging to a particular avlod can be lost by the individual's own behavior. The *obru* can be bestowed to one by certain manifestations of respect towards their representatives of power. Thus the individual can either enlarge the family *obru* through their merits, or reduce it through misbehavior and transgressions.

Every person in the community is judged according to the *obru*. In the case of committing a serious misconduct, person can lose good reputation and no longer be allowed to have a positive oburu. For instance, positive *obru* can be irreparably lost by mistreating and disrespecting parents or elderly people ('oki padar' is the Tajik word for someone who does not respect his father), or by doing something immoral that immediately lose his father's reputation in the community. People call such a person benomus (without honor) or beobru ('without face' or 'lost face'). Therefore, every member of the community tries to keep their *obru* positive. The Tajiks will at all costs avoid losing their *obru*. Losing face can generate strong reactions within the community. For better understanding the role of *obru* in Tajik culture, I find it necessary to refer to the following Persian-Tajik saying:

> *Obest obiru ki naoyad ba juy boz,* (Obru is the water which will not come back to the rivulet)*Az tashnagi bimiru marez obu rui khud.* (Better die of thirsty than to lose your face[165])

---

164 Olimova, Saodat. (1999). Political Islam and Conflict in Tajikistan', in Lena Jonson and Murad Esenov, *Political Islam and Conflicts in Russia and Central Asia* Conference Paper no. 24. The Swedish Institute of International Affairs: Stockholm.

165 Author's translation.

One of my respondents expressed his opinion concerning obru:

> *Obru is very important in our community. Every person is responsible not only for his oburu, but for his entire family and avlod's reputation. If someone does something wrong against his community's code of behavior, automatically he/ she loses his/her avlod's oburu. Of course, people are not perfect and everybody does some mistakes. Avlod loses its reputation in the case of serious immoral actions. I can tell you one story in our mahalla. Approximately 15 years ago, one mahalla member had stolen money and some valuable things from a small factory. When they caught him, it was very hard for his father, because he lost the reputation of whole family. In one meeting in the village mosque, his father said that since that day, he disowned his son, and he later on added that he did not want to see him in his house. Hence son has left our mahalla and now he is living in the capital. When his father was sick and before his father's death, he came, but he did not stay in our mahalla. Sometimes he is coming to visit his mother, however, people still remember him as a person who did not respect the community's rule. (male, 52 years old. September, 2011).*

A man who loses his *obru*, simultaneously loses the moral right to live within community. *Oki padar* loses any possibility to expect a respect from other mahalla members. No Tajik in his community will bend a helping hand to him. One of my interviewees, the head of an avlod, urges that Avlod does not merely offer important physical security, but also provides considerable emotional protection by a sense of belonging to a particular group. In addition, avlod materially supports its members by providing financial assistance for the needy, and also by various services such as physical labor or legal assistance.

For instance, during the civil war of 1992-1997, avlod members gave shelter to their relatives fleeing from the battleground areas. Nowadays, avlods still play an important role in the labour migration of Tajiks. As a rule, avlod's members searching for a new place of living, usually prefer to settle down nearby family members. This will ensure the care and supervision from the side of the avlod members. Members of avlods financially support those who intend to establish a business. They provide the required capital for its opening, and in the case of urgent need, they help financially in order to stimulate the development of it. They also try to take part in solving any problematic situation that may arise, and are ready to help in paying for the business' creditors in the case of bankruptcy.

In addition, avlod plays an important role in education the younger generation. The members of avlod gather and decide which professions their young members should choose. They do not enforce their opinions, but merely suggest various specializations. The members of avlods try to include within their kin various specialists, such as lawyers, doctors, policemen, economists, mullas, teachers, and etc. Furthermore, the elders of avlod financially support the younger members during all study. They also transfer money to such members who study abroad. Upon the completion of studies, they even help them throughout their professional career.

In the large mahallas inhabited by the representatives of several avlods, the authority of the mahalla is chosen throughout the course of negotiations run by the elders of the specific avlods. As it has been practiced from previous centuries till the present day, the mulla announces the candidacy of the head of the mahalla. The conflicts within the mahalla have traditionally been resolved in meetings of the elders of the avlods. As a way to resolve conflicts, the recognition of the interests of the individual is subordinated to the principle of communal harmony.

2.3.2 Qawm

There are different views about the meaning of term qawm in Western science. It is a traditional institution which exists in Afghanistan and in agricultural societies in Central Asia. The very term qawm is derived from Arabic meaning any form of solidarity that might be based on kinship, residence, or occupation. However, according to other researchers, for example, Tapper, qawm involves exceptionally the identity of regional, linguistic, or tribal character. However, it is possible to meet some qawms whose members are not from the same linguistic group.[166] For instance, considering this, Canfield claims that qawm consists of people who are supporting each other commonly, whose who have been grown up in one territory or have become bounded with some inhabitants of this territory through marital ties.

Traditionally, the members of such a group call each other *qawmi*. *Azoi qawm* is translated as qawm members, whereas *berun az qawm* or *begona* means a person out of qawm or not qawm member, an outsider. These are terms referring to people living in one territory and are tied with the feeling of solidarity to each other. They should collaborate and help each other in any kind of work. The term qawn bears an especially religious meaning in Tajikistan and is colored with aspect, however, is that they must be religiously united. All the qawm members celebrate Muslim holidays together. They usually pray together and listen to Al-Quran recitation, the Islamic hadith, and morals during prayer time. In all events, including weddings and funerals, the members must gather together. According to Canfield, in its spirit term qawn is close to the meaning a "solidarity unit".[167]

166 Tapper, R, & Tapper, N. (1988). Ethnicity, Order and Meaning in the Anthropology of Iran and Afghanistan. In Digard, J.-P. (Ed.). *Le fait ethnique en Iran et en Afghanistan*. Paris: Editions du Centre Nationale de Recherche Scientifique., pp. 21-35.

167 Canfield, R. L. (1973). *Factions and Conversion in a Plural Society: Religious Alignments in the Hindu Kush*. Ann Arbor: University of Michigan Press.

Roy claims that qawm is not an union of people on the basis of ethnicity, but is rather a solidarity unit formed on the base of life in the same territory. Thus, as Richard Tapper and Nancy Tapper argue, qawm is "a highly ambiguous and flexible concept allowing scope for strategic manipulations of identity"[168]. In any case, in Afghanistan, the term of qawm is used to denominate a large diversity of different social groups. In the rural areas of Afghanistan, all important social relations take place through the qawm. Every qawm is headed by *jirga* or *shura* (council of elder males). It is more or less similar to the council of elders in the mahalla institution of Tajikistan[169].

As it might be noticed, in Tajikistan, the term qawm is a commonly used as a synonym to term avlod. If one asks the Tajiks about the meaning of word qawm, they unhesitatingly answer that this is avlod. It should be emphasized that the Tajiks always lived in isolation from each other because of the geographical peculiarities of the country. The rule was that an avlod residing in a particular territory was related to another through marital ties. By living in one territory, avlods are united to fight for their common purpose, (for example, during the civil war). It is during this time that the solidity between them is expressed as qawm, and it is still a solitary unit. Due to the cultural idea of all human relationships being built upon the model of family ties, the term qawm was the most likely to express this essence of solidarity.

2.3.3 Gashtak or Davra

Gashtak or Davra (in Tajik meaning 'circle turning out') is an institution described in cultural anthropology as the class of age. In the past, gashtak was considered as consisting of a specific age range. Nowadays, davra is the gathering of people of similar age connected by friendship or kinship ties within their neighborhoods. Davra is often a gathering of former classmates. It is worth noting that such institutions are met within female groups as well.[170]

The name originates from the fact that such a group meets regularly. Depending on the season and the region, this could be anywhere from every week to every couple weeks, or sometimes just once a month. The number of gashtak

168 Tapper, R, & Tapper, N. (1988). Ethnicity, Order and Meaning in the Anthropology of Iran and Afghanistan. In Digard, J.-P. (Ed.). *Le fait ethnique en Iran et en Afghanistan..*, Paris: Editions du Centre Nationale de Recherche Scientifique, pp. 21-35.

169 Wardak, A. (n.d.) *Jirga - A Traditional Mechanism of Conflict Resolution in Afghanistan*. University of Glamorgan: UK.

170 Giffen, J., Earle L & Buxton. *The Development of Civil Society in Central Asia*. The International NGO Training and Research Centre.

participants may vary from anywhere between 15-30 people. The meetings are held at various members' homes, with the host changing upon each meeting. Therefore, it operates like a circle. The gashtak meetings are usually organized on Saturdays or Sundays. The gashtak host prepares different kinds of meals: rice, meat, tea, including traditional dish – palav. The guests start talking and discussing some issues after the meal[171]. Such meetings can last from several hours till all night long. They talk and discuss religious topics, and each participant exchanges information about their own life. They collectively decide how to solve common problems. They also gather money from each member to support any needy participant. This instance is also present during weddings or funerals.

The participants of gashtaks not only help one another financially, but they also participate in the organization of various ceremonies. They will also provide important assistance to participant, for instance, in building a house. Each gashtak, or davra, has its own leader. Likewise, as with the leader of the mahalla, the gashtak leader is also called *rais*. *Rais* is an unofficial title bestowed only by gashtak members, among whom he is chosen. He must be distinguished by his moral behavior, education, and the authority obtained among other members. Rais is also the institution's treasurer, and he reports on the group's finances every meeting. Rais has the right to punish participants even on matters extending beyond their behavior at meetings. This punishment may be allotted in either beatings or fines. The most severe penalty is removal from gashtak. Punishment is also administered to participants who miss three meetings without excuse.

According to Matveeva, in the northern part of Tajikistan where life is more urbanized, gashtaks are organized in local *choykhonas* (teahouses), and the host is changed each time. In my opinion, this is typical custom in the larger cities, but in the rural area, gashtak meetings are organized in the members' homes. There are also regional differences concerning the age of the gashtak participants. From my experience in the western part of the country, gashtaks are organized by classmates that are about 16 years old. The same is also true for the female organizations[172].

Gashtak and davra are horizontal networks in Tajik society that significantly limit the capacity of state power. From the other side, they fulfill the most important role of sustaining social unity and solving problems in an informal

---

171 Karimov, Sh. (n.d.). *NGO Development in Tajikistan: Traditions and Current Situation.*

172 Matveeva, A. (2009). *The Perils of Emerging Statehood: Civil War and State Reconstruction in Tajikistan. An Analytical Narrative on State-Making.* Crisis States Research Centre.

way. They are used, among other means, as a rapid transfer of information. It is a well-established tradition that people who are studying or working in other cities will come to their villages to attend gashtak meetings. During such meetings, the participants willingly exchange information about the current situation of other parts of the country. Even if someone of the members of the gashtak is studying abroad or is engaged in migratory labor, he or she regularly calls other members and informs them of their situation. Thanks to the gashtak institution in Tajik society, even without the modern means of spreading information (for example, the Internet), information is still rapidly transmitted. As one of my respondents said:

> *I started my participation in gashtak meetings when I was 15 years old. Usually, gashtak meetings begin from this age in our village. This is because after the ninth year, pupils starting enter lyceums and technical colleges and they go to the cities to continue their education. The aim of gashtak is not gathering and eating. Its main aim is in keeping us united and preserving the relations which we had during school years. In the cities, life is different from villages, therefore, such meetings always help people to remember the unwritten code of their community.*
>
> *We help each other as much we can. Thanks to such gatherings, we know about each other's problems. We have our own funds. In every meeting, we gather money and we give it to our rais. It is not a lot of money, however, it is enough for urgent needs. Every person can give as much as he can. People who are working in a good position, of course, their contribution is bigger. It general, it is a symbolic amount, but it is better than nothing.*
>
> *In addition, it is very interesting that, for example, during my student years in the capital, every week I came to my village to participate in gashtak gatherings. We were studying in different universities, and every week we gathered together and exchange information with each other. It was also useful and interesting for our classmates who were living in the villages. Because not all of them in the local areas had access to the latest technology.(Male, economist, bank worker, 36 years old. July, 2011).*

As the participants and members of gashtak can confirm, this institution is very active in my region. I have been abroad more than six years, however, I am still in contact with my gashtak members. In set gashtak days, I being in Europe do not forget it and speak via mobile phone with my former classmates working as labour migrants in Russia. We all keep in touch with each another, and we always inform everybody about the latest news from our mahalla.

2.3.4 *Mushkilkusho*

Mushkilkusho is a female equivalent to the jam'omad. The term derives from Tajik and literally means 'solving a problem' (mushkil-problem, or difficulty, and kusho- solving). These are women's regular meetings in which they discuss the problems of religious life in the mahallas. They usually gather on Wednesdays. Women also perform pilgrimages to mazars (the tomb of saintly people), which is an important institution of so-called folk Islam[173]. This institution plays a significant role in the exchange of information about the issues of the mahallas, and women can utilize it as an intermediary in public life.

2.3.5 *Shinosbozi or jurabozi*

This term is a combination of two Tajik words, shinos (jura) – friend or college – and bozi – game or play. It is a group of people who are obliged to mutually help one another, and of whom one's help can be depended on in every circumstance of life. The closest equivalent of the Tajik 'jurabozi' is the Chinese 'guanxi'. Some people continue their relationships with their father's friends and their family even after father's death. A good 'shinos' or jura of avlod is a kin to a friend for all avlod members. They can be friends from school, the workplace, or merely people who had established close relationships while in another area or country. The authority of such a group depends on how influential its state administrational area is. Some members of this group are represented in various ministries, law enforcement bodies, courts, tax authorities, intellectual groups, and well-known specialist positions.

It is an ideal to have close relationships with others. Even if someone's friend is long distanced for a period of time, still he can rely on help due to this institution. Group members maintain friendly relations with one another due to regular meetings, under which common causes are discussed. There are no fixed dates for such meetings. This type of meeting is strengthened by the expected reciprocity of personal contacts by each member.

Sufi Clerics

Sufi *tariqats* (the followers of the Sufi brotherhood) has played an important role in the Islamization of pre-soviet and soviet society. Sufi followers, because of their sophisticated networks, could organize confrontational forces against ag-

173 The term of folk Islam has been invented in the Soviet Union after the religious education reforms. It had initially been carried out by the creative power of the reformist Jadids, of whom after Great October Revolution many outstanding representatives later became allies of the Bolsheviks. The opposition to the folk Islam is originated from the official Islam represented in the Soviet Union. Currently, some authors use term high Islam, meaning Islam as represented by scholars, theologians, and Islamic jurists, as opposition to folk Islam.

gressors. Therefore, fierce confrontation against the Russian invasion had been led by the followers of Sufism. The followers of Sufi tariqat, because of their ardent anti-Bolshevik movement, has turned to be the number one enemy for the communist regime. During the period of Stalin's "Great Purges", many followers of Sufism have been imprisoned or sent into exile[174]. Even under such anti-religious persecution, the Sufis have still been propagating against atheist regime, and even have managed to increase the number of their *murids* (adepts). By accepting new *murids,* the Sufi clerics has increased and sustained their influence and the religious – meaning also anti-Soviet- feelings among Tajik Muslims. This is because of their role as the guardian of Islam and protector of the poor from the unfair policies of the authorities, the respect towards Sufi clerics -experienced throughout Tajik history – has continued even during Soviet era. The Sufi adepts could easily infiltrate among the people and run their underground institutions[175]. There cases of the activities among Sufi followers have happened to be reported and documented in Soviet regime. For instance, in a particular case, it was pointed out that:

> *eshons* (Sufi clerics usually were dubbed like so in Tajikistan and Uzbekistan) went around rural areas in late 1940s enlisting murids. One Kolkhoz chairman in Tajikistan invited a well-known *eshan* from another *oblast*, offering him good conditions and even building him a house. Two further eshans wielded considerable influence in the central parts of the republic in the early 1950s: one who was over seventy and did no traveling, but was visited at his *kishlak* (village) by a large number of *murids*; and another who traveled around Vaksh Valley and was thought to have between 500 and 1000 *murids*[176].

The future Sufi murids have been educating in unofficial rural schools. For entirely security reasons, the Sufis got accustomed to use any place as a secret gathering destination. In underground conditions, the *murids* have got education, performed their *zikrs* (remembrance of God), read the Al-Quran and hadith, listened to the *amri maruf*[177] (enjoying what is good), and prayed collectively

174 Mullojonov, P. (2001). The Islamic Clergy in Tajikistan'. In Stephane A. Dudoignon and Komatsu Hisao (Ed.), *Islam and Politics in Russia and Central Asia*, Kegan Paul International Limited: London, pp. 221-250

175 Shapoatov, S (2004). The Tajik Civil War: 1992-1997.

176 Ro'i, Yaacov. Islam in the Soviet Union: From the Second World War to Gorbachev, Hurst and Company, London, 2000, p. 396 in Shapoatov, S (2004). The Tajik Civil War: 1992-1997.

177 Amri maruf is from the Arabic "Amr bil Ma'ruf wa Nahy an al Munkar (امر بالمعروف و نهی عن المنکر)", which means 'commanding to the right/honorable and forbidding the wrong/dishonorable'.

(namozi jamo'a), in a word, have not failed to forget any obligatory practice but under the veil of absolute conspiracy and silence.

One attribute of the *eshons* has concerned the inheritance of the title from their ancestors. Every *eshan* in turn, has tried to educate his offspring in theology. These old-aged practices have been carefully kept alive throughout centuries, and the members of the families guarding them have enjoyed a respectful position in Tajik society. *Eshons* are regarded to be the offspring of the Prophet, the *Sahabas* (companions of Prophet Muhammad (BPUH)), and famous Sufi clerics. According to this tradition, the anti-communist feelings of the *eshans* could be passed on to their offspring and could spread among the Tajik Muslims. In the past, the Sufi leaders - called *pirs*- as clergy or teachers from these brotherhoods, has directly influenced the behavior of their students (murids) in political life. As such, at the end of the nineteenth century and also in 1916, the leaders of the brotherhoods in the Ferghana Valley (the northern region of contemporary Tajikistan) have turned to be the ardent initiators of the anti- Russian revolts.

The Sufi brotherhoods play an important role in the religious and political life of the Tajik people. The most popular in Tajikistan is the *Naqshbandiya brotherhood* [178]. There are *Qadiriya*[179] and Jahriya brotherhoods as well. People in such brotherhoods search for a spiritual connection with God and do not directly participate in social life, preferring the inner sphere of life above the socially-determinated duties and obligations.

As one of my respondents has noticed:

> *It should be noted that the eshons and sufi clergies played a vital role in preserving Islamic rituals. During the Communist regime, they propagated against the atheist regime. They did this usually through increasing their murids (adepts). Some of them taught youngsters for free. An example to this kind of eshan is my uncle. Currently, he is 82. He was the mulla of our village. He had almost 100 students. He had a big house. His students were accommodated at his house and his neighbor's house. In addition to accommodation, the mullah provided them with a free meal.*
>
> *He did not accept any rewards from the parents of his students, and such behavior was upsetting him. As we know, he took care of his students individually, one by one. Such students from unofficial schools became very competent. There are more examples like this.*

---

178 The Naqshbandiya is a tariqah named after Baha-ud-Din Naqshbandi (d.791H / 1389CE). According to Shaykh Ahmad al-Faruqi al-Sirhindi (d.1034H / 1624CE) Naqshbandiya is described as the "Mother of all Tariqah's".

179 The tariqah of Qadiriyyah is one of the oldest tariqas of Sufizm. It was named after Abdul-Qadir Gilani AH 470 (1077-1166), from Iranian province of Gilan. There are several Spiritual Order's albeit Naqshbandiya, Qadiriya, Chistiya and Suhrawardiya, are considered as the four main Silsila's of the Ahl as-Sunnah wa'l Jama'at.

I brought you an example of only one of them. (Male, 52 years old, electrician, member of mahalla. August, 2011).

To sum up, the abovementioned institutions such as mahalla, avlod, qawm, gashtak and jamomad represent the quality of the lifestyle of an ordinary Tajik. It spreads a range of relationships with other people that Tajiks can rely on in understanding and support. These institutions provide with a material assistance for Tajiks: for instance, in study and business, protection against arbitrary actions, as well as spiritual support in all other circumstances of life. However, the existence of them is related to the attitudes and behavioral patterns that, for instance, in the West might be regarded as sources of corruption. For Tajiks, however, these attitudes and behaviors are among the most important ideals of their moral culture.

Chapter 3: Theories of civil society in Western social science

The concept of civil society is understood as all the organizations and associations that exist outside of the state (including political parties). It includes the gamut of organizations that political science labels interest groups — NGOs, labor unions, professional associations, chambers of commerce, ethnic associations, and others. It also incorporates the many other associations that exist for purposes other than advancing the specific social or political agendas. This includes religious organizations, student groups, cultural organizations (from choral societies to bird-watching clubs), sports clubs, and informal community groups[180].

The modern idea of civil society has emerged in the late 18th century. The term has been an inter-alia for Thomas Paine, an English-American political activist and philosopher, and for Georg Wilhelm Friedrich Hegel, German philosopher, as a realm where citizens, independent from the state, associate according to their interests and wishes. In the 20th century, the very concept has become in intellectual vogue not in last degree because of the writings of Antonio Gramsci, the Italian Marxist. For the later fate of the idea, great importance was placed into introducing the concept of cultural hegemony by Gramsci. According to Gramsci, the state is not pure force and violence, nor is it merely the dictatorship of one class over another.[181]

Gramsci's notion of hegemony stressed the importance of the relationship between the state and cultural institutions of society disseminating of ideological systems of values and beliefs. The works of Gramsci have been indeed influential in the 1970s and 1980s circles, especially among leftist intellectuals in the West. In their regard, the opposition members of Eastern European countries, such as the Czech Republic, Hungary and Poland have also acted as advocates of civil society opposed to the communist dictatorship. In the 1990s, the concept of civil society has achieved an exceptionally popularity from politicians to political scientists as a label or concept of hot debates. The collapse of Soviet Union has immediately opened up a room for the development of the preconditions for the civil society to flourish in the former communist countries. Yet, in the United States and Western

---

180 Carothers, T. (2000). *Think Again: Civil Society.* Foreign Policy, winter 1999-2000.

181 Fontana, B. (1993). *Hegemony and Power: On the Relation Between Gramsci and Machiavelli.* University of Minnesota Press: USA.

Europe, the disappearance of a mass party has sparked interest in civil society as a means of social renewal. According to above mentioned Thomas Carothers, civil society has become a key element of the post-cold-war zeitgeist[182].

In opinion of number of contemporary sociologists, the concept of civil society has been understood in diverse ways. For instance:

Arato and Cohen (1995) urge that the civil society like an area of social communication between economy and state, over all consist of the intimate area (particularly the family), the area of associations (especially voluntary associations), social movements, and different kinds of public communication.[183] Diamond defines civil society as the domain of planned social life that is open, voluntary, self-generating, at least partly self-supporting, and sovereign from the state, and that is bound by a legal order or a place of common collective rules.[184] For instance, these authors emphasize the social orientation of the domain distinguished as civil society.[185]

Chandhoke (2004) reviews six explanations on civil society. According to the first version, every one which does not belong to the state is belong to civil society, including families, religious, associations, communities, work places and other organizations can be named as private.[186] Secondly, civil society is regarded as a private area, in opposition to state as a public sphere. Furthermore in the other side of liberalism it is a family which is private, and all else, together with civil society, is public. Thirdly, it mediates as the site of the public dialogue among public opinion and the state. The fourth, civil society is the place where the state interferes to form and influence on public opinion, so that it can form consent for its own rules. The fifth, civil society as a political debate becomes the field of political democracy that produces a society which is occupied in participative and deliberative functions. The sixth description include the institutions

182 Thomas Carothers (2000). *Think Again: Civil Society.* Foreign Policy, winter 1999-2000.

183 Cohen, J. L., & Arato, A. (1992). *Civil Society and Political Theory.* Cambridge: MIT

184 Tusalem, R. F. (2007). A Boon or a Bane? The Role of Civil Society. In *International Political Science Review,* 28(3), pp. 361-386.

185 Hearm, J. (2001). Taking Liberties: Contesting Visions of the Civil Society Project. In *Critique Of Anthropology,* 21(4), pp. 339-360.

186 Chandhoke, N. (2004). *State and Civil Society: Explorations in Political Theory.* New Delhi: Sage Publication.

of the market that form civil society for that reason civil society is measured as an economic debate.[187]

Habermas believes that civil society as institutional sphere has been formed through voluntary associations like churches, independent media, ethnic, race and sexuality cultural organizations and sport clubs, outside the area of the state and the economy. [188] Regarding Habermas' theory civil society and the public sphere are depended on each other. Habermas divides society in two areas; private (include two areas; close area or family and private economy) and public area (include public area and public authority area or state) which civil society in some sense addresses to the area of the personal and bourgeois economy as well in the broader sense it means all the area of society contrast to the state.[189]

A perfect public area declares itself as a protection against the systematizing effects of the state and the economy. The public area is placed in civil society and it is where citizens can discuss issues of common concern as peers, and learn about details, events, and the views, interests, and outlooks of others in a free atmosphere or equalities that individuals would eager to agree or be silent. This participation develops the autonomy of citizens and is a learning procedure. This dialogue or discussions on morals, ethics, values, norms and laws creates politically applicable public view. These debates can happen inside different units of civil society. However, there is also a bigger public area that mediates between the different mini-publics that appear in and crossways institutions, movements, religious organizations, local associations of concerned individuals, and informal social networks in the formation of public opinion.[190]

Habermas considers that the civil society should be believed as shaped of those more or less instinctively "emergent associations, organizations, and movements that, regulated to how societal problems resonate in the private life spheres, distill and transmit such reactions in amplified form to the public sphere".[191]

---

187 Vahid Amani Zoeram, & Jayum Anak Jawan, & Lee Yok Fee (2010) The Epistemology of the Concept of Civil Society in the West and Iranian Interpretations. In *Canadian Social Science* Vol. 6 No. 4.

188 Flyvbjerg, B. (1998). Habermas and Foucault: Thinkers for Civil Society? In *The British Journal of Sociology*, 49(2), pp. 210-233.

189 Cohen, J. L., & Arato, A. (1992). *Civil Society and Political Theory*. Cambridge: MIT

190 Fleming, T. (2000). *Habermas, Democracy and Civil Society: Unearthing the Social in Transformation Theory*. Retrieved 25 January, 2008, from http://adulteducation.nuim.ie/department_staff/documents/Habermas democracyand civilsociety.pdf

191 Staats, J. L. (2004). Habermas and Democratic Theory: The Threat To Democracy of Unchecked Corporate Power. In *Political Research Quarterly* 57(4), 585-594.

Generally Habermas addresses civil society to the sphere of social relations free from intervention of political power. Self-governing civic institutions like as political parties, unions, academic associations, social institutions, free media and others in civil society protect individuals' rights against political and economic powers. In reality civil society guarantees public area against digressions since public area has been suppressed by state and economic forces. In Habermas theory deliberative democracy like ideal state requests a influential and active public area and ideal public area is placed in civil society.

According to Keane the concept of civil society started from the 18th century begun to be perceived in opposition to state, as a sphere institutionally far-fetched from the government including "market exchanges, charitable groups, clubs and voluntary associations, independent churches and publishing houses[192]". First and foremost, the sphere of civil society implies the nonviolent, creative, initiative, democratic moods in the society. In fact this definition is still actual in contemporary world, when for instance for Poland, Hungary it turns to be associated with the all nation resistance to the totalitarian regimes.

Moreover, Keane accentuates the key issues characterizing the particularity of the concept of civil society. The civil society above all gives a priority to the individual freedom from violence, arbitrary conduct of the authorities, and social injustices. It struggles thus for the providing the individuals with the law basis and non-state communication media for free expression of social identities and realization of the freedom of communication. A kind of friendly political framework for the development of the key principle of civil society might be regarded a democratic regime. In Keane's view for the first time in the history of development of the civil society, namely in the middle of 20th century, the language of the democracy and civil society have become conjoined. Under democracy, the government and civil society tend to conduct separately, but contiguously, enjoying as public monitoring, compromise, and agreement as the newly experienced content of the dialogue.

To sum up, the concept of civil society is widely defined as one of the crucial pillars of Western mentality, type of behavior, social structure, to say more Western civilization, in the academic discourse it has broken the boundaries and has entered the realm of research interests of the Asian scholars. As Keane underlines: "A measure of the "emigration" of the term from its European birthplace is the way that the contemporary renewal of interest in civil society first began during the second half of the 1960s in Japan[193]". To the contemporary non-European

192 Keane, J. (2009). Civil Society, Definitions, Approaches. In *Springer-Ver* (promoted by the lag Berlin Heidelberg), pp. 34-40, p. 35

193 Ibid., p. 37.

inquiries on concept of civil society one might add: Norton, AR. ‘s *Civil society in the Middle East,* Bratton M. ‘s *Beyond the State: Civil Society and Associational Life in Africa*, Mardin S. ‘s *Civil Society and Islam.*

However, the spreading of the international popularity of the concept of civil society causes the ambiguities and confusions: the difficulty to define one meaning of the civil society, the variety of the approaches overlapping and completing each other, the search for reconciliation between the triad of approaches: 1) the theoretically-inclined interpretation, i.e. normative standpoint; 2) and empirical-analytic-interpretative approaches, preoccupied with the intellectual tasks, close to the methodological tools, such as “naming, categorizing, observing, theorizing, comparing, and understanding[194]” 3) the pragmatic and strategic usages urge for the clear definition of the necessary and unnecessary actions/steps on the route to the achieving the proper political aim.

Jan Kubik and Grzegorz Ekiert before approaching the understanding the phenomenon of the civil society distinguish its tree basic types: one normative and two analytical types. The concept of civil society as a normative concept is predominantly formulated by western thinkers. Moreover, it is a conceptual tool and one of the hallmark of the proving the uniqueness of the Western civilization. Civil society from the first analytical point of view is a practical sphere in-between, balancing between the society and the state that possesses an immunine against its interference and state’s arbitrary encroachment. Yet civil society from the second analytical point of view is perceived as a set of the united groups or organizations of people acting collectively in order to reach the similar aim. The character of activity runs by the organization is different thus many scholars distinguish the following type of organizations:1) if family as a primary organization so the civil organization is the secondary organization coming after the institution of the family. Above all, the members of civil organization might adopt its space by the opposing themselves to their background, i.e. family ties, cultural roots (Ekiert and Kubik exemplify Gellner’s modular man). 2) The openness and transparence of civil organization vis-à-vis public organization. 3) The tolerant, moderate, anti-radical direction of the civil organization’s activity makes their strategies and accompanying actions to be welcoming to the popular government and proctoring of individual rights. 4) The civil organization’s merit is also acclaimed in the promotion of the networks of relationships based on trust and reciprocity as a key factors of stabilizing the social capital (here Ekiert and Kubik refer to the chef figures in the promotion of the concept of social capital and trust, e.g. James S. Colleman, Alejandro Portes and Robert D. Putnam)

---

194 Ibid., p. 38.

As it is seen from the analytical perspective the authors selected two criteria: space and set of the group. The civil society is thus a space inhabited by the groups promoted its ideals and strategies, albeit that is flexible vis-a- vis social and political changes: in democratic regimes the space of civil society is "institutionally established, stabilized, and guaranteed usually, though not necessarily, by legal (particularly constitutional) regulations, although the boundaries of this space are usually contested and fuzzy[195]". It is worth mentioning the non homogeneous content of the groups, besides the protectors of civil society such groups as enemies and free rides are also presented. In the communist and fascist - like regimes, the space of civil society is more inhabited by the enemies than supporters. In official way, the space of civil society might be proclaimed as an under protection, but, in fact, the goal is the destruction and not supporting the further strengthening and enlargement of its boundaries.

For instance, under state socialist regime the space of civil society has been severely hemmed in and the groups have enjoyed a little autonomy and freedom. However, in post-totalitarian states in example of the countries in transition (e.g. post-soviet countries) the tendency to semi-autonomous climate has been noticed. The authors term this situation as institutionalized autonomy. There might be formulated the three forms, in their view: (1) pseudo-autonomous (e.g., official trade unions or professional associations); (2) semi-autonomous (e.g., some churches and religious organizations); and (3) illegally autonomous (e.g., dissident groups or black-market networks)[196]. The combination of all these form constitute in author's understanding the incomplete civil society comparing with legal transparent civil society, the type existed in democratic regimes.

All above mentioned historical review shows that there have been several consensuses on the meaning of the civil society. Furthermore, it was not always considered as a positive concept even traditional Marxism had not optimistic vision on civil society. In recent times, the role of civil society in the development of democratization has led to creating a positive view on the idea. In minimal understanding of civil society in recent decades, it is believed in general as an area of social communication separately from market, state and family sphere that consist of the non-governmental organization, social institutions, movements, free media, and voluntary associations. In these sphere people pursuit their personal interests in peaceful independent groups, separately of states and

---

195 Ekiert, G., Kubik, J. (2000). *Civil Society from Abroad: the Role of Foreign Assistance in the Democratization of Poland.* Weatherhead Center for International Affairs: Harvard University: Cambridge, p. 7.

196 Ibid., p. 8

market's oppressions. Civil society in its turn protects citizens' rights in opposition to state and economic forces. In methodological term in the context of Western philosophy the idea addressees to differentiate among: forms of authority other than the state; non-state forms of organization and associations, which are intermediate among the state and the family; voluntary associations; non-governmental associations; economic pressure groups; different kinds of professional organizations and social movements.[197]

The issues of civil society have been a matter of interest in Polish works of sociologists being in opposition to state in 1980's. The subject of sociological research as an academic science became only from 1989. However, I did not find one common definition of this concept in the works of Polish authors which I have been reading. For example, one of the most well-known Polish sociologists, Andrzej Siciński, considers civil society as a "spider web" of various types of links between individuals, through which citizens have an impact on the state. Such bonds formed from the initiative of citizens themselves, who operate independently from the state apparatus and are guided only by the motive of service for their social environment. Siciński defines the network as "authentic local government." In his opinion, civil society epitomizes such values as: openness, horizontal institutional and social bonds, also civic activity which involves responsibility, solidarity and obligation to the well-being of the community[198].

According to Wictor Osiatyński, civil society is "an autonomous being able to balance the power of the state", allowing the public to manifest their interests and needs, uniting them for the issues of common concern and also influencing on the public decisions. In order for civil society to play this role, it must have the viable internal forces and own structure, inter woven into a network, that is not controlled by the state and its associated apparatus. In this definition, civil society has a political character. According to the author, the state is necessary, however, it is always prone to degeneration, which in turn can, and should, counteract civil society as an autonomous entity[199].

Meanwhile, the authors of the texts have published the website of the Stefan Batory Foundation, defines civil society as a society where citizens feel co-responsible for the shape of democracy and do not expect that all their affairs will be arranged by the state. It also states that they organize themselves around their

197 Hudson, W. (2003). Problematizing European Theories of Civil Society. In D. C. Schak & W. Hudson (Eds.), *Civil Society in Asia*. Hampshire: Ashgate.

198 Gawin, D & Gliński, P. (2006) Civil Society In the Making. Warsaw. IFIS Publishers.

199 Osiyatiński, W. In Krasnodębski (2010) *Społeczeństwo obywatelskie i jego przyjaciele.* (Civil society and his friends).

needs, beliefs and desires. From this definition, the authors derive the postulate to support various "forms of social activity, mainly of independent non-governmental organizations, to take action where the role or the capacity of the state are inadequate, which helps to engage citizens in public life and create equal opportunities for socially vulnerable or disadvantaged groups [200].

In my opinion, all authors defining the concept of civil society would agree with Marta Lampart who lists the basic elements of this notion in clear and concise theses:

1) civil society is a group organization of society;
2) is based on a voluntary basis;
3) it represents the collective interests and serves for the common purpose;
4) it is located outside the structure of public authority and market, as well as outside the framework of a family or clan[201].

Qua case study of national example one might refer to a particular country and its peculiarities of the development of civil society. As Jacek Kurczewski and Joanna Kurczewska urge in article *A Self-Governing Society Twenty Years After: Democracy and the Third Sector in Poland* discusing the Polish debates on civil society the two approaches might be figured out. The first one presents civil society in purely Western vision as a society based on associational structure with the ruling liberal type of economy. The second approach is prone to a community model absorbed both by traditional and democratic traditions. (In my view, the second approach is closer to the theme of dissertation, i.e. juxtaposing of mahalla as a specific type of community of Tajik culture with the meaning of civil society developed within European culture).

In the belief of Jacek Kurczewski and Joanna Kurczewska, the civil society implies the supporting concept, the idea of citizenship. Taking into consideration, the thesis that people composed society play the pivotal role in the processes and events underwent in it, so in the case of defining the core of civil society as firstly a particular type of society, the members and the feeling and moods inspiring them to take part in the carrying out the changes to betterment must be clearly emphasized. "A civil society is composed of citizens who enjoy the rights of full social citizenship[202]" state Jacek Kurczewski and Joanna Kurczewska where the social citizenship signifies the certain kind of feeling toward community including the willing to act actively according to the dominance of political, social, and participatory rights. Later on the authors clarify their statement on the concept of citizenship: "If the key to citizenship is independence (as in the sovereignty of the community at the group level), then civil or legal rights are fundamental to such citizen-

200 Dudkiewicz, M. (2009) Technokracji Dobroczynności. Wydawnictwa Uniwersytetu Warszawskiego. Warszawa

201 Olejniczak, M. (2005) Europejskie społeczeństwo obywatelskie?(European civil society?)

202 Kurczewski, J. and Kurczewska J. (2001). A Self-Governing Society Twenty Years After: Democracy and the Third Sector in Poland. In *Social Research*, Vol. 68, No. 4, p. 968

ship; yet with its development other rights—political, social, and participatory—are an important, though not necessary, element"[203].

Joanna Kurczewska in the article *Local Civil Societies in Poland in the Nineties A Diagnosis* formulates triad:"state – the nation - civil society[204]" as a necessary condition for the transformation on qualitatively advanced level of social development. With the accent on local civic communities, Kurczewska views civil society as the last and not less important stage in the process of reconstruction local democracy in Poland.

Piotr Gliński, in the article *Operational Model of Civil Society,* is looking for elements of this concept that are common to different authors, despite having differences in theoretical approaches. In his view, the concept of civil society in literature is often ambiguous, and the considerations on it are complicated by referencing past authors without awareness, to the historical context in which this concept was present. He intends to define civil society by clarifying and structuralizing its theoretical history.

Gliński differentiates four theoretical trends in the study of concepts of civil society that are associated with various historical traditions of this concept. The first tradition is civic tradition that embraces the civic virtues: civic efficiency, responsibility and the capability of taking an active part in public life. The second tradition represents liberal tradition based on the doctrine of natural rights, including the emphasis on the idea that economic freedoms are crucial to the functioning of society.

The third tradition views civil society as an opposition to the state. In this perspective, civil society is considered as a sphere of independent citizen's activity, whereas the state is viewed as oppressive, and democracy is seen as prone to degeneration. Civil society, however, is quite the opposite and is regarded as a power able to exert pressure on the state in order to defend the rights of citizens. This is precisely because of the view of civil society that Adam Michnik, in his concept "new evolutionism", has included as the idea of the development of the civic communities among Polish dissidents in 1970s. In my view, a similar situation and – during the same time span of 70s and 80s – has been characterized with the occurrence of the movement of the dissidents in the republics of the USSR.

The fourth tradition, "communitarian", emphasizes the active engagement of the political or apolitical, local or non-governmental, social communities in the organizing of the social life of the citizens. In my opinion, the case of mahalla might fit this type of tradition, primarily for the reason that mahalla's leader and members are responsible for the living conditions of mahalla members.

203 Ibid.

204 Kurczewska, J. (2002). Local Civil Societies in Poland in the Nineties A Diagnosis. In *Polish Sociological Review,* No. 139, pp. 297-314, p. 312

As a result of his analyses, Gliński sums up nineteen descriptive characteristics, or as he calls it, dimensions, of civil society. 1) the first one describes the nature of civil society, the specific position – residence – it holds in society. Civil society is residual by definition. It is located among other groups – for example family, as a small social group, or model of Gramscian political society, as a large group. Whereas Aristotle identifies civil society and political community, John Locke and Thomas Hobbes tend to separate civil society form the state. Later, starting from the second half of the XVIII century, the civil society and state have been seen as separate spheres fulfilling different functions.

The second dimension concerns the horizontal nature of structural ties characterizing civil society. Such a structure guarantees the independence of both the individuals and the institutions involved in interactions between equal social and institutional partners. Thirdly, the civil society emerges only from the initiative of the free communities or individuals, which are capable of self-organization and implementation of Aristotle's ideal of political autonomy of citizens. Fourthly, the communities in general and the individual in particular must be conscious of the ideas they aim to reach, the project they intend to realize. For example, it is obligatory that they must be mature, motivated, pro- social form factors of social identities.

The fifth dimension is based on the principle of openness of the society. This means that civic groups and individuals formulate their identities on the ground of the broad spectrum of values. The sixth dimension supplements the fifth one: the spectrum of values must be limited by the social acceptance. This limit implies the acceptance of some axiological borders, which can be either human rights, citizens rights, Christian values, Koranic law or Confucian values.

The seventh feature of civil society includes the acceptance of the democratic "rules of the game". Gliński states that civil society aiming to co-operate with the state institutions that can function only in a democratic state, however, adding as a footnote, the civil society can also exist in a non-democratic state being as an opposition to the dominant regime. For instance, such an oppositional type of civil society functioned in Poland under the communist regime.

Next, the eighth feature concerns the respect of law. Good laws and the citizens that respect them constitute the firm basis for the civil society. The ninth feature presents the activity of the social group and individual. The social activities vary from the simple ones, such as an individual's promotion of some needs and interests, to complex ones such as lobbying the authorities, including the most serious, such as participation in politics.

The tenth characteristic concerns the level of tolerance toward the groups of "others". Civil society's tolerance moves from affirmation and respect for otherness through neutral acceptance, to consent to let these "other" group enjoy equal rights with the rest of society. The eleventh feature constitutes the capacity of the negotiating and mediating institutions which mitigate differences arising between various social groups. The role of these institutions is of much importance, since it aims to minimize and solve the conflicts that arise in the society. The twelfth characteristic is constant, dynamic public debate." The aim of this debate is to define different values and interests in the society, identify arguments and vantage points of the sides involved, and to broaden the scope of the understanding of the common good"[205].

The thirteenth and fourteenth features complement each other. Civil society, in order to function effectively, needs to have a solid economic base. This idea belongs to Adam Smith and Adam Ferguson, who believed that economic entrepreneurship enhances the promotion of civic values. The later feature implies the existence of ethical order, an awareness of the existence of social justice and acceptable living conditions for everyone. In civil society, there must be an equal access to occupying governmental positions or social goods such as knowledge, information, or the media. In the opposite situation, this may occur in social conflicts and dysfunction of public institutions. It can create feeling of deprivation and favorable conditions for the emergence of underclasses.

The fifteenth feature, in Gliński's opinion, is of very importance, and implies the implementation of civic virtues. This implementation, if it is direct, contributes to the common good, whereas the indirect facilitates the realization of the common good. One should understand civic values as being such values that inspire positive relations between people, thereby enlarging the feeling of civic responsibility for the community. Civic virtues exhibiting direct influence on civil society can be said to represent all individual attributes that are instrumental in establishing positive relations between people that in turn enhance citizens' responsibility for the community[206].

The sixteenth feature applies to the citizen's feeling of being represented in political life or feeling of "civic efficiency". As Gliński emphasizes: "Trust and the conviction that one can influence the decision-making processes in the country condition the evolvement of civic spirit". The seventeenth feature refers to the knowledge of civic issues. One of the most crucial conditions of the enhancing of civil society is the familiarity of citizens with their rights and the possibility to use them in the process of planning and implementing social changes.

---

205 Gliński,, P. (2006). Operational Model of Civil Society. In *Civil Society in the Making*. IFIS Publishers: Warsaw, pp. 62-77

206 Ibid.

The eighteenth feature concerns the principle of envisaging the self-organization of society in order to address social needs on the lowest level of local community or neighborhood. The organizational entities of the higher rank should support local initiatives by providing them with public resources. The last feature relates to the level of social capital in civil society. Gliński in this case refers to Robert Putnam's understanding of the concept of social capital, which means the generalization of norms of reciprocity and social trust that has been formed during the period of historical and cultural development. Gliński concludes that the operational model of civil society "identifies the different dimensions of civil society, whereas social practice determines whether these theoretical constructs will find their empirical confirmation and whether they will support or undermine one another[207]".

The democratic changes in Poland record the exclusively positive image of civil society[208]. Polish authors operate on the concept of civil society extensionally without exception, including all non-state forms of organization and associations in which people pursue their personal interests separately from the state and the market. With such a broad meaning of the concept of civil society, criminal organizations such as the mafia could also be within its scope. As far as I know, Piotr Gliński is one of others Polish authors – specializing on the concept of civil society – who introducing the concept of public benefit, narrows the scope of this concept. In his view, civil society represents only the organizations and associated activities that are related to the activity of the "common good". The concept of public benefit allows for the exclusion from the concept of civil society certain organizations which, for the most part, are opposed to the public good[209].

Piotr Gliński as a representative of the civil society in Poland, believes in constituting of so-called 'third sector' of Non Governmental Organizations. NGOs are specific, contemporary forms of social self-organization. They are structures to integrate groups of citizens that are characterized by a relatively mature social identity, a certain degree of organization, the private nature of the initiative, voluntary participation, independence and non-commercial and, usually, a substantial share of voluntary and important roles in shaping human

---

207 Ibid. p. 72.

208 On the base of literature available to me, I found the work of historian Sheri Berman titled Civil *Society and the Collapse of the Weimar Republic* that demonstrates the role played by civil society in the rise of power by Nazis in Germany in 1930s.

209 Gliński, P. Stylu działan organizacji pozarządowy ch w Posce. Grupy interesu czy pożytku publicznego (Styles of activities of NGOs in Poland. Interest groups or public benefit?). Wydawnictwo IFIS PAN.

attitudes (both those involved in organizations, and those having any contact with them). According to the aforementioned definition given by Piotr Gliński, NGO's are private institutions in the sense that they are set up for functioning through a common will associated in its citizens. It is not as a result of the decisions of public institutions, such state, government, local government.

The activity of NGOs is closely connected with the public sphere. The concept of public benefit is critical in understanding the role of NGO's in the public sphere. Public benefit is generally defined as an activity that meets noble or socially useful targets, or as having socially useful objectives conducted in the area of public tasks. However, not all researchers in Poland would agree with the view that the third sector meets the expectations of civil society. An example of such a position is read in the article *The Trap of Civil Society* by Agnieszka Graff[210]. Graff expresses the blunt statement, "We dreamed of a civil society, and we have a whole bunch of NGOs[211]". In her opinion, NGOs do not stimulate the activity of society and do not pursue the realization of one common social purpose. According to Andrzej Rychard, in studying non-governmental organizations we should not limit ourselves to NGOs as the basic most visible form in which civil society manifests itself. It should take into consideration civic ties and initiatives with a much less formal character[212].

It is a fact that American conservatives and leftist thinkers draw inspiration from the writings of Antonio Gramsci, who has believed that the institutions of civil civil society will be multiplying the number of people involved with social associations and their related activities for the realization of some important interests. According to Graff NGOs cannot fulfill this role because they are created on the grounds of philosophical ideas in which social activists should be replaced by the professionals. So, idea of NGO'S is to institutionalize the activities that should be grassroots and spontaneous. In her opinion NGOs act as small capitalist companies, seeking only specific goals and financial sources[213].

210 Graff, A. *Pułapka społeczentswa obywatelskiego* (The trap of civil socjety) Krytyka polityczna.18.10.2010

211 Ibid.

212 Rychard, A. (2004). *Entrepreneurs, Consumers and Civility: the Case of Poland.* IFIS: Warszawa.

213 Ilona Iłowiecka-Tańska expresses similar views on the role of NGOs

Chapter 4: Can mahalla be considered as a counterpart to Western civil society?

4.1. The problem of legitimacy of comparison civil society and mahalla

For the Western reader, the intention to present the idea of mahalla as a counterpart for the existing concept of civil society in the West might be seen as ambiguous one. I am convinced that I could defend my purpose by paying attention to what I believe to be a poor Western understanding of Tajik social institutions. To begin with, I would like to respond to a few views I found in the works of civil society which seem to exclude the possibility of mahalla being an equivalent of civil society.

4.1.1. Equality versus Hierarchy- casus Putnam

Until the eighteenth century, in European culture there was no idea of human equality. The people were diverse in terms of strata, and inequalities between stratas seemingly justified the alleged inequalities. Inherent moral qualities characterize each of their representatives. In Poland, people can still be found who claim that the word noble "*szlachcic*" comes from the word "*szlachetny*"[214].

Therefore, as a kind of the social convection to attribute high moral values to these representatives of high class. Not accidently, until now, in the Polish language, the word peasant is called *cham*[215] that is also the name of the Biblical Noah's son who treated his father in a morally repulsive way. The existing social inequalities and their corresponding moral values of differences are presented by the adherers of the various of Christian theology are explained as the consequences of the original sin committed by Adam and Eve. In Enlightment Pope, representing Catholic Church, and Voltaire, philosopher representing fervent anti-Church position, had worked to discredit the views most popular in the second half of the eighteenth century. In their poetry, they laughed at the notion that original

214 Zapaśnik, S. in his lectures.
215 Ibid.

sin may affect the differences of moral quality of the contemporary human[216]. The merits of Puritanism should be emphasized. Religion has proclaimed the existence of a link between the moral character of man and his work. In any case, in the late eighteen century, Western philosophers have rejected the notion that the moral values man are innate. It begins to spread the notion that moral character is created and is not fully determined by its origin constitutes.

The Western value of equality permeates the entirety of social life. Its symptom is the institution of democratic elections(today everyone adult has the right to vote), as in everyday social relationships ("Just call me by my first name"). According to Liu, most of the main social relations within a family are based on equality rather than hierarchy. Formality is not significant, and children are usually treated as adults, in that they can call their parents by their given names. Kinship relations are far from being felt as an important tie among members of society. Generally, kinship relationships are seen as important barriers to individual's self-development and progress. Liu observes that in secondary relationships, it is possible to notice that most friends and co-workers are also treated as equals. Subordinates believe that the superiors are the same kind of people like them, and superiors distinguish their subordinates the same way[217].

However, in the Eastern culture it is quite in contrary. According to some ethnographers, almost all relationships in Asia are hierarchical. Every person should behave according to his social status. The concept of hierarchy has been very strong in Asian culture. One can notice that even today most Easterners are quite aware of hierarchical differences in any interaction. For instance, when meeting a stranger, the conversation begins by explaining who is older and who is younger. The level of one's educational attainment is also important that helps to differentiate who is a teacher and who is a student. Especially, they are very conscious of relationships inside family structure. The members of the families should know how they should behave with others in the family. In Eastern countries, especially in the case of Tajikistan, it is possible to observe the signs of social hierarchy in nearly every setting: in the family, schools, streets and etc.

In the family, parents possess the highest status. Sons and daughters have to obey their parents. They should not interrupt them when they are speaking or disagree with them. In the streets, every person, when meeting someone who is their elder, should demonstrate respect by stopping and greeting the stranger

216 Zapaśnik, S.(1982). Kultura a filozofia Francii XVIII wieku (French culture and philosophy of the eighteenth century).

217 Liu Qingxue (2003). Understanding different cultural patterns or orientations between East and West. Shijiazhuang Mechanical Engineering College Hebei, China.

with the word "*Assalamu Alaykum*" (or *assalom, durud*), which means peace be upon you. Additionally, one should also include in greeting this greeting the person's title, if they are of high esteem. If a person whom one meets is older than him from between one month to about ten years, he will call him as *Barodari kalon* or *Aka* (means "older brother"). However, if the person is older by more than 15 or 20 years, he will call him *Amak* which means uncle. In the case of females, the habit is similar, except that they use other words, such as *khohar* (younger sister) or *apa*, which means older sister and *khola*, which means aunt. In Tajikistan like other Central Asian countries, there exist the custom of greeting others by shaking right hands, but it may take place between representatives of the same gender.

The behavior of Tajiks confirms that Tajik society also can be applied to the observations of other researchers of Asian countries that none of the members of these societies do not have a chance to meet in his life a person equal to him. Therefore, every Tajik is sensitive to the status of the person with whom they have contact with, and he/ she will behave according to the place in the hierarchy.

Robert D. Putnam in his well-known and often cited book, *Making Democracy Work: Civic Traditions in Modern Italy* challenges the view that in a hierarchical society, there might be an authentic institution of civil the society[218]. Interestingly enough in the fourth chapter of the book called *Explaining Institutional Performance,* the author starts with the question: What differentiates the successful regions in the North from the unsuccessful ones from the South? Trying to answer to this question, he points out that the economic development of the North was stimulated by the rising of civil society institutions. This leads to the process of economic and social transformation that in other Western European countries has led to an increasing of living standards, level of education, and etc and what in case of Italy has happened the end of the nineteenth century.

The changes touched all regions of Italy, but the results have been different. Since the beginning of the transformation, contrasts can be noted in the development between the northern and southern regions. And this condition does not change even though in Putnam's opinion, the poorer regions receive substantial dots from the central regional government (southern regions have more funds available that they are able to expend). In Putnam's view, differences in economic performance are consequences of differences in the condition of "civic society".

218 Putnam, R. D. (1994). *Making Democracy Work.* Princeton University Press: New Jersey.

In his analysis, the author was inspired by the idea of "civic virtue" (the term is derived from Nicolo Machiavelli's thought) and the observations of Alexis de Tocqueville on American society contained in the often quoted by Putnam book, *Democracy in America*. Putnam describes what civic community means in practice. The starting point for him is the notion of citizenship. This concept implies, first and foremost, active participation in public affairs. In other words, the state of being devoted to the political activity is the manifestation of the abovementioned civic virtue. Secondly, citizenship in the civic community implies equal rights and obligations for everyone. Speaking about the civil organizations that, according to Tocqueville, differ from political ones. Thus it is relevant to notice that their existence is the condition of effectiveness and stability of the democratic institutions. In Putnam's words, members of civic organizations represent the political sophistication, social trust and skills of cooperation.

Putnam underlines four indicators of "civic-ness" that later he unites in one Civic Community Index. The first two correspond with Tocqueville's concept of the civic community, and the later two refer to the particular political behavior. First indicator is, in Putnam's opinion, vibrancy of associations. In other words, the presence of a variety of local and national associations such as amateur soccer clubs, hiking club, bird-watching groups, literary circles, hunter's associations and sport clubs that lead among others in the sphere of activity. Explaining this criterion, Putnam notices the important role of mass media in informing people about community affairs. In any case, it is the continuation of the Tocqueville idea of the connection of civic associations with local newspapers. Another measure of "civic-ness" is political participation in the form of electoral turnout. The civic activity showed significant results of attendance in referenda on anti-terrorism (1981) or nuclear power (1987). However, turnout in general election is not a relevant indicator of "civic-ness", because of the system of voting where voters have to choose from a single party list. Actually, it is not an indicator of civic community. In Putnam's words; it is more about personalism, factionalism, and patron-client politics.

Speaking about Italy's twenty regions, the most civic and average civic index is represented in the North, with the least civic area being in the South. The citizens from the most civic regions are involved in all kinds of local associations, and they also express interest in the local press. Putnam uses the following example, where he illustrates that when two citizens from civic regions meet on the street, both of them have a topic for conversation from the newspaper they have read earlier. People from less civic regions hardly do it. Later, Putnam prefers to name regions, using labels more or less civic instead of antagonism -North and South. In this sense, he underlines "civic-ness" as a main criterion of the difference[219].

In the following discussion, Putnam draws attention to the differences in the character of the political elites. He says that the politics of less civic regions is realized in patron-client networks. He also notices that the educational level among politicians is higher in less civic regions. In other words, the representatives of the regional elite in the less civic regions are taken from the privileged stratum of the population, while political leaders from the most civic regions come from middle- class background. The political leaders in the more civic regions are distinguished by their ability to compromise, thus Putnam characterizes them using the concept of an openness of partisanship. Putnam also characterizes the civic community by three significant affiliations for majority of Italians: unions, Church, and political parties. In Italy white collar and agriculture unions are common and, in general, political motivation and ideological tradition are more important than economically oriented motivation.

In Putnam's opinion, the presence of the Papacy in Rome influences civic life of all the Italian regions. Data show that religious sentiments and civic activity are not identical. Practicing Italians are not interested in public affairs, they rarely read newspapers and do not discuss politics. In the first two decades after World War II, the Catholic Action, a federation of Catholic associations, has appeared. In his view, it can be treated as an example of the attempt to combine religious and civic duties in one homogeneous behavior. It has remained in history as a mass organization, that at its peak enrolled about tenth of all Italian men, women, and children in cultural, educational activity. The Catholic Action was more present in northern, more civic regions, than in the southern ones. In the 1960's, because of the of secularization of Italian society, the federation collapsed. Putnam returns again to Machiavelli by noticing that in contemporary Italy, as in the Italy of Machiavelli's time, the civic community is a secular community.

The presence of Italian political parties characterizes all Italian regions. Therefore, citizens from more and less civic regions are active in political affairs and interested in the politics as well. Furthermore, the less civic regions, despite the small amount of civic associations, are characterized by a highly developed political capacity. However, citizens in the less civic regions, in spite of their political capacities, feel powerless. In Putnam's opinion, the level of education does not underlie the security. For him, honesty, trust, and law-abidingness are the most crucial criteria of civic virtue, and all should be manifested in the civic attitudes.

---

219 Ibid.

For these reasons, collective life in the civic regions is eased by the expectations that others will follow the rules, and the mutual trust will be performed in such a way. Summarizing all the above, Putnam presents the results of a nationwide survey where twenty-five thousand people were asked about satisfaction with their own life. Surprisingly, the citizens of more civic regions are much more satisfied with life.

The fifth chapter called *Tracing the Roots of the Civic Community*, begins with the attempts to point out the roots to the civic community in the history of Italian regions. Putnam once more asks the question: What makes one region more civic than another? He underlines that from a millennium and a half ago, from the fall of Rome Empire until the middle of the nineteenth century, Italy was a conglomerate of separate city-states. Traditionally, the Middle Ages are treated as the Dark Ages in the historiography of many countries. According to Putnam, in Italy it is quite the opposite case. He feels that the differences between the development of the northern and southern regions are inherent to the history of Middle Age Italy.

From the eleventh century, both the North and the South developed differently. In the beginning of the fourteenth century, in Italy two patterns of governance functioned: feudal autocracy of the South and fertile communal republicanism. Both systems were different in accordance to their structure and consequences. In the North, for instance, feudal bonds of personal dependence were weakened, but conversely, in the South, they were strengthened. In the North, the people were citizens, but in the South, they were subjects. In the northern regions, the legitimate authority was by citizens delegated to public officials. In the southern regions, the legitimate authority was monopolized by the king[220].

The North has succeeded in establishing the civic associations since Medieval times (in the twelfth century new local organizations such as neighbourhood associations, parish organizations, and politico-religious parties played the dominant role in local affairs). The same tendency has been prolonged in the nineteenth century, when in the post-unification period, new associations appeared like their analogues in France (France provided an example of Masons lodges, choral societies and peasant clubs). In this case, Putnam makes a conclusion that regions that have been civic in the last centuries remain the same in present time.

Answering the main question about the crucial reason of these differences, Putnam again combines two criteria. From the one hand, it is economic development, and from the other, civic community. He questions what has come first –

220 Ibid.

economics or civics? Despite the different level of economic success, northern regions have remained as civic ones throughout its history. In his opinion, economics does not predict civics, but civics does predict economics. For example, Emilia-Romagna, contemporaneously the most civic city in Italy in the last centuries in terms of political participation and social solidarity, is holding similar leading positions. Generally speaking, in the case of Italy, is relevant to claim that the most economically successful regions are the most civic ones.

To sum it all up, Putnam in the fourth and fifth chapters asks about the criterion of visible difference in the successful North and the unsuccessful South. Underlining the level of presence of civics as criterion, he calls regions more and less civic. Exploration of the question of differences in development has made him look to history. Taking into account establishing civic organizations as one of the characteristics of civics, Putnam firstly noticed the role of the past, because northern regions succeeded in both the last centuries and today.

I do not have sufficient competence to write about the history of Italy. However, in my opinion, Putnam overlooked that the North and South have belonged to different cultures for almost the whole of Italian history. The history of the North, the territory of where Lombards have been settling, connected with the history of Germanic peoples, and the influence of Western Europe always been strong here, while the South has long been associated with Byzantium, for a short time it has been occupied by the Arabs (and still the influence of Arab culture is present), and almost in its entire history, it has been connected with the history of Habsburgs, beginning with the Spanish, and later the Austrian monarchy. Therefore, the North and South are not different in terms of civics, but rather in terms of cultural values. Putnam is further wrong in claiming that the condition of honesty, trust and law abiding comprising the concept of civic virtue is the existence of the idea of equality between men and that they cannot develop in a hierarchical society. In my opinion, as I shall argue further, they are more strongly developed in Tajik society than anywhere in the West even though, as I have stated, is very hierarchical.

4.1.2 Mahalla and modernisation projects

The concept of civil society remains alien for the Tajiks until the systematic change that have been began in 1991 before the collapse of the USSR. The Tajiks were introduced to these concepts only with the appearance of the first Western aid organizations that have already started to work there during the Civil War. For the managers of the Western organizations coming to Tajikistan during that time and now, NGOs have been the equivalent to civil society. Also, the idea of association of civil society with the NGO's brought with them resulted in changes to the legislation imposed by the Western countries and organizations such as OSCE. In the Tajik Law regarding civil society as an institution of such society, takes into account the sole NGO's.

Such an understanding of the concept of civil society did not arise the opposition of Tajik elites striving to constitutional changes. They have been the product of the Soviet times, and in their opinion - as taught by Soviet Marxism – modernization could be made only by the complete elimination of tradition.

It is true that the opposition of traditional elements of society to modernization hads been described from the 1970's. However, because of the isolation of the Tajik science from the Western science, this change in views on the role of traditional institutions in the process of modernization has been unknown in Tajikistan. The vast majority of Tajik intellectuals, as carried out by the results of my interviews, is still deeply convinced that the institution of traditional society can be a hindrance in the process of modernization. At the same time, they pointed out that even in the USSR there had been some forms of the organizations corresponding to the idea of civil society. Precisely, they were the first to point out the role of such traditional institutions such as mahalla, avlod or gashtak in providing social protection to members and resolving community problems[221].

This is a case of the authors of the reports, for instance from such organizations as the Aga Khan Foundation and UNDP, thematically touched the issue of civil society that kinship and clan can serve as a base for organizing civil society in Tajikistan[222]. As in one of the examples, Freizer, explains the significance of traditional institutions such as the mahalla and avlod in providing social safety to members and resolving neighborhood problems[223]. On this basis, she proposes the idea of a 'communal[224]' civil society reflecting the social relations in Central Asia. She believes that exactly this in the future will contribute to betterment of the social conditions than any of Western neo-liberal models. Nevertheless, by these considerations, traditional Tajik institutions are treated as a potential ally of the NGO's, but not as the institutions that could play an equally important role as the NGO's in regime change.

---

221 Giffen, Earle & Buxton (n.d.). *The Development of Civil Society in Central Asia*. INTRAC.

222 Ibid.

223 Freizer, S. (2004). Central Asian Fragmented Civil Society: Communal and Neoliberal Forms in Tajikistan and Uzbekistan. In Glasius, M., Lewis, D. and Seckinelgin, H. (eds.) *Exploring Civil Society: Political and Cultural Contexts*. London and New York: Routledge.

224 Ibid.

In my opinion, such an attitude towards the mahalla in the Western projection of civil society in Tajikistan is a consequence of the fact that the institution of mahalla is based on Islam. Already in the 1980s, Samuel Huntington has provocatively pointed out that in any of the countries where the main religion is Islam, there is no democracy. This view ahs been echoed in the immensely influential book *The Clash of Civilizations and the Remaking of World Order*[225] published in 1996. Under the influence of this book, it has become a popular view – and a basis for a bias - in the West that Islam is the enemy for Christian civilization and its values. I believe that this thesis in its turn has deeply influenced on the views of politicians, lawyers and Western managers who reject the idea that mahalla could be an important instrument for building civil society.

Reflecting on democracy in Muslim countries, the Westerners have usually adopted a misconception that religion is one of the crucial impediment on the route to democracy. Both representatives of the extreme Christian rights and the followers of the ideology of liberalism believe that their values are universal. In turn, in general in the theories of social change adopted in Western science, culture is not considered as an agent of social change. For these two reasons, the dangers of political change in Central Asia are proved to be susceptible to Huntington's assertions about the role of Islam. Although Huntington himself, by criticizing the views of social sciences on the development of the Third world societies, has postulated the necessity to consider culture as an important factor in the processes occurring them. In my interpretation, Huntington has not manifest the deep knowledge of cultures he has been referring to. This is shown in the concept of civilization he operates wiht. Till now as a result, the concept of civilization is overlapped with the concept of culture, perceived a high level of development of human race.

The point is what criterion will assist to distinguish cultural attribute in every level of development of humanity. According to the tradition of the nineteenth century, the attribute of civilization would be literacy. In the twentieth century, following Australian archeologist Gordon Childe, the attribute of civilization started to be the process of urbanization. Recognizing religion as the only attribute of civilization, Huntington has demonstrated that he neither understands the culture, nor the relationship between the concepts of culture and civilization. In my strong opinion, he has not avoid the prejudice against Is-

225 Hungtington S. (1987). *The Goals of Development*. In Wiener, M. & Huntington, S. (Eds.). *Understanding Political Development*. Boston Little Brown and Co.

lam presented in Western culture since the era of the Crusades. His vision of the world – as constant conflicts between cultures – has formulated present reality as the conflict between Islam and Christianity. In this way, Islam in his discussion is a potential enemy to Christianity, and Islamic civilization is a negation of the values upon which Christian Western civilization rests.

It is also needed to present a large number of the critical feedbacks *Clash of Civilizations* has invoked in the milieu of the scholars and researchers. I would like to sketch those that in my opinion are significant and reflect my own interpretation of main theses of this work. Firstly, such grand works as Fukuyama's *End of History* and Huntington's *Clash of Civilizations* have attempted to provide answers to the central political questions of the post Cold War world. However, both theses have faced criticism for their particular assumptions. Fukuyama's analysis has been disparaged for not sufficiently weighing the national and religious revival that had taken place in the former Soviet Union and the wider world as societies emerging from the Cold War sought to reclaim their pasts and their cultures. These "spiritual" movements reflected the continuing appeal of alternatives to liberalism, and many have been openly hostile to the West, rejecting Western liberalism as arrogant, exploitative, morally bankrupt, and obsessed with the satisfaction of individual material needs. The *End of History* thus represents an unjustified assumption of liberalism's superiority and destiny as the universal civilization to that all would ultimately subscribe.

Secondly, there are two basic problems with the Clash of Civilizations theory. First off, the methodological foundations of the thesis involve a program of categorizing the peoples of the world according to one, supposedly objective system. To classify individuals unhesitatingly as members of civilizations (for example as members of "the Western world," or "the Islamic world", or "the Buddhist world") is overly reductionist and ignores numerous other affiliations, such as by profession, industry, politics, and education. Second off, the civilizational categories are far from clear-cut; the misreading of history attached to this categorization overlooks each culture's complexities and neglects historical interactions between them. There is almost one and a half billion Muslims, most of whom are not Arabs, and whose priorities and cultures are very diverse. Moreover, the Islamic world, just like other civilizations, is divided into states, each with its cultural and traditional traits, and often is engaged into inner rather than external conflicts, i.e. accent on the inside when outside perspective [226].

Thirdly, in the view of Fouad Ajami, it is fair to urge that states control civilizations rather then opposite: civilizations control states [227]. During last several decades, the governments of two states in the Middle East that have most frequently invoked religion to legitimize their rule had been the Saudi Arabia and Iran. Yet Saudi Arabia has remained a staunch American ally while Iran still tries to oppose itself to the U.S. foreign policy. Moreover, following the Iraqi invasion of Kuwait in 1990, many major Muslim countries, including Saudi Arabia, Syria, and Egypt, acted against Huntington's formula by joining the United States in a war against their fellow Muslim state of Iraq[228].

Fourthly, among the recent publications there is the accent on the identity problem. In view of Chaklader Mahboob-ul Alam, an author of article *Huntington Was Wrong*[229], the very attitude to the Muslims is prone to form the image of the "others" where otherness is inevitably hostile, politically dangerous. The identity of Muslims constructed by Huntington is based on the religion – that is correctly plays a crucial role in the life of the Muslims – but the very approach is one-way, and as a result the one-side identity is seen disadvantageous, and mistakenly, the Muslims are denied from the possibility to build democratically-based society, to open dialogue with other nations from other parts of the world, in a short they become isolated and deprived from the goods enjoyed by Western world.

In my interpretation, the clash of civilizations implies the clash or old-aged confrontation between the East and the West, the very idea and as leitmotif brightly and detailed has been presented by prominent scholar Edward Said in *Orientalism*. The orientalistic biases which in Said's view are of political explanation still are not removed from the agenda of the international arena. The bipolar vision of the world despite its cultural narrowness and explicit ignorance of the diversities, multicultural background is in a way a justification for breaking up the conflicts from local to global scale. Apropos, Chaklader Mahboob-ul Alam refers to Said as a open critic of Huntington's theses. He cites Said explaining the core of his critique: the confrontation between two extremes is prone to the

---

226 Shireen T. Hunter In *The Future of Islam and the West* (1998). Westport, Conn.: Praeger, p. 411.

227 Fouad Ajami (1993). The Summoning. In *Foreign Affairs* 72.4.

228 Shibley Telhami, (2001). American Foreign Policy Toward the Muslim World In *SAIS Review* 221.2 pp. 139-154. See also Roy Mottehedeh, (1995). The Clash of Civilizations: An Islamicist's Critique. In *Harvard Middle Eastern and Islamic Review* 2.1 p. 126.

229 An article has been recently published on this issue in *The Daily Star* (31.03.2011)

ignorance of the interdependencies, multi-identical and multicultural context of the constant-changing world. Chaklader Mahboob-ul Alam writes "Huntington's categorisation of the world's fixed "civilizations" omitted the dynamic interdependence and interaction of cultures over the centuries.[230]"

Reading the works of the Western authors, I almost have not meet any more or less objective understanding of the relationships that exist between the cultures of Muslim societies and the religion of Islam. Only a very few Western scholars are aware of the fact that Hanafi school of Sunni Islam is tolerant towards tradition. It accepted local customary *adat* and accordingly adapted to it, and did not change them. If there are no democratic institutions in Muslim societies, it is always characteristic of the culture, and it is not the fault of the religion. It is the fact that Islam encourages certain organizational and associational forms in that authority is chosen, as is the case of mahalla. Even such radical forms of Islam such as Islamic fundamentalism, above all, seeking to restoration of the Caliphate apply to the view that the Caliph, as a ruler, would be chosen by the believers.

Emphasizing that religion is a basis of the mahalla institution I should warn against any possible misunderstanding. Independence of NGOs lies in the fact that their choice of targets and methods of action are unfettered from the government institutions, business, sponsors, etc., but also from religious institutions. I think that there is a great misunderstanding of Islam in the West. Moreover, in my opinion, there is a tendency in the West about not fully awareness about differences between Islam and Christianity. In all its versions, Christianity exists as a church, as a hierarchical organization. However, Islam is a religion supporting the self-governing communities. It is a historical fact that the Tajiks underwent not one attempt to subdue religious communities. For instance, in Tsarist Russia and later in the Soviet Union for that purpose such institution as D*uchownoe Uprawlenie Muzułman Sredni Azii i Kazachstana* (Spiritual Directorate of the Muslims in Central Asia and Kazakhstan) has been launched. Yet, as I have mentioned above, such attempts could not subordinate fully mahalla which, despite discussed repressions, amazingly has remained as a partially independent social institution. This striving to independence mahalla tries to keep till now. In my interpretation, mahalla is different from the Polish parish organization, called *parafia*, this is because its religious leader, imam, is chosen by community and its funding source is a charity collected by mahalla members. Imam is working first of all for the interest of his community escaping the command completed by the designated national hierarchy.

---

230 Ibid.

4.1.3 Is Mahalla a public benefit organization?

The reports prepared for the Western organizations, by Western experts and their Tajik counterparts, repeated the negative evaluation of NGO's as a tool for the development of civil society in Tajikistan. Akiner, for example, believed that Western concepts of civil society are unsuitable for Tajik society[231]. Oliver Roy, in contrast to Akiner, argues that the efforts of international donors to endorse civil society will eventually fail in Central Asia" if NGO's continue to ignore a traditional [...] social fabric"[232]. In turn, a critical evaluation of NGOs in Tajikistan are contained in the report of the Polish authors Zapaśnik, Cieślewska and Marszewski and based on the empirical research in different regions of Tajikistan conducted in 2010[233]. The authors establish fact of the usage of mahallas as the most important instrument of constitutional political transformation in Tajikistan. They invoke the memorandum prepared by the Tajik managers working in international aid organizations in Tajikistan. This memorandum challenges the assertion that NGO's in Tajikistan contribute to the creation of civil society, and it suggests instead the utilization of mahallas for this purpose.

Characterizing NGO's as organizations of civil society, Piotr Glinski, in his work *Style działań organizacji pozarządowych w Polsce. Grupy interesu czy pożytku publicznego?* (Styles of activities of NGOs in Poland. Interest groups or public benefit?) introduces the concept of public benefit. Earlier, when writing about Glinski's views, I expressed the conviction that the concept of public benefit is also important for the presentation of mahalla as civil society institutions. Albeit, with one exception: NGO's are working for the realization of rather narrow scope of objectives mentioned in the statute defining the legal framework of its activities. The aim of mahalla is a social protection of its members and solving community problems in the changing historical conditions. Thus, the scope of its activities is extremely broad, and the priorities are not determined.

Not many researchers will question the fact that the activity of mahalla is useful, in the sense that it is providing a certain good or services for mahalla residents. In this way, it is also useful in the sense that it contributes to the development of common good and positive characteristics of society. Mahalla's model

231 The views of the author I know from Roy's *Civil society In Central Asia.*

232 Roy, O (1999). Kolkhoz and Civil Society in the Independent States of Central Asia. In Ruffin, M.H. and Waugh, D. (eds.) *Civil Society in Central Asia*, Seattle: University of Washington Press/Center for Civil Society International.

233 Zapaśnik, S. & Cieslewska, A. & Marszewski, M. (2010). Relationship between self-governments and Informal, Traditional institutions, and International and Local NGOs in Tajikistan.

is derived from tradition. If its activity is in accordance with this model, it helps to strengthen it in society.

Secondly, mahalla is not an organization created for the realization of narrow purposes. Surely, it works primarily for the benefit of its members. Mahalla care of people at risk, weak or socially disadvantaged. It supports the special talented representatives of youth among its members by providing for them, for instance, financial support for their studies. All of these activities are related to their own members. Quite often, though mahalla, cooperate with other mahallas to implement general social goals. For instances, mahallas in a particular areas build sports facilities to satisfy the needs of all the residents of the whole region.

Another example is collecting money for the purchase of vaccines aimed to protect all children living in one territory from the epidemic polio. Consistent with the tradition of Islam, the faithful are obliged to spend 2.5 percent of their income to help needy people. This kind of charity, as it was mentioned before, is called *zakat* in Islam. Well, I have personally witnessed several times where wealthy people from one mahalla divide the collected *zakat* not only among its poor members, but also some poor people from neighboring mahallas. In the mahalla where I am from, the well-to-do people usually help mahallas where Uzbeks live, and also Uzbeks help to mahallas where Tajiks live, despite the ethnic antagonism that exists between Tajik and Uzbeks. In the case of some other mahallas that were formed by a population who flooded to this territory recently, and who did not have enough land of their own, other mahallas allowed them to use part of our cemetery to bury their dead. For these reasons, none of the divisions of non-governmental organizations presented in the above-mentioned Glinski's book apply to mahalla. It is not an organization that provides exclusive service to its members, because many of its activities involve a wider audience.

4.1.4 Cultural values of the Tajik people

The gist of the traditional patterns of behavior and institution of Tajik social life consists of the complex values hiding under the concept of humanity (odamiyat or insoniyat). Nowadays, odami komil is a significant notion in Tajik Islamic culture, which means a true human being. In English translation, odami komil means "Perfect Human Being". The names of *insoni komil* and *odami komil* are used as synonyms. *Insoni komil* derives from Arabic word (الاسان الكام), that has been rendered in Persian (انسانِ کامل), Tajik *Инсони комил* and in Turkish *İnsan-ı Kamilı.* The Arabic name has been used also by the Sufi brotherhoods. The perfect human being should implement in his life such important values of humanity as *adab, hurmat or ehtirom, nomus, obru, mehmondusti* and etc.

Possessing these values distinguishes man from animal. However, to embody the certain ideal of humanity is a rigid lifelong struggle. It may happen that a man had committed the particular condemned moral offense, so immediately he loses his complete humanity in the eyes of his community. He loses the right to be regarded by others as a human being. Thus, such a saying is popular among Tajiks:

> *Olim shudan oson, Odam shudan mushkil.* (It is easy to be scientist but it is very difficult to be a human person)[234].

Adab derives Arabic word ادب means behavior, politeness, morals, manners, decorum, decency, good breeding, respect, discipline, learning, doctrine. This is a highly polysemantic word. Under the concept of adab, one must envisage the patterns of particular behavior. For instance, it might mean good manners, but I believe that in its core it is a pure moral concept. Therefore, it is not complex to find an equivalent word in English that would embrace the whole multi-sided meaning of adab. Generally, under the concept of adab, the attitude based on *tarbiyat* (good breeding) might be understood. In this religious and cultural context it is a quite significant duty for the Tajiks to provide a good upbringing for their children. Therefore, Tajik people always mention *tarbiyai farzand* (children growing up) as a basic duty of parents. If someone commits a bad deed, in some mahallas or in public places, the people will say that it is the fault of his parents. They call such person *beadab* (person without adab, i.e. good manners).

From the religious perspective, adab is a moral quality meaning "breeding", "decency", also, it is a steadiness of the spirit after being conjoined with true faith. It is possible to state that adab elevating from the religious level has been endorsed to the human being as one of important characteristics to honored man such as striving to in the various affairs of daily life. Islam teaches man the highest moral norms of daily behavior on the basis of the life and achievements in prophetic and socio-political aspects of the Prophet Muhammad (BPUH), whose example serves as the first and the brightest to follow. Undoubtedly, being a challenge to human nature, adab implies all life-long self-training and self-discipline in order to meet the requirements. For instance Muhammad Fertullah Gulen, the contemporary Turkish theologist, in *The Doubts Caused by the Century*, cites the following wisdom sayings: "Abad is that always hides nudeness of man… Without this robe man is like a nude… in other words, the breeding of

234 Author's translation.

man is similar to the robe that hides the nudeness and protects from the strange looks. If man is not breed, he is like someone without robe[235]".

The concept of adab in Tajik culture also bears a religious significance. In the process of the domestic upbringing of children, parents often quote the words written by Prophet Muhammad (BPUH). "Good breeding is a part of faith. The beauty and propriety of all affairs, religious as well as temporal, depends on a certain discipline of good breeding. Humanity, it consists in noble- mindedness; religiously, in observing the Sunnah (Prophet tradition); in love, good breeding is reverence. A person who neglects this discipline cannot ever possibly be a Saint, for The Prophet said 'Good breeding is a mark of those God loves [236]". The great number of the proverbs on adab proves the significance of its value in the Tajik culture. One of the most frequently used proclaims:

> *Az beadabi kase ba maksad narasad, Zero, ki adab toji sari mardon ast.*
> (Without good breeding anybody will not reach his aim, because adab- good breeding is the crown of men[237]).

Another concept in Tajik culture which plays an important role in interpersonal relations is *Ehtirom*. *Ehtirom* is the plural of the word *hurmat* and applies to the relation to people in old age, that thus can be interpreted as evidence that such men are subject of the respect accumulated during lifetime and maintained by the kin, they belong to. The word *ehtirom* also can mean honor, but to its connotation the concept of obligation should also be added. Children must have *ehtirom* for "*buzurgon*" (great or big personality) someone who is older or possesses higher social status. The source of cultivation of ehtirom is the education achieved at home. Children learn the responsibilities of *ehtirom* in their relations with parents, brothers, sisters, relatives and community members. This is especially the case in their relationship with their parents, who have the highest status in the family. Children should not interrupt their parents when they are speaking or disagree with them. When parents enter the home, children have to stand up and welcome them. The obligation of such behavior is also justified by the following proverbs:

Padaru Modar rozi- Khudo rozi (if parents are content on you, so God is also content on you). On the basis of these attitudes, children are well aware that they

235 Author's translation from Gulen, F. (2010). Somneniya Porojdennye Vekom. (The Doubts Caused by the Century) Kokjiev-B: Almaty, p. 215.

236 Sahragard R.(2008) *A Cultural Script Analyses of a Politeness Feather in Persian*, p. 8.

237 Author's translation.

should not be disobedient to their parents. As the sayings from Hadiths express the moral doctrine of Islam:

> *Jannat, ki rizoi mo dar on ast,* (Paradise that we want to reach it),
> *Dar zeri kudumi Modaron ast.* (Lays under the mothers feet).

If someone did not respect older people, the Tajiks call such men *beehtiromi* (men without respect). Apropos, respect should be given not only to the elders but everybody has right to it. Therefore, the Tajiks stopped by a foreigner on the street and asked about directions must, as I wrote above, greet them in a certain way before giving an answer. This greeting includes saying "good day" and asking about his health and his family.

In the Tajik society *Ustod* (teacher, professor, or religious teacher) is considered as the person most worthy of respect As in times of Ayni who wrote in his memoires that his father says to the teacher: you can do with him what you want, his body belong to you and bones belong to me. By the way, today this attitude is still actual. Therefore, every Tajik respects his teachers like own parents, and in some cases, even more. In illustration, this proverb says:

> *Qadri ustod az padar besh ast,*
> *W-az Padar Ustod dar pesh ast.*
> (The value of teacher is more than father, because teacher in life stays before the father[238]).

There is also another proverb concerning respect for the teachers. *Javri ustod beh az mehri padar* (a teacher's cruel discipline is better than the love of the father). It means that the education is very significant and should be sought even under harsh circumstances.

Another important value for Tajiks is *nomus* (honor). An honorable Tajik never thinks solely about himself. In making any decisions, he always considers what consequences the decision will have for his family, avlod and mahalla. On this ground, the importance of honor in the life of the Tajiks is confirmed by the instance of credit organizations providing mini- credits. Western organizations working in Tajikistan require guarantors as a mandatory condition to providing loans, whereas Tajik organizations do not stipulate such conditions. This is because of the belief of family honor, and the potential repayment of the loan by members of the family.

Every Tajik is obliged to defend the positive reputation of his family and his avlod. The man has to defend the *nomus* of his house against any threats (physical and verbal) to the members of his family from others. *Nomus* of a man is also

238 Author's translation.

related with the honor of all the women in his family (mother, wife, sisters and daughters). According to tradition, an honorable man has to be ready to fight in any situations where a woman of his family becomes the object of slander or gossip. In Tajik culture, the concept of honor coincides closely related with the concept of shame (*ayb or sharm*).

A woman who violates certain moral standards, as defined by the religious concept of *haram*[239] (a forbidden act), brings shame not only to her family and the entire avlod. For example, it shall be considered *haram* behavior for a woman to dance in the presence of men who are not family members. This type of behavior can have very serious consequences for the family's face (reputation) if the dancing took place in the presence of men outside of the family. An unmarried woman's virginity is an especially important topic for the honor of the family. In the case of married women, suspicions of marital infidelity may arise if a man's wife speaks longer with a man than she does with her husband or other family members.

The custom of honor killings is alien in Tajik culture, although it does occur in some ethnic groups living in neighboring Afghanistan. However, due to the importance placed upon moral offenses related to sex and their consequently strict observance by the community, they may occur in order to preserve family honor. A Tajik who exposes himself to shame in the eyes of his mahalla members by, for example, not showing the proper respect to older people, may avoid public places for some time. Forgiveness of his action by the community will depend on whether or not he will go to the injured person's house to apologize (the act of apologizing is called *tawba* in Tajik). However, despite the significant role of shame in the culture of the Tajik, it should not be regarded as a culture full of shame which is highlighted by the Ruth Benedict in her work *"The Chrysanthemum and the Sword"*[240]. The Tajiks, in fact, experience - and sometimes even very strongly - feelings of guilt when they commit a bad behavior to a close acquaintance, family member or friend.

The last of the aforementioned important cultural concepts is the notion of *mehmondusti* (hospitality). Tajik believes that a guest is sent from God. The best food and the most comfortable conditions for the guest are always reserved by the members of the hosting family. In the case that difficulty arises in accommodating a guest, the host's neighbors will help him with the arrangements. For

239 Haraam is an Arabic word (حَرام) that means sinful. In Islam haraam acts are acts prohibited in religious texts and possess the highest status of prohibition given to anything that would result in sin when a Muslim commits it.

240 Benedict, R. (1946) *The Chrysanthemum and the Sword: Patterns of Japanese Culture.* Boston: USA.

instance, the foreigner or outsider coming to the village will not have any difficulties in finding a place to rest, because all the members of the community are happy to invite him into their quarters. These traditions are still practiced in Tajik society to this day. One of my interviewers said:

> *We all must to be very hospitable. For the main reason that it is our duty. Throughout history of our descendants they always respected their guests. Because, guest is send to us by God. By the will of God he comes to our house. That is why we have to meet them with smile and provide him the best what we have (man 48 years old. July, 2011).*

4.1.5. Education

As it had been mentioned above, *tarbiya* is a local term that means education and upbringing. This includes a diverse assortment of practices, all of which concern the conscious, intentional education of norms, values and moral codes. Moral education is found in personal religious courses (*sabaq*), taught in ethics courses (*odobnoma)* in schools[241], and practiced and negotiated among individual Muslim families (*oila*).

According to Manja, the parental generation strives to use education as a means to safeguard and protect the traditional order and its norms, values and moral principles, with the objective of guaranteeing the survival and unity of its own social group. The moral teaching is carried out by parents in families, by teachers in the schools, and by mulla in religious courses.

The traditional Muslim family and the association of personal religious courses followed the early tradition of the *maktab* by providing basic knowledge about the fundamental tenets of Islam for boys and girls, with the moral and religious fields overlapping. In most rural and urban families, the systemized education of religious knowledge is a significant pillar of moral education in Tajikistan. Whether offered in the conditions of respect for the parents or as an expression of a recently revived spiritual consciousness, the so-called 'religious method' of teaching essential religious knowledge is mainly planned to prepare the young generation to perform (*namoz*), the formal prayer.

This is because of the need for moral education and to support parents' efforts, religious books and a wide range of religious tapes are producing and marketing. Nowadays there is an easy access to religious books. The lessons on ethical and religious teaching for young people have become very popular in the both urban

---

241 Manja S (2010) Moral Education, Islam and Being Muslim in Tajikistan. In *Religion, Identity, Post Socialism*. The Halle Focus Group 2003-2010. Max Planck Institute for Social Anthropology Halle/Saale (Department II)

and rural neighborhoods, though the state has not assigned them.[242] Rooted in the neighborhood environment of the urban locality, these lessons are a supplement to the domestic learning of religious topics. Particularly for people who have recently migrated to cities in some degree loosing contact with their traditional institutions, these lessons are a valuable method to guarantee for their children a religious and social adulthood under the guidance of spiritual authorities, and that they are protected against the immoral negative influences of 'the street' [243].

In ethical lessons, moral teaching is presented in a circumstance that fuses the spiritual and secular spheres. The courses, though secular, make regular mention to religion; spiritual symbols are an important part of everyday education practices. This is not only the result of the desolation of secular pedagogy, but also a fact of the return of Islam to the public domain. Religion provides education in a new secular moral way. Therefore, as opposed to their intended principle, ethics lessons did not present a secular option to the established religious teachings in the region, but rather prompted their continuity by reinforcing Islamic consciousness among the local population.

4.2. Mahalla as a source of social capital

In a general perspective, trust is regarded as a feeling that one man expresses to another man. When one man trusts another, it implies that he believes in what another man says, and he takes promises seriously. He is sure that they will be realized in the future. Trust is a crucial precondition for the union of people. Such a belief can usually be found in relation to people with whom we have common contacts, as for example, our neighbors. As a Tajik proverb says: *hamsoyai nazdik beh az kheshi dur* (a close neighbor is better than a distant relative[244]). It is one of the most important conditions for collective activity in a community. Without trust, a real community would not exist. As Georg Simmel notes, trust is one of the most vital unifying powers in society. Trust unites people and builds social interaction, thereby making collaboration achievable. It presents an expectation of others that we can rely on them.

Not accidently, Fukuyama discusses trust as the central component of social capital. In his opinion, social capital is not possible without trust. These two concepts are correlated with one another. Fukuyama clams that trust as a conviction

242 Ibid.
243 Ibid.
244 Author's translation.

expecting others that we will not be disappointed in collective action. According to him, people will consequently realize these goals and encourage them, and in a case of difficulties, they can count on friendly help and later on reciprocate it. This expectation may arise on the grounds of the faith that they share in common values, and, therefore, that certain moral standards would be acceptable to determine the success of the operation.

Francis Fukuyama in article *Social Capital and Development: The Coming Agenda* discusses the interconnection between successful development and social capital: social capital is a precondition of successful development of democracy and economy, while the strong law and basic political institutions are the precondition for the building of social capital. Even if the social capital primarily implies the moral component – trust according to definition elaborated in the article is the" shared norms or values that promote social cooperation, instantiated in actual social relationships[245]" – its development depends on the institutional constructions. Francis Fukuyama in this essay provides definition of social capital as a norm, embracing the whole spectrum of social life – as a sphere of its attribution emphasizing the spirit of trust – as an emotional attitude of one toward another one capable to unit people and promote common work:

> "social capital is an instantiated informal norm that promotes cooperation between two or more individuals. The norms that constitute social capital can range from a norm of reciprocity between two friends, all the way up to complex and elaborately articulated doctrines like Christianity or Confucianism. They must be instantiated in an actual human relationship: the norm of reciprocity exists in potential in my dealings with all people, but is actualized only in my dealings with my friends. By this definition, trust, networks, civil society, and the like which have been associated with social capital are all epiphenomenal, arising as a result of social capital but not constituting social capital itself[246]."

James Colleman, who in Fukuyama's expression has put the concept of social capital in wider use in sociology[247], defines social capital in *Foundations of social theory* as ""Social capital is defined by its function. It is not a single entity, but a variety of different entities having two characteristics in common: They all consist of some aspect of social structure, and they facilitate certain actions of individuals who are within the structure"[248]

245 The Social Capital Foundation", Citizendium, The Citizen Compendium.

246 Fukuyama, F. (1999). *Social Capital and Civil Society.* An essay prepared for delivery at the IMF Conference on Second Generation Reforms.

247 Ibid.

248 Colleman, J. (1990). *Foundations of Social Theory.* Cambridge: Harvard University Press, p. 302.

In my view, Fukuyama's reflections on traditional societies and trust are applicable in the case of mahalla, for the main reason that in example of traditional type of society the trust can be measured. The level of trust is depicted by Fukuyama with the help of concept "radius of trust"[249]. The size of radius depends on the positive externalities produced by social unit. Thus, in this context, the traditional societies characterized by the large number of self-contained social units like villages and tribes – in my interpretation, the mahalla can prolong this list – are tended to present a widening radius of trust

The notion of social capital has originated from sociology and political science, illustrated the resources obtainable to individuals by their individual behaviors and their relationships within the community networks [250]. The academic history of the term of social capital dates back to 1918 when L.J. Hanifan in article *The Rural School Community Center* has underlined in social capital a kind of immaterial component of goodwill, fellowship, sympathy to each other in contrast to material goods seek by the members of community. In the 1960's Jane Jacobs used the term of social capital in relation to value of networks albeit not strictly defining it. It has been on behalf of sociologists of recent years to define the social capital. Contrary to financial capital, which exists in bank accounts, or human capital, which is personified by a person's investment in education, social capital is explained by the quality of social interactions among individuals and the presence of their social structures[251]. The term of 'social capital' is comparatively new, however the elements of it, such as the significance of social networks and the relationship of specific communities have been previously the subject of a great deal of study. In this part of my thesis, I will mainly use the works of two authors: Pierre Bourdieu and Robert Putnam.

Pierre Bourdieu was quite possibly the first researcher to bring the concept of capital from the economic sphere to the spheres of culture and society. His idea of social capital is related with his theoretical reflections on class. Bourdieu classifies three dimensions of capital – all are linked with concept of class: economic,

---

249 In Fukuyama's words, the very idea of this concept belongs to Lawrence Harrison. See in *Underdevelopment is a State of Mind: The Latin American Case.*

250 Kawachi, I. (1999). *Social capital and community effects on population and individual health.* Annals of the New York Academy of Sciences.

251 Kawachi, I. (1999). Kennedy, B.P.; Glass, R. Social Capital and Self-Rated Health: a Contextual Analysis. In *American Journal of Public Health.*

cultural and social capital. His notion of social capital is related to class conflict and class power[252].

In his turn Robert Putnam's idea of social capital is also threefold, but the leitmotif differs: moral obligations and norms, social values, and social networks (especially voluntary associations). His central idea is that a well-functioning economic system and political integration are the product of a successful growth of social capital. One of the most important components of Putnam's notion of social capital are trust and voluntary associations[253]. The more trust that exists in society, the stronger the social capital will be within that society. For instance in his book, Putnam classifies social capital as "features of social organization, such as trust, norms, and networks that can improve the efficiency of society by facilitating coordinated actions"[254].

Robert D. Putnam in *Bowling Alone: The Collapse and Revival of American Community* defines social capital as "the collective value of all 'social networks' and the inclinations that arise from these networks to do things for each other". Moreover, in this book the sub-types of his vision of social capital are also presented. Under detailed examination, Putnam distinguishes two sub-types of social capital: bonding social capital and bringing social capital. The first sub-type implies the common value assigned to social networks and shared by the homogenous groups, while the second – common values shared by the heterogeneous groups. The examples of the first sub-type are the criminal gangs, while of the second sub-type – chorus, associations, and for example bowling clubs. Personally Putnam believes that bringing social capital is beneficial for the societies, governments, communities, and individuals[255].

4.2.1. Trust and cultural values of Tajiks

There is definitely the level of trust that in my view is exceptionally high between members of the mahallas of Tajikistan. As it has been mentioned in one of the earlier chapters of my work, in Tajik culture, the individual in every situation puts the interest of the group above self-interest. In this regard it is possible to

---

252 Ottebjer L. (2005). Bourdieu, Coleman and Putnam on Social Capital. Karolinska Institutet. Master of Public Health Education. Department of Public Health Sciences.

253 Siisiäinen M. (2008). *Two Concepts of Social Capital: Bourdieu vs. Putnam.* Department of Social Sciences and Philosophy University of Jyväskylä.

254 Ibid., p. 58.

255 Putnam, R.D. (2000). *Bowling Alone: The Collapse and Revival of American Community.* New York: Simon and Schuster.

image the following situation: the Tajiks in every situation ask themselves, "What will be the consequences of my actions in regards to the honor of my avlod and mahalla?". This results from the consciousness of the fact that any negative actions could possibly effect the loosing of face (*obru*), i.e. the reputation individual enjoys in the group he/she represents.

The growth of social position is one of the subterranean aims of many community members. As is the case with a typical person in the West, the typical Tajik tries to actualize his goals, be they increasing his personal wealth or achieving a respectable position in society. Such respectable social positions may include the title of mulla (spiritual teacher), teacher, or the sufficient government worker. However, unlike an ordinary Western man, a Tajik is aware of the fact that purely a social position does not guarantee him with strong authority among community members. Property is important, but every Tajik knows the proverb: n*imtai non rohati jon, jak tai non baloi jon*. (He who eats half of the bread is the lucky one, he who eats all of the bread has problems).

Owing to the position of education and work, governmental jobs are obviously very important for the prestige of the family, conversely, they do not provide oneself with respect and authority. Every mahalla member who values opinions of other members knows that authority can only be achieved by the observing cultural codes of behavior. It is important to highlight that the authority of kin and the mahalla is built up by non worn out ties from generation to generation. Some negative characteristics of the earlier generation will negatively affect the recent representatives of the kin. Referring to this situation, the Tajik proverb says: *Okibat gurgzoda gurg shawad, garchi sad odami buzurg shawad* (After all, a wolf pup will become a wolf, even if it will be a great person[256]).

In Tajikistan, like most Asian countries, people do not appreciate relations that are based on contracts. Also, in business relationships, agreements are all based on trust among the people. This is because the knowledge about moral qualities of a partner can be obtained from the elders of the mahalla where this person lives. It never occurs that in such causes the community elders will give false information. The Tajiks traditionally say that the honor of men is in their tongue and words. The symbol of the obliging promise is to shake the right hand, and such promises are not permitted to be broken by anyone. As Tajik, a proverb clatifies: *Agar ba'di va'da va dodani dasti rost va'dakhilofi kuni, natanho obrui khud balki obrui zanu farzandatro merezoni* (If you do not meet the obliga-

256 Author's translation.

tions endorsed by giving the right-hand, you scale the good name not only of your own, but also of your wife and children[257]).

A good illustration of the role of trust in business is the system of *hawala,* the system is widely met and promoted in Asian countries. The word derives from Arabic "*hawala*", which basically means "transfer", but it is frequently rendered as "trust". It is an informal transfer system grounded on the honor of money brokers. It has its origins in classical Islamic law. In this system, money is transferred via the hands of *hawala* brokers. The Tajik labour migrants usually send their money through this network. A person approaches a *hawala* broker and gives some sum of money to be transferred to a receiver in another place.

Such a transaction is done without witnesses, and the transferring money broker does not receive a receipt. In the case if the broker is not a resident of the same mahalla, the transferring person has to pay the broker a small commission for his services. The *hawala* system based on customer confidence in the broker, and in the confidence of the broker to his partner in another place. In my view, it could be fair to call it an honor system.

4.2.2. Not only trust

The living conditions of the Western societies do not favor the formation of pro-social attitudes. It is no accident that psychologists in their studies in the last quarter of a century have devoted much attention to empathy. Empathy is a feeling that in some cases leads people to act altruistically. The possibility of altruistic behavior cannot be justified on the basis of the rational decision-making model of human behavior by those who specialize in the study of man and society, which is borrowed from neoclassical economic thought. In views of the American conservatives, western intellectuals of leftist-like orientation and dissidents of the former soviet bloc, the civil society, as well as social institutions should motivate people to action in a wide social environment. Their goal was to become an instrument replacing the State by taking over its functions in society. Successful implementation of the idea of civil society depends on the creation of the broadest possible range of people ready to work for broader objectives, rather than in self-interest.

Western individualism is alien to Tajik society. Typical Western individualistic behavior is morally condemned in contemporary Tajik society. It rather arises disgust among the people. I have mentioned in the above the hashar-community of work. No Tajik will accept the outside imposition of hasher. The obligation to pro-

257 Author's translation.

vide to the community, or, if necessary, to the whole of society, is so strongly enrooted into the inner structure of the Tajik culture that every Tajik considers it inseparable from the essence of humanity. At the time that I am writing these lines, my local mahalla's members are building a sport complex that will be used by residents of the mahallas in the surrounding countryside. Almost all of the young residents of the mahalla are participating in its construction, and nearly every house in the mahalla prepares meals two or three times a week to support their efforts.

As in the past, today the basis of Tajik economy is agriculture. In this part of Asia, cultivated fields require irrigation. This requires creating and maintaining the complex network of irrigation canals, so called *ariks*. These canals must be cleaned annually, and not only the section that brings the water directly to the fields, but all of the sections. It must be constantly replenished. This is one of the reasons why the ordinary inhabitant of a mahalla will consider the welfare of the wider community, for example, the residents of the valley. (It should be pointed out that the size of a valley in Tajikistan cannot be compared even with the valleys in the Swiss Alps. For example, Hisor Valley, where I am living, has a length of more than 100 km).

The residents of the mahalla and of other mahallas in our valley in Hashar were participated in repairing the Great Hisor Canal. It was built during World War II with the work of all the inhabitants of the valley, and from the moment of its creation, it has contributed to the common good of all the inhabitants of the whole valley. Among other things, even people from distant mahallas do not treat one another like strangers. This necessity of taking care of the common good encourages the ideals of Tajik culture, specifically the quest to transform the interpersonal relations that unite the closest members of the family. This ideal arises on the basis of cultural beliefs which are so beautifully expressed by the phrases of the Persian poet Sa'di Sherozi, that are often repeated by Tajiks:

Bani Odam a'zoi yakdigarand,
Ki dar ofarinish zi yak gawharand.
Chu uzwe ba dard owarad ruzgor,
Digar uzwhoro namonad karor.

Human beings are members of a whole,
In creation of one essence and soul.
If one member is afflicted with pain,
Other members uneasy will remain.

However, the circle of people to which the ideal of culture extends is significantly wider than the inhabitants of the valley due to religion. In my opinion, the Islamic concept of *ummah* (community of the faithful people) implies the existence of a significantly stronger ties with other co-religionists than is possible in the community of Christians. In many situations, the duty of *zakat* – the obligation of a voluntary tax on every Muslim to help poor people – might include even residents from the distant geographical locations. For example, after the floods in 2010 in Kulob, a town about 200 kilometers from my place, all the residents of our mahalla and other neighboring mahallas offered assistance. These operations were completely spontaneous, and the initiative was adopted without any incentives from the state authorities. Such assistance is also delivered to mahalla residents after the death of the head of their family. In mahalla, such actions are the norm.

In Putnam's approach, one of the most important components of the concept of social capital is social network. As a result of tradition, voluntary social networks promoted by the managers of Western NGO's could not be created without dividing the model of civil society already in place. It has happened in other societies that active local organizations have formed some goals to create a social network. For instance, organizations set up to bring drinking water to others may meet the obstacle of corruption, thereby necessitating the creation of officials to fight corruption in nationwide scale. In analogous situation, the mahalla is looking for informal support structures, such as those earlier mentioned in my work: jamomad, qawm and gashtak. The problem is not solved by the organization per se, but rather through the influential members within the structure. Depending on the importance of the problem, it could be grown from a local problem to a generalized social issue. The same mechanism is used by a mahalla to create bases of support for candidates for Parliament.

The social networks in the West utilize the political mechanisms of democratic states, and in the case of necessity, intervene with the instruments of law. Such interventions, as we can note, are not always effective. This can be exemplified, for instance, by the American Human Rights Watch actions after September 11, 2001. From the Western perspective, the social networking activities in Tajikistan would be classified as a phenomenon of corruption. Their essence is based on purely personal actions, mostly confidential, and do not have the characteristics of formal action under the applicable law in the state. We cannot change the fact that they are often very effective. However, the assessment of this behavior as corruption is the result of ungrounded evaluations of behavior in Asian cultures, especially when they are compared to the West. In this regard, in the eyes of the Tajiks, nepotism and obligation to accelerate the provisioning of help to members of own community - regardless of the resources that are needed to make this happen, so long as they are not against the dictates of religion - expose the honor of the highly valued ideals of the whole avlod.

4.2.3. The role of the mahalla in relations with the state

It is in some degree possible to state that the Eastern countries mentally differ from the the Western countries in the issue of human dignity that is understood as the dignity of the individual, and – that is important – individualism turns to be an invention of the West. The Eastern societies do not view the individual as an autonomous being who possesses rights that go above those of society. The individual is regularly considered as an integral part of a group, family, clan, tribe or the local community, that are regarded as the basic unit of society[258]. For this reason, as far as the West goes, human rights are interpreted as the right of every individual, but in the East, it is as the exclusive right of groups. Furthermore, in Asian cultures there are similar values of Western human dignity, such as the category of Chinese *lian* (guarantees everyone the right to be respected in society), and these values are transitive. The individual may lose his dignity if he commits a serious moral offense such as neglecting his responsibilities towards his parents. Yet, in Western culture, human dignity is understood as a non-transferable quality.

In the Eastern cultures, man cannot separate his being from other people. For most Easterners, and it is fair for the Tajiks, the true human essence fully develops only in natural social groups, such as family and community, where relationships are based on mutual interests and a sense of collective responsibility. In these cultures, rights cannot be treated as independent from obligations, as they are perceived in Western culture. There must be a symmetry between them. This is why the Easterners believe that the dignity is a sense of debt, to which every man is born. The ties among people are based on trust, duty and responsibility, not on the rights and claims.

These cultural differences are reflected in the concept of Asian[259] values which are preached by some Eastern scholars. In their opinion, there are certain common values in all Asian cultures. They are the following:

---

258 Pathak, Raghunadan Swarup (1989) Introductory Report on Universality of Human Rights, in Universality of Human Rights, Council of Europe, Strasbourg.

259 One of the most famous proponents of Asian values is the former Prime Minister of Malaysia, Mahathir Mohammad, who ruled the country from 1981 till 2003. He refuted Western universalism and the liberal idea of human rights, which, he supposed, can corrupt Malaysian culture and religious values. Being preoccupied with the possibility of negative influence of the idea of western individualism for the future of Asian values and traditions, he launched the "Look East" strategy in 1982 as a broader movement against "Western values". The foundation of this strategy is postulated by him model of the society known as the "The Mahathir Model". The most important

- placing society above the self, upholding the family as building block of society;
- resolving issues through consensus instead of contention;
- the importance of duty as counterpoint to right;
- the obligation of the community to look after its disadvantaged members[260].

This complicated personal network in which Tajiks live serves to defend his interests just as effectively as does the Western civil societal concept of formal law defend those of Westerners. This is one more reason that Tajik will not accept the idea of bending of human rights as individual rights. However, that interpretation of these rights will also interfere with a citizen's understanding of the concept of power and the role of power in society.

In my view, the idea of civil society is an expression of the attitude of Western individuals to state authority. The mission of civil society is to replace the state in its functions, not only because the state is unable to meet all the needs of its citizens, but also to serve the best interests of the community. Additionally, the state officials often make mistakes, and government units are subject to degeneration. Sometimes, they even act outside of their Constitutional mandates. There is also something more significant involved. The postulate of citizens taking over state functions, and thus limiting the scope of the government's presence in the community, arises from belief that the state restricts the freedom of its citizens and could become an obstacle to the implantation of the autonomous entity of some of the routes chosen in a person's life.

Such an attitude to state authority is completely alien to the Tajiks. In all Asian cultures, power is understood as an intermediary between the higher order, in the case of the Tajiks, order is laid down by the law of God and society. Islam does not allow the separation of religion from the state. In the early history of the Islamic states, the head of the state was the Caliph, who ruled by religious law and was its protector. His role as the promoter of Islamic law, and simultaneously, as the supervising guard of this law in the community, was the only legitimacy of his power. The Caliph was elected by the ummah, a Muslim community of believers. If the Caliph did not fulfill his role as the guardian of Islamic law, the duty of the ummah was to deprive him from power.

---

characteristics of this model are a strong authority, prioritizing the community above the individual, and a strong family based society. Mahatir expressed his opposition to the concept of individualism by rejecting Western interpretations of human rights. Therefore, according to his vision, human rights are culturally relative, not universal".

260 Ghai, Y. (1994). Human Rights and Governance: The Asia Debate. in *Center for Asian and Pacific Affairs, Occasional papers*. The Asia Foundation, San Francisco, November, pp. 8-9.

In Bukhara and Eastern Bukhara (the present territory of Tajikistan), the state was ruled by the Amir. The Amir was a supreme authority, both religious and political. According to the Tajiks, the Amir, as a ruling authority, was the shadow of God upon the Earth[261]. They attributed to him magical powers, and they believed that he knows everything and can never be wrong. In the general opinion of the Tajiks, any individual revolt against the ruler brings not only the anger of God upon that individual, but also upon the whole community. The divinity of the Amir or Khan did not deprive him of humanity (the ruler was considered to be the prototype of man and the shadow of god, and other people were "shadow of Amir").

The Amir was the mediator between God and people, he belonged to both worlds (although more closely associated with the world of humans), and with ritual, he provided the harmony between them. The Amir defended the country and frightened its enemies. He was a source and norm of justice, with justice being what he wanted and what he announced[262]. In the eyes of the people, the Amir was their protector and responsible for prosperity and peace. Therefore, people, in spite all of the loads incurred by the State, such as high taxation or military conscription, were praying for "the continuity of the state and the stability of the Amir's kingdom". One of the Persian sayings that Tajiks often use should be especially noted: "Religion and kingship are twins, and there is no consolidation for the one except through its companion, as religion is the foundation of kingship, and kingship becomes its guardian. Kingship needs its foundation, and religion needs its guardians[263]".

In many situations, the Amir sought to maintain and strengthen his authority, and acted primarily in the interest of his dynasty. However, in the eyes of the people, he always was the basis of social order. As a propagator and performer of religious law, he guaranteed the existence of harmony within social relations. And what is more to note, he protected people and the world from demons, which in the case of weakening religious law, could penetrate this world.

The Tajiks know several types of demons. In Tajikistan and other Central Asian countries, there is a general belief in jinn[264], which are malicious spirits that hang around in buildings, cemeteries and lonely highways, where they then

261 Ayni S. *Yodostho.* Moskow.

262 Donish, A. *Kratkaya Istoriya Manghitskikh emirom Bukhari*. A short history of Manghit dynasty in Bukhara.

263 *Tārikh-e Sistān*: تتعاالطط// تتسسویویوا اهمایاسس وو ایاددخ االتتککت یتججحح ننااققررفف تتآیآ ببججااووهددررکک وواا. The history of Sistan.

264 The word of Jinn is derived from Arabic (جن) which means to hide, be hidden or conceal. In case of Tajiks, they usually use *jinn* and also sometimes incorrect plural form *ajina*. There are another synonyms for them like: *pari, dev, balo, ofat, ajina, ghull* and etc.

attack humans. In folk tradition, there is a belief that jinn haunt houses and play all kinds of naughty tricks on people. Many natural sicknesses, which fail to respond to normal medication, are recognized as the actions of such jinn. Jinn are physically invisible to humans. They are beings created with free will, to live in a world parallel with humans.

Similar to mankind, the Jinn can be good, evil, or impartially benevolent. There are two kinds of jinn: white jinn and black jinn. The white jinn is benevolent, the black is violent, angry, and cruel. People believe that jinn are able to cause humans to suffer in many different ways. They are able to enter a victim's body and make him or her insane[265]. Jinn appears as different animals, for example, as snakes, dogs, dragons and others. They have the power to travel long distances with extreme speed. They form a similar organization of the state like humans do. For instance, jinn also have kings, judges, weddings and mourning rituals. There are Muslim jinn and Kafir jinn (pagan), because the Prophet's Muhammad (BPUH) mission has been addressed to the jinns as well as humans[266].

---

265 It usually happens at night, when people sleep. A person wakes up unexpectedly to find himself unable to move, speak, or even utter a sound. In order to avoid jinn, or as Tajiks call this case, *balo*, or to make them leave, it is excepted that one recites "*bismillāh al-raḥmān al-raḥīm*" (in the name of God, the Compassionate, the Merciful). Usually the family of victims hires a mullah to recite selected surah from the Al-Qur'an, or even the complete Book, over the victim (this called khatmi Qur'on). Such recitation usually continues late into the night. At the end, they beat the victim with willow branches while calling upon the malicious jinn to depart from the body of patient. In some extreme situation, the intervention of a Shaman is necessary. Shamanism in Central Asia was under the influence of Siberian shamanism, but between them there are some important differences. In both Siberia and Central Asia, shamans serve as intermediaries between mankind and the spirit world. Their role is in doing tasks such as healing, divination, appealing to ancestors, controlling the elements, leading lost souls and managing religious rituals. In most Central Asian countries, the term *bakhshi* is usually employed as the equivalent to shaman. Bakhshi means shaman, magician, doctor, savant, sage, and etc. In some regions of Afghanistan, shamans are called *malang*.

266 Islam recognizes and accepts the existence of the jinn. Jinn are regularly mentioned in the Qur'an. For example, Surah - chapter 72 (Surat-al-jinn)is named after the jinn. According to Al-Qur'an, jinn are made from the smokeless flame of fire (Al- Qur'an. Surah Al-Hijr 15:26-27).

According to Muslim scholars, jinn are of different types:

1. Jinn living alone are known as*jinni.*
2. Jinn that live among mankind are called *aamir,* of which the plural is *Umaar* or *Awaamir.*

Commonly, the Muslim jinn are illustrated as beautiful, while the pagan jinn are described as ugly monsters with a long head and a single eye in the middle of the forehead.

Another type of dangerous demons for people is *dev* (in English Dev is *demon, monster, field*[267]). Folk tradition blames them for several mental and physical troubles. The Persian word devona (insanity) betrays the association of all mental sickness with demonic possession. People call such sicknesses ofati dev (the demon's malady), thereby attributing them to demons. A religious ritual, gesture and phrase, or prayer (such as those conducted before eating) can be used to protect people from the demons. These rituals are performed in the family. The family is not only the basis of social order, but also one of the centers of harmony in the world. We can imagine a society as a field consisting of a large number of centers such as harmony. These centers are diverse, and the differences between them arise from the degree of their distance from sources of life, which is the light of God. The most important centers have more lights, and they are mullahs, imams, ishons and rulers, unless their actions manifest commitment to the faith[268].

Each family is like a separate center, but also part of the larger field in which harmony depends on the family ritual. Continuity of the field stems from the fact that the relations in the family constitute a model that should be followed in all human relations in society. The role of the ruling is only to be the personification of order formed through the implementation of this model. This is why when discussing the concept of power, the Tajiks cannot think abstractly without relation to a specific person, realizing in the relations with his subjects the ideal of the father's ties with the children. In other words, the source of authority is not a formal office, but it is always the same ruler as a human being. These are not the personality characteristics which allows his subject to regard

---

3. Jinn that antagonize young children -or young adults are known as *arwaah.*
4. Evil jinn that show hostility to human beings are called *shaytan* (in the singular) and *shayaateen* (in the plural).
5. If they harm human beings, they are called *Maarid,*
6. And if they cause intense harm and become strong as a result of this, they are called *ifreet,* of which the plural is *Afaareet.* afreet (Umar Sulaiman al-Ashqar 1998, p. 13)

267 In the Persian classic literature the devs are often described as black (for example in Shah-nama)with long teeth, large bodies and some of them has several heads, although others have monstrous teeth and black lips.

268 Zapaśnik in the lectures.

him as an outstanding individuality. Authority in the family accounts for people whose unique virtues certify that they walk the path indicated by their ancestors. Authority in the country belongs only to the representatives of the families whose life force was confirmed by the elevation of some ancestor to the position of the founder of the state, and which guarantees that their descendants would maintain harmony in nature and society.

As I have already written above, in Central Asian societies, Western ideas of equality are alien. They believe that people are different because of their inherent moral quality. The Tajiks believe that the head of the state has some talent or gift from God. As a Tajik proverb says:

> *Bo Khudododagon siteza makun,*
> *Ki Khudododaro Kudo dodast.*(Do not argue with the people with talent, because this talent is given them by God[269])

Therefore, in the tradition of the region, the authority of the tribe or the country could only serve someone who has been either a descendant of Chingiz Khan or, as Khoja or Said, a descendant of the first Caliphs and whose from Prophet Muhammad's surroundings. The state of Bukhara was formed in the XVII century, and was for its existence a tribal state that was ruled by Khans who were descendants of Chingiz Khan, or Amirs, Khojas or Said, descendants of Prophet Muhammad (BPUH).

The attitude of the Tajiks towards Western democracy demonstrates the fact that they believe the authority of the power does not form simply as a result of voting. Authority is always built on the attributed personality of the ruler and his innate moral qualities, and the function of voting can be only a public acknowledgment of its existence. A king was assigned the role of intermediary between the divine order and society, and given the high virtues placed upon him, one could never accuse the ruler of bad intentions. The Western attitude of relying on civil society as the basic element of power was alien to the king. The Tajik sought authority with confidence, and they lived in the belief that the king has moral obligations to society for its paternal care, forming the basis of harmony in society.

If we reject the popular stereotype of the West – oriental despotism – we can see that the Tajik had less reasons to feel threatened by the authorities than an inhabitant of any of the European absolute monarchies. The horizontal network of informal links, such as mahalla, avlod, gashtak, jamomad, qawm, etc., limited the despotic intentions of the authority described above. The

269 Author's translation.

Amir showed his concern for the population not only by building mosques and madrasahs. He also visited different parts of the Emirate, and during such visits, acquainted himself with the local situation and the needs of the residents. This gesture showed the people that he was taking care of them. One of the ways he obtained consensus was by distributing the positions and privileges. Also, the time was his gif to people(for the people Amir found time for the people, and that was gift for them) the time was his gift. He distributed it participating religious festivals and local celebrations in different places. Even visiting various mahallas. During such visit even he did not dismount from the horses.

It was enough to greeted the elders of mahalla and this sign was highly appreciated. For the same reasons, regarding any decision concerning the population of the mahalla, state authorities entered into agreement with the elders of the mahalla, for instance in the meetings being held in the mosque. Sometimes facing strong opposition from the authorities often departed from his intention still he was compelled to pay for permission, even at high price.

Today, Tajiks still trust the national authority, despite the difficult tragedy that took place after independence in 1991, and do not suspect it of bad intentions. This is an inheritance of the traditional image of authority as a source for social justice and as a protector of the nation. This notion is still alive in Tajik culture. The relations of the President towards the population, and the relations of the people towards power authorities, remain similar to how it was during the era of the Bukhara Emirate. Throughout history, the head of the state was treated as a father. The head of the state thus was always considered a caring father of the nation, and people also consider him as a father of all of them. Every year, the head of the state visits different regions of the country, one after another. Usually, he participates in the meetings with the intelligentsia in order to discuss the important problems of the region and advises how these problems can be addressed. He promises to use the Presidential fund to build hospitals, schools and other public buildings.

The President participates in traditional and religious holidays and in this way he was sharing his happiness with the people. This is especially widely appreciated during the yearly Navruz (Persian New Year, dates 21 of March), whereby the President designates one city to host the Navruz celebration. Traditionally, every city and region celebrates this holiday, but in the chosen city, the celebration is arranged in significantly high level, with the participation of governmental elite and the representatives of foreign embassies and international organizations. This has significant meaning for the people, because the head of the state is finding time to come to them and take care of their problems. I have heard several times that in the regions where people were criticizing government and its policy, their moods change after the visit of Head of State. People declare that they are happy and very proud of the state authority.

As I mentioned before, in the Eastern cultures where people consider the power authority to be like a Great Father, people are born with a debt and obligation towards the head of state. Here I can bring up a lot of examples which illustrate the relations of contemporary Tajiks towards state authority. One of the most recent examples is the issue of financing the construction of the Rogun dam[270]. So as not to ask foreign investors for financing, the Tajik government called upon the population to make a financial contribution to the project by means of voluntary donations. The Tajik authorities appealed to a feeling of honor, common pride and the patriotism of the population in justifying it, as well as a desire to avoid asking other countries for help. It was emphasized that each family should buy stocks for the construction of the dam, and the appeal was broadcast by all state media. Almost every family, be they rich or poor, has bought donations for Rogun. I have heard that in the beginning, in local areas, some people have even sold their properties (for example: cow, sheep, or land) in order to buy stocks. The pensioners have given their pensions for the construction, and there were also cases where Tajik students from abroad have sent money to their country for the construction of Rogun. I have been witness to many people in local areas buying donations voluntarily and with a great pride.

The fact that ordinary Tajiks still believe in the good intentions of the authorities, as a result of the role of cultural tradition, is one of the reasons they do not attach great weight to the fact that the government has preserved almost all of the Soviet-era restrictions and laws about the traditional functions of mahalla. The Tajiks do not ever accuse the authority of bad intentions due to the role of the authority as the intermediary between God and the order of society. It is alien to the attitude of Western people, whose relations to power are reflected in the idea of civil society. Tajiks seek the authority's power with confidence, and have lived with the belief that he has a moral obligation to use his authority to display his parental care for society, which establishes the basis of harmony in society. I asked one of my respondents about his relations to the authority and what he answered:

We are not politicized. I dare to say it on behalf of majority people of Tajikistan. The most important thing for us is peace and stability in our country. We do not want to have a lot

270 Rogun Dam is now under construction. It is expected to be a dam on the Vakhsh River in the southern part of Tajikistan. Should it be completed, it will be one of the world's tallest dams, with a height of 335 meters and with 3,600 megawatts of hydroelectricity, allowing the country to solve its energy crises and to also become the region's largest exporter of electricity.

of problems. If we have something to eat for us and for our family it is enough. As Tajiks says: nimtai non rohati jon, jaktai non baloi jon (who has half of bread is enjoying his life but a who has a whole bread has more problems). What is the benefit gathering in the street and protesting against government? One time by mistake we had civil war and it was a good lesson for us. We did not appreciate what we had that time. In regions where was going civil war almost from every family someone died. Also in some family they lost all men of their family. We do not want such brutal war anymore. Thanks to God, now we have not war, we have something to eat and we are healthy. It is the most important thing for us. Nowadays, in television we see that wars and instability are happened in different parts of the world. I do not want to any country of the world such war. Because I have seen it with my own eyes and I have experienced it and now I know how horrible it is. For example, for myself, I do not mind who is a head of the state. Where he is from and how long he is in this position. How long he will be in future, I do not mind. What I do mind is peace and stability in our country (man, 45 years old. September, 2010).

Until recently, the legal status of mahalla was undetermined by the laws of Tajikistan, despite the fact that the rebuilding of traditional social institutions has continued since the end of the civil war. In 2008, a new act on the organs of social initiatives was established. It decreed that civil society institutions (such as mahalla) can be formally registered and have a stamp on the institution, its own legal status and bank account, and the option of keeping separate stock records. According to this act, mahalla has to be the smallest state unit regulating the life of the residents in local level. Therefore, the mahallas are de juro capable to work with governmental bodies and international organizations in official level, and in economic aspect are allowed to gain income from other sources.

The new law also regulates the activity of mahalla committees, acting as a body representing the resident's matters to local authorities. The Tajik government has explained its transformation of the traditional mahalla institutions into formal administrative units by stating the need to strengthen its capacity. Henceforth, rais is intended to be a unpaid civil servants because he does not receive any salary from government (perhaps in near future will be paid for work). Theoretically, the new law expands the operational capability of mahalla in obtaining funds for investment or in cooperating with state institutions and NGOs. Albeitt, after careful analysis of the act, as well as the implementation process, it raises many questions and controversies.

According to Polish authors S. Zapaśnik, A. Cieślewska and M. Marszewski[271], who conducted empirical research in different regions of Tajikistan in 2010,

271 Zapaśnik, S& Cieslewska, A. & Marszewski, M. (2010). Relationship between Self-Governments and Informal, Traditional Institutions, and International and Local NGOs in Tajikistan.

the new law reminds them a similar regulation already operating in Uzbekistan since 1993, the Act On Local Government Institutions. Since 1999, raisi mahalla is a civil servant paid by the state and elected for a period of 30 months. Uzbek government policy in relation to the mahalla describes the term as *mahallization*. There are many reasons to believe that *mahallization* seeks to subordinate mahalla to state power. The Tajik state seeks to introduce a similar model. Similar to the government and authorities of Uzbekistan, the Tajik government's transformation of the legal status of mahalla can be explained by their willingness to counter the danger of terrorism. The question arises as to what extent the state power is able to control mahalla, because this depends on the region, the degree of integration of the same community and informal factors influencing the relationship between the various actors involved in the distribution of power.

Mahalla theoretically has to function as a formal executive body of state power, but its actions are still based on informal social relations. The possession of executive attributes such as bank accounts or official stamps can help mahallas in performing financial transactions. However, for many centuries, each mahalla had an informal joint fund, which had been used in request to the needs of the community, and most importantly, was independent from state control. Also, the banking requirements imposed upon the mahallas work towards the interest of the state, due to the fact that it gives the authorities the possibility to access and control the mahalla's finances, thereby exercising control over their activities.

Despite the above-mentioned act, the status of mahalla still is not clear, and state power has no concept of how to manage its local development. For example, the act stipulates that mahalla projects would be funded by the government. In practice, the state does not have sufficient financial resources to cover the basic needs of local government, so it is unlikely that it will fund the local initiatives at the level of mahalla. On the one hand, the mahalla committee has limited powers to gain their own funding resources, such as the implementation of projects jointly with international and local NGOs. This means that cooperation with mahallas is only possible through a local partner who knows the modalities of this type of community.

On the other hand, mahalla is now the lowest-level body of state administration, however, in the villages and as well as in the cities, mahallas today have still preserved many of their traditional functions. The community always appears as a collective whole in carrying out some type of work for the mahalla. For instance, in the organization of feasts and ceremonies such as funerals or weddings, community members take all the responsibilities associated with receiving guests. In the minds of the residents of mahalla, the mahalla functions like a big family, even if not all of its members have a blood connection with each other.

The happiness of one family on the occasion of a circumcision ceremony or a wedding, for example, is the cause of happiness for all mahalla members. Likewise, mourning on the death of any member leads to mourning for all residents.

According to the observation of Polish authors in the villages where strong and powerful avlods are living, is existence of dual power. Formally, rais and councils rule a mahalla, but in fact, the mahalla is governed by a council of elders (*shuroi muysafedon*), whose decisions every person must accept. Paradoxically, the government's ally, Western aid organizations working in Tajikistan might be exemplified as well, in fact are opposite to mahalla for its mass popularity.

Mahalla protects the most vital interests of its residents, initiates collective action in order to eliminate their problems, and to some extent, more or less, today as in the past, also protects them from the abuses of power. It has a few unquestionable advantages over Western civil society. In mahalla, participants are engaged in the most important events in the life of each resident. This can include weddings, childbirth, circumcision rites, sickness, bereavement and mourning. By reason of living together for generations, many families are related to each other and have formed special bonds of solidarity. There is also a huge capital of trust. But from the institutions of civil society in the West, mahalla also differs in that it is not exposed to the fluctuation of participants in joint activities or their withdrawal, depending on the whim of the individual.

According to Bryant[272], the mahalla includes some of the crucial characteristics of the concept of civil society, including autonomy from the state, self- organization and legalized existence. The feature of the autonomy of the state is expressed in ways which mirror democratic institutions, such as free elections that are based on the will of all members of the community. The decision making process is realized in the regular meetings that are organized in order to discuss the important issues of the community. The financial ground of the mahalla is based on the resources generated through the voluntary contributions from the members of the mahalla. This charitable ground provides the mahalla with the status of economic independence that in turn determines political independence.

Therefore, mahallas provide a hotbed of incomparably higher social capital than could be achieved in the West. Regrettably, the stereotypes embedded in the thinking of the managers of the Western organizations do not allow them to recognize the existence of this capital. The implementation of assistance projects involves employees whose candidacy has not been consulted with the local ma-

---

272 Bryant, C. (1995). Civic Nation, Civic Society, Civic Religion. In Hall, J. A. (Ed).: *Civil Society Theory, History, Comparison*. Cambridge: Polity.

hallas. This demonstrates the full disregard of local authorities, creating a new aristocracy of gainful employment that consists of people competing for the donor's favor. The provisioning in the form of hashar is included in the project's costs, but it created mechanisms of action that in no way contributes to the activity of members of mahalla, and even more for their political education. In the opinion of above cited Polish researchers, through an appropriate legal basis, mahalla could be an instrument of political transformation in bringing Tajikistan closer to the Western democratic standards. This will sound reasonable to anyone who is acquainted with the history and traditions of Central Asian societies, and on such historical basis one might propose the need for changes in legislation concerning mahalla as a condition of accelerating political changes in the countries of the whole region.

4.3 Conclusion

The primary aim of my work has been a description of the mahalla as an old traditional institution of a specific form close to civil society in this part of Central Asia. For this purpose, I have compared this traditional social institution with the concept of civil society adopted from the West tradition. Such an idea is also required the discussion of the differences of Eastern and Western cultures. These differences are best characterized by the concept of collectivism and individualism. From distinguished citations in the work of Steven Lukes, the five basic ideas constituting the very concept of individualism are examined: the dignity of man, autonomy, privacy, self-development and abstract individual[273]. In my opinion, none of them are known and are comparable with collectivist cultures. As it is called by Mohammad Mahathir, "Asian values that create an Eastern man's identity in society are collective and expressed by the pronoun "we". The individual in these cultures does not have the mental capability of distinguishing themselves from his family and community as much as their Western counterparts do. It is usually assumed that "Asians tend to be more aware of the connections they have as members of their social groups, and therefore, they tend to be more conscious of the consequences of their actions on their members of their groups"[274].

The subsequent development of European thought generated such key concepts as liberalism, civil society, and universal human rights, has been to a large extent influenced by the development of the concept of individualism in the

273 Lukes, S. (1990). *Individualism*. Basil Blackwell Ltd: Oxford

274 Liu Qingxue (2003). *Understanding Different Cultural Patterns or Orientations between East and West*. Shijiazhuang Mechanical Engineering College Hebei, China. p. 25.

Western societies. Meanwhile, the ideas of human dignity, individual autonomy, privacy, and many others, linked with individualism, are still alien and almost incomprehensible to the representatives of the East.

Characteristics of mahalla as the civil society institution has required to prolong discussion with the reference to the typical cultural values of the Tajiks: *adab, ehtirom, nomus, oburu* and trust. Adab is a moral quality that means a good upbringing, politeness, morals, and in general, good behavior. It is the responsibility of the parents to bring up children well, i.e. to cultivate the adab. The next value taught by parents is ehtirom, the respect of teachers, neighbors, and older people. The ehtirom concerns the attitude to guests, who are welcoming and hospitably treated. Nomus is an honor, a hallmark distinguishing young men and women. The presence of this value is highly approved by society, and the absence of it is taken as the opposition to the norms and is reproved. Finally, obru is an authority which earns every individuals. Altogether these values represent the particularity of Tajik culture, the norms that are capable of regulating social relations. Overall, these fundamental values of Tajik society allow to sketch out a comparison between mahalla as Eastern specificity and civil society as Western particularity consequently.

To understand the concept of civil society in the West, I owe particular respects to Polish scientists. In my work, I mainly have been focuing on Piotr Glinski's works. This author, in the article, "Operational Model of Civil Society", is looking for such elements of this concept that are common to different authors, despite differences in theoretical approaches. In his view, the concept of civil society in literature is often ambiguous, and the considerations on it are complicated by referring to past authors without awareness on historical context in that this concept was present. He intends to define civil society by clarifying and structuralizing its theoretical history.

Glinski introduces the concept of public benefit organizations. In my opinion, the concept of public benefit is also important for the presentation of mahalla as civil society institution, however, with the exception being NGO's working for the realization of rather narrow objectives mentioned in the statute defining the legal framework of its activities. The aim of mahalla is social protection for its members and solving community problems under dynamic conditions. Thus, the scope of its activities is extremely broad and does not have a predetermined priority.

Thus, independent from some similarities between mahalla and the institutions of civil society in the West, there are differences in the purpose of their functions. Nonetheless, mahalla produces a significantly higher level of trust between its members than is possible in the institutions of civil society in the West. Additionally, mahalla differs from Western civil society institutions in not exposing to the fluctuation of participants in joint activities or their withdrawal, depending on the whim of the individual. In my opinion, it has a few unquestionable advantages over the Western civil society. In mahalla, where the members participate in the most important events in the life of each residents, such as marriage, birth of a child, the rite of circumcision, sickness, and bereavement, and where by reason of living together for generations, many families become related to each other by forming special bonds of solidarity. As it has been abovementioned, there is also a very huge capital of trust.

The recognition of mahalla as a civil society institution, in my opinion, interferes with the convictions of managers of Western organizations, who hold the believe that modernization is necessarily opposite to tradition. Mahalla is a traditional institution, however, due to its historical role in Tajik society, mahalla is capable of protecting the interests of its members better than the Western institutions (such as NGO's) that have recently been introduced.

Such a conclusion has also been arrived at earlier cited authors of the report, *The Role and the Place of Social Institutes in the Process of Development of Rural Communities*[275]. Therefore, among the recommendations that are presented as conclusions of the research, the authors of the last report wrote among others: "If foreign practice is going to be used, it should without fail be adapted to the Tajik environment, its national context, way of life, and culture of the people". I think that this opinion is one more argument strengthening my conviction that the appropriate legal basis of mahalla might be used as an instrument to enact constitutional changes to bring Tajikistan closer to Western ideas of democracy.

275 Abdullaeva, M. & Tuyryaev, F. (2004). *The Role and the Place of Social Institutes in the Process of Development of Rural Communities* (the outcome of sampling of 19 Jamoats of the Northern Tajikistan. Khujand.

References

Abdullaev, K. (2006). Current Local Government Policy Situation in Tajikistan. *In Tajikistan at the crossroad: The Politics of Decentralization.*

Abdullaev & Akbarzaheh (2010). *Historically Dictionary of Tajikistan.* Second edition.

Abdullaev, E. (1997). *Islam i Islamskiy Faktor v Sovremennom Uzbekistane (Islam and Islamic Factor in Modern Uzbekistan)*. Central Asia and the Caucasus № 6, Sweden. Retrieved from: http://www.ca-c.org/journal/cac-05-1999

Abdullaeva, M. & Tuyryaev, F. (2004) The Role and the Place of Social Institutes in the Process of Development of Rural Communities (the outcome of sampling of 19 Jamoats of the Northern Tajikistan. Khujand.

Alexander, J. C. (1997). The Paradoxes of Civil Society. In *International Sociology, 12(2),* 115-133.

Alkhazraji, K. M., Gardner III, W. L. *The acculturation of immigrants to U.S. organizations.* Management Communication Quarterly, 11, 1997, pp. 217-265.

Ayni, S. (1956). *Dokhunda.* Moscow.

Ayni, S. (2009). *Memories.* Dushanbe.

Babajanian, B. V. (2004). *Poverty and Social Exclusion in Tajikistan.* World Bank.

Baccaro, L. (2001). *Civil Society, NGOs, and Decent Work Policies: Sorting out the Issues.* Geneva. International Institute for Labour Studies Geneva.

Baker, G. (1998). Civil Society and democracy: In *The Gap between Theory and Possibility. Politics, 18(2),* 81-88.

Bartold, V. (1920) A Short History of Turkestan. In *Four Studies on the History of Central Asia* (Leiden: E.J. Brill) 1956 (Trans. V. & T.Minorsky).

Benedict, R. (1946). *The Chrysanthemum and the Sword: Patterns of Japanese Culture.* USA: Boston.

Berlin, I. (1969). Two Concept of Liberty. In *Four Essays on Liberty.* New York: Oxford University Press.

Bertelsmann S.(2010), *BTI — Tajikistan Country Report.*

Bhabha, H. (1994). *The Location of Culture.* Routledge: New York.

Birnbaum P.& Leca J. (1990) *Individualism. Theories and methods.* Clarendon Press: Oxford.

Bradley, F. H. (1927) My Station and its Duties. In *Ethical Studies.* Oxford.

Brill's E.J. (1913-1936). *The First Encyclopedia of Islam.* Netherlands.

Bryant, C. (1995*). Civic Nation, Civic Society, Civic Religion.* In Hall, J. A. (Ed).: *Civil Society Theory, History, Comparison.* Cambridge: Polity.

Bushkov, V.I. & Mikulsky D.V. *Anatomiya Grajdanskoy Voyni v Tadjikistane (Anatomy of Tajik Civil War).* Institute of Ethnology and Anthropology of the Russian Academy of Sciences, Moscow, 1993, p. 87.

Canfield, R. L. (1973) *Factions and Conversion in a Plural Society: Religious Alignments in the Hindu Kush.* Ann Arbor: University of Michigan Press.

Canfield, R. (1996) 'Ethnic, Regional, and Sectarian Alignments in Afghanistan'. In *The State, Religion and Ethnic Politics: Afghanistan, Iran, Pakistan,* Ed. by A. Banuazizi and M. Weiner, New York: Syracuse University Press.

Chandhoke, N. (2004). *State and Civil Society: Explorations in Political Theory.* New Delhi: Sage Publication.

Civil society and human development in Tajikistan. (2006) Retrieved 24, April, 2009, from:http://cfapp1-docs-public.undp.org/eo/evaldocs1/adr/eo_doc_597030542.pdf

Cohen, J. L., & Arato, A. (1992). *Civil Society and Political Theory.* Cambridge: MIT.

Coleman J. (1988). *Social Capital in the Creation of Human Capital.* American Journal of Sociology, pp. 94: 95-121.

Constitution of the Republic of Tajikistan (1994) Dushanbe. Retrieved from: http://unpan1.un.org/intradoc/groups/public/documents/untc/unpan003670.htm

Cook, D. (2001). Muslim Messianic Movements and Astronomical Phenomena In *Revue du Monde Musulmane et de la Méditerranée,* pp. 29-51.

Cook, D. (2001). *Hadith, Authority and the End of the World: Traditions in Modern Muslim Apocalyptic Literature.* Oriente Moderno.

Creese, G., Dyck, I. and McLaren, A. (1999). *Reconstituting the Family: Negotiating Immigration and Settlement in Research on Immigration and Integration in the Metropolis.* Working Paper Series 99-10, Vancouver Centre of Excellence, Vancouver.

Dadabaev, T. (2006). *Changing nature of the mahalla: Outcomes of the project.* Tokyo: Ricas.

David C., Thomas, K. A. (2002) The Effect of Cultural Differences on Behavioral Responses to Low Job Satisfaction. In *Journal of International Business Studies*, Vol. 33, No. 2 (2nd Qtr., 2002), pp. 309-326. Published by: Palgrave Macmillan Journals. Stable. Retrieved from: http://www.jstor.org/stable/3069546

Dudkiewicz, M. (2009). *Technokracji Dobroczynności.* Wydawnictwa Uniwersytetu Warszawskiego. Warszawa.

Ehrenberg, J. (1999). *Civil Society the Critical History of an Idea.* New York New York University Press.

Ekiert, G., Kubik, J. (2000). *Civil Society from Abroad: the Role of Foreign Assistance in the Democratization of Poland.* Weatherhead Center for International Affairs: Harvard University: Cambridge, p. 7.

Ekiert, Grzegorz and Jan Kubik. 1999. *Rebellious Civil Society: Popular Protest and Democratic Consolidation in Poland, 19891993.* Ann Arbor: The University of Michigan Press.

Elliott & Gray, (2000). *Family Structures a report for the New Zealand Immigration service.* New Zealand Immigration Service Te Ratonga Menene.

Falkingham & Vlachantoni (2010). *Pensions and Social Protection in Central Asia and South Caucasus: developments in the post-Soviet era. Centre for Research on Ageing, School of Social Science.* University of Southampton: UK.

Farhadi, R. (2000) 'Tajikane Afghanistan wa Qadamhaie Ashti Bain Aishan' in *Qadamhaie Ashti wa Masauliate ma Afghanistan,* Kabultec: Falls Church, VA.

Ferguson, R., Gever, M., Minh-ha, T., & West, C.(1990). *Out There: Marginalization and Contemporary Cultures.* MIT Press, Cambridge, MA.

Finlay, C. J. (2004). Hume's Theory of civil Society. In *European Journal of Political Theory 3,* 369-391. Press.

Fleming, T. (2000). *Habermas, Democracy and Civil Society: Unearthing the Social in Transformation Theory.* Retrieved 25 January, 2008, from http://adulteducation.nuim.ie/department_staff/documents/Habermas democracy andcivilsociety.pdf

Flyvbjerg, B. (1998). Habermas and Foucault: Thinkers for Civil Society? In *The British Journal of Sociology,* 49(2),pp. 210-233.

Fontana B (1993). *Hegemony and Power: On the Relation Between Gramsci and Machiavelli,* University of Minnesota Press.

Fouad A., (1993). The Summoning. In *Foreign Affairs* 72.4 (Sept./Oct. 29.

Freizer, S. (2004). Central Asian Fragmented Civil Society: Communal and Neoliberal Forms in Tajikistan and Uzbekistan. In Glasius, M., Lewis, D. and Seckinelgin, H. (eds.) *Exploring Civil Society: Political and Cultural Contexts.* London and New York: Routledge.

Fukuyama, F. (1995) *Trust.* Penguin books.

Fukuyama, F. (1999). *Social Capital and Civil Society.* An essay prepared for delivery at the IMF Conference on Second Generation Reforms.

Gafurov, B.(1972). *The Tajiks: Prehistory, Ancient, and Medieval History.* Moscow.

Galnoor, I. (Ed.) (2001) *International Encyclopedia of the Social and Behavioral Sciences (Vols. 3).*

Gawlikowski, K. (1999) *Indywidualizm a kolektywizm.* (Individualism and colectivism)Warszawa: IFIS PAN.

Geiss, P. G. (2001) "Mahalla and kinship relations: A study of residential communal commitment structures in Central Asia of the nineteenth century," In *Central Asian Survey*, 20 (1), pp. 97-106.

Gellner, E. (1994) *Conditions of Liberty. Civil Society and Its Rivals.* Allen Lane/ The Penguin Press.

George C. Lodge and Ezra F. Vogel (1987). *Ideology and National Competitiveness: An Analysis of Nine Countries.*

Ghai, Y. (1994). Human Rights and Governance: The Asia Debate. In Center for Asian and Pacific Affairs. Occasional papers. The Asia Foundation: San Francisco.

Ghobar, M. (2001). *Afghanistan dar Maseer –e- Tareekh*, (Vols. one and two). Peshawar: Maiwand Publishing Centre.

Ghyathul-Lughat (1871) Edited by Maulana Gheyathoddin, Kanpur Press: New Delhi.

Giffen, J., Earle L & Buxton. *The Development of Civil Society in Central Asia.* The International NGO Training and Research Centre.

Gliński,, P. (2006). Operational Model of Civil Society. In *Civil Society in the Making*. IFIS Publishers: Warsaw, pp. 62-77.

Gliński, P. (2006) *Civil Society In the Making.* Warsaw. IFIS Publishers.

Gliński, P. Stylu działan organizacji pozarządowyh w Posce. Grupy interesu czy pożytku publicznego. Wydawnictwo IFIS PAN. Str.

Grabowska, M. (1995) Civil Society after 1989 - Rebirth or Decease, in *After Communism. A Multidisciplinary Approach to Radical Social Change*, Edmund Wnuk-Lipinski. (Ed.) Warsaw: ISP PAN.

Grabowski, T. (1996). The Party That Never Was: The Rise and Fall of the Solidarity Citizens Committees in Poland. In *East European Politics and Societies*, 10(2), pp. 214-54.

Graff A. (2010). *Pułapka społeczentswa obywatelskiego* „ (The trap of civil socjety). Warszawa: Krytyka polityczna.

Guanipa, C. (1998) *Culture shock. Department of Counseling and School Psychology.* San Diego State University.

Gulen, F. (2010). Somneniya Porojdennye Vekom. (The Doubts Caused by the Century) Kokjiev-B: Almaty.

Gunda, W. (2009). *Socio-Political Change in Tajikistan The Development Process, its Challenges Since the Civil War and the Silence Before the New Storm?* University of Hamburg Faculty of Social Sciences Institute for Political Science.

Habiba Fathi Otines. (2007). *The unknown women clerics of Central Asian Islam.* The Institut National des Langues et Civilizations Orientates, Paris.

Hall, E. T., & Hall, M. R., 1990. *Understanding Cultural Differences: German, French and Americans*, Yarmouth, ME: Intercultural Press.

Hall, J. (1995). *Civil Society. Theory, History, Comparison*. Cambridge: Polity Press.

Hann, C. (1992). Civil Society at the Grass-Roots: A Reactionary View. In Paul G. Lewis, (Ed). *Democracy and Civil Society in Eastern Europe*. New York: St. Martin's Press.

Harris, C. (2004). *Control and aversion: Gender Relations in Tajikistan.* Pluto Press.

Harkin, J & Skidmore, P.(2003). *Grow-up trust.* A scene-setting paper for the Demos/ Nationwide seminar series on trust

Hearm, J. (2001). Taking Liberties: Contesting Visions of the Civil Society Project. In *Critique Of Anthropology, 21(4)*, 339-360.

Hudson, W. (2003). Problematizing European Theories of Civil Society. In D. C. Schak & W. Hudson (Eds.), *Civil Society in Asia.* Hampshire: Ashgate.

Hungtington S. P. (2003). *The Clash of Civilizations and the Remaking of World Order.* USA.

Ilolov, M. &Khudoiyev, M. (2000) Local Government in Tajikistan. Local Governments. In report *Eastern Europe, in the Caucasus and Central Asia.*

Ilolov, M. & Khudoiev, M. (n.d.). *Local Government in Tajikistan, Developing New Races in the Old Environment.*

Janoski, T. (1998). *Citizenship and Civil Society*. Cambridge University Press: Cambridge.

Jasiewicz, Z. *Machalla w Uzbekistanie. Tradycyjna Społeczność dzielnic miejskich w życiu współczesnym.* (Mahalla In Uzbekistan. Tradition and Urban social districts In modern life).

Kania, R. (Ed). *Post-communist Transformations. A New Generation of Perspectives.*

Karajah, S. (2007). Civil Society in the Arab World: The Missing Concept. In *The Middle East: Senior Research Fellow Papers.* International Journal of Not-for-Profit Law / vol. 9, no. 2.

Karimov, Sh. (n.d.). *NGO Development in Tajikistan: Traditions and current situation.*

Kawachi, I. (1999). *Social capital and community effects on population and individual health.* Annals of the New York Academy of Sciences.

Kawachi, I., Kennedy, B.P., Glass, R. (1999). Social capital and self-rated health: a contextual analysis. *American Journal of Public Health.*

Keane, J. (2003). *Global Civil society?* Cambridge: Cambridge University Press.

Khamagayev, A. (2002) *Media and language policies in Central Asia countries.* Media Insight Central

Kim, Myung-Hye (1993) Transformation of family ideology in upper-middle class families in urban South Korea. In *Ethnology,* Vol. 32 No. 1 Winter.

Kim, Myung-Hye (1996). Changing Relationships Between Daughters-in-law and Mothers-in-law in Urban South Korea. In *Anthropological Quarterly,* Vol. 69 No. 4.

King J., Noble J. and Humphreys, A. (1996). *Central Asia, A Lonely Planet Travel Survival Kit.* Lonely Planet Publications, Oakland p. 429.

Kipling, R. (1940) The Ballad of East and West. In *Rudyard Kipling's Verse.* Definitive edition: London.

Ku, A. S. (2002). Beyond the Paradoxical Conception of `Civil Society without Citizenship. *International Sociology 17(4),* 529-548.

Kubik, J. (1997). Institutionalization of Protest During Democratic Consolidations in Central Europe. In David M., Tarrow, S. (Eds.) *A Movement Society? Contentious Politics for a New Century*. Boulder, CO: Rowland and Littlefield.

Kubik, J. (1994). *The Power of Symbols Against the Symbols of Power. The Rise of Solidarity and the Fall of State Socialism in Poland*. University Park, Pennsylvania: The Penn State University Press.

Kurczewska, J. (2002). Local Civil Societies in Poland in the Nineties A Diagnosis. In *Polish Sociological Review*. Warszawa: IFIS.

Kurczewska, J. & Kurczewski, J.(2001). *A Self- Governing Society 20 Years After: Democracy and the Third Sector in Poland*. Warszawa: IFIS.

Kymlicka, W. (1993). Two Models of Pluralism and Tolerance. In Heyd D. (Ed.). *Toleration. An Elusive Virtue*. Princeton: Princeton University Press.

Lavalette, M., & Ferguson, I. (2007). Democratic Language and Neo-Liberal Practice: The Problem with Civil Society. In *International Social Work 50(4)*, pp. 447-449.

Leo, O. U. (2005). *Beyond Liberal Political Morality: A Critique of State Colonization of Civil Society in Canada*. University of Alberta: Edmonton.

Leung, K (1987). Some determinants of reactions to procedural models for conflict resolution In *A cross-national study. Journal of Personality and Social Psychology*. 53, pp. 898-908.

Liu Qingxue (2003). *Understanding Different Cultural Patterns or Orientations Between East and West*. Shijiazhuang Mechanical Engineering College Hebei: China.

Lukes, S. (1990). *Individualism*. Basil Blackwell Ltd: Oxford.

Manja, S. (2010). Moral Education, Islam and Being Muslim in Tajikistan. In *Religion, Identity, Postsocialism* The Halle Focus Group 2003-2010. Max Planck Institute for Social Anthropology Halle/Saale (Department II).

Marx, K. (1953). *Capital*.

Masov R. *(1991). Istoriya Topornogo Razdeleniya*. (History of Clumsy division), Dushanbe Irfon

Masov, R. (1995). Tadzyki: Istoriya s grifom "Sovershenno sekretno" (The Tajiks: history with signature stamp "top secret"*)*. Dushanbe.

Matveeva, A. (2009). *The Perils of Emerging Statehood: Civil War and State Reconstruction in Tajikistan. An Analytical Narrative on State–Making*. Crisis States Research Centre. Working Paper no. 46

Matveeva, A. *External Democracy Promotion in Post-Conflict Zones: Evidence from Case Studies: Tajikistan*. Freie Universität Berlin

Matveeva A. (2004). *Association of Scientific and Technical Intelligentsia*. Khujand.

Milikbekova, M. (2005). *Irregular Migration and Human Rights: Tajik Irregular Migrant Workers in Russia*. Lund, Sweden.

Mond Azizuddin (n.d.). *Mahathir Mohamad as a Cultural Relativist: Mahathirism on Human Rights*. 06010 Sintok, Kedah, Malaysia

Moryakova, E. (1998). Mahalla: The Traditional Muslim Neighborhood Community in the Development of Uzbek Civil Society. In Dornisch, D., Elvin, P., *Post-Communist Transformations*. IFiS Publishers Warsaw, 1998.

Muhutdinova, R. (2007). *Nations in Transition 2007*. Tajikistan.

Mullojonov, P. (2001). The Islamic Clergy in Tajikistan. In Dudoignon S.A., & Komatsu H. (Ed.), *Islam and Politics in Russia and Central Asia*. Kegan Paul International Limited: London, pp. 221-250.

Müller, K. B. (2006). The Civil Society-State Relationship. In *Contemporary Discourse: A Complementary Account from Giddens' Perspective*. BJPIR, 8, 311-330.

Muminov, A.K. (1999). Traditsionnie i Sovremennie Religiozno-Teologicheskie Shkoli v Tsentralnoy Azii (Traditional and Modern Religio-Theological Schools in Central Asia). In Central Asia and the Caucasus № 5, Sweden. Retrieved from: http://www.ca-c.org/journal/cac-05-1999/st_13_muminov.shtml

Narshakhi, M. (1979) *Tarikhi Bukhoro* (History of Bukhara). Dushanbe: Donish.

Nemeth, C. (1985). Dissent, group processes and creativity. In E. Lawler (Ed.) *Advances in Group Processes Theory and Research* (pp. 57– 75). Greenwich, CT: JAI Press.

Niyazi, A. (1999). Islam and Tajikistan's Human and Ecological Crisis. In *Civil Society in Central Asia*. Ruffin, M. H. & Waugh, D. (Eds). (pp. 180-198). University of Washington Press: Seattle.

O'Brien Rory. (1999). *Philosophical History of the Idea of Civil Society*.

O'Hara, S. L. (2000). Lessons from the Past: Water Management. In *Central Asia. Water Policy*, 2, 365-384.

Olejniczak, M. (2005) Europejskie społeczeństwo obywatelskie?(European civil society?).

Olimova, Saodat (1999). Political Islam and Conflict in Tajikistan. In Lena Jonson and Muradsenov (Eds.). *Political Islam and Conflicts in Russia and Central Asia*. Conference Paper no. 24, The Swedish Institute of International Affairs, Stockholm, 1999.

Olimova, Saodat. (1999).'*Politicheskiy Islam i Konflikt v Tajikistane* (Political Islam and Conflict in Tajikistan)', In *Central Asia and the Caucasus* № 5, Sweden. Retrieved from: http://www.cac.org/journal/cac-05-1999/contcac_5_99.shtml

Olimovy, Saodat and Muzaffar (2003). *Мусульманские Лидеры: Социальная Роль и Авторитет* (Muslim Leaders: Social Role and (Degree of) Respect), Sharq Centre and Friedrich Ebert Foundation Roundtable: Dushanbe.

Osiyatiński, W. Krasnodębski (2010) *Społeczeństwo obywatelskie i jego przyjaciele.* (Civil society and its friends).

Ottebjer L. (2005). *Bourdieu, Coleman and Putnam on Social Capital.* Karolinska Institutet. Master of Public Health Education. Department of Public Health Sciences.

Oyserman, D., Heather M. Coon & Kemmelmeier, M (2002). *Rethinking Individualism and Collectivism: Evaluation of Theoretical Assumptions and Meta-Analyses.* University of Michigan.

Pathak, Raghunadan Swarup (1989) Introductory Report on Universality of Human Rights. In *Universality of Human Rights.* Council of Europe: Strasbourg.

Bergne, P. (2007). *The Birth of Tajikistan: National Identity and the Origins of the Republic.* London and New York: I. B. Tauris.

Putnam, R. D. (1994). *Making Democracy Work.* Princeton University Press: New Jersey.

Putnam, R.D. (2000). *Bowling Alone: The Collapse and Revival of American Community.* New York: Simon and Schuster.

Rakhmatullaev, S. A., Bazarov, D. R., & Kazbekov, J. S. (2003). Historical Irrigation Development in Uzbekistan from Ancient to Present: Past Lessons and Future Perspectives for Sustainable Development. In *Proceedings of the Third International Conference of International Water History Association.* Alexandria: Egypt, pp. 79-80.

Rasuly-Paleczek, G. (1998). Ethnic Identity versus Nationalism: The Uzbeks of Afghanistan and the Afghan State. In: *Post-Soviet Central Asia.* T. Atabaki and J. O'Kane, eds., pp. 204-230. London: Tauris.

Reykowski, R. (1999) (*Kolektywizm i indywidualizm jako kategorie opisu zmian społecznych i mentalności*) Collectivism and individualism as a description of the categories of social change and the mentality. In *Indywidualizm a Kolektywizm.* IFiS PAN, Warszawa.

Roashan, R. (2001). *Loya Jirga: One of the Last Political Tools for Bringing Peace in Afghanistan*. IAS. Retrieved from: www.intitute-for-afghan-studies.com.

Roskin, M. G., Medeiros, J. A., Cord, R. L., & Jones, W. S. (2008). *Political Science an Introduction*. New Jersey: Printice Hall.

Ro'i, Y. (2000). *Islam in the Soviet Union: From the Second World War to Gorbachev*. Hurst and Company: London.

Roy, O. (1992). Ethnic Identity and Political Expression in Northern Afghanistan. In: *Muslims in Central Asia: Expressions of Identity and Change*. Jo-Ann Gross, ed., pp. 73-86. Durham: Duke University Press.

Roy, O. (1995). Civil War in Tajikistan. Cited In Rubin, B. *Causes and Consequences of the Civil War in Tajikistan*. Columbia University: USA.

Roy, M. (1995). The Clash of Civilizations: An Islamicist's Critique. In *Harvard Middle Eastern and Islamic Review* 2.1.

Rousseau, J-J (1947). *Les Confessions*. Paris.

Rubin, B. (1995). *Causes and Consequences of the Civil War in Tajikistan*. University of Washington Press: Seattle.

Ruffin& Waugh, (1999). *Civil Society in Central Asia*. University of Washington Press: Seattle.

Rychard, A. (2004). *Entrepreneurs, Consumers and Civility: the Case of Poland*. IFIS: Warszawa.

Sahragard R.(2008). *A Cultural Script Analyses of a Politeness Feather in Persian*.

Said, E. (1978). *Orientalism*. New York.

Sangren, P.S. (1997). *Myth, Gender and Subjectivity*. National Tsing Hua University, Hsin-chu: Taiwan.

Seleny A. (1996). Old Political Rationalities and New Democracies: Compromise and Confrontation in Hungary and Poland, In *Pew Papers on Central Eastern European Reform and Regionalism*, No. 9., Center for International Studies, Princeton University.

Shapoatov Sayfiddin (2004). *The Tajik Civil War:1992-1997*. The Graduate School of Social Sciences of Middle East: Technical University.

Shibley, T. (2001). American Foreign Policy Toward the Muslim World. In *SAIS Review* 221.2 (Summer-Fall 2001): 139154.

Shireen T. (1998). Hunter in The Future of Islam and the West. Westport, Conn.: Praeger.

Shishov, A. (2006) *Tadzyki* (The Tajiks). Almaty.

Sievers, (2002). Uzbekistan's Mahalla: From Soviet to Absolutist Residential Community Associations. In *The Journal of International and Comparative Law*. Chicago-Kent: Volume 2.

Siisiäinen M. (2008). *Two Concepts of Social Capital: Bourdieu vs. Putnam*. Department of Social Sciences and Philosophy University of Jyväskylä.

Smith, A. (1991). *National Identity*. Penguin Books: London.

Spinoza, B. de (1966). *Letters to friend and Foe*. Philosophical Library: New York.

Staats, J. L. (2004). Habermas and Democratic Theory: The Threat To Democracy of Unchecked Corporate Power. In *Political Research Quarterly 57(4)*, 585-594.

Stanowski, K. (1998). Teaching Democracy in Postcommunist Countries. In *Journal of Democracy*, 9, pp. 157-65.

Sukhareva, O.A.(1976). *Квартальная община позднефеодального города Бухары* (Quarterly community of late feudal city Bukhara). Nauka: Moscow.

Sulek, M. (2008). Aristotle and Civil Society Theory. Paper for: WIMPS presentation. Indiana University Center On Philanthropy.

Szelenyi, I. (1988). Socialist Entrepreneurs. Embourgeoisement. In *Rural Hungary*. Madison: The University of Wisconsin Press.

Tangad, O (2009). *Przemiany ustrojowe w Mongolii a kategorie tradycyjnego myślenia w kulturze* (Political changes in Mongolia and the categories of traditional thinking in the culture).

Tapper, R, & Tapper, N. (1988). Ethnicity, Order and Meaning in the Anthropology of Iran and Afghanistan." In Digard, J-P. (Ed.), *Le fait ethnique en Iran et en Afghanistan*. pp. 21-35. Paris: Editions du Centre Nationale de Recherche Scientifique.

Tapper, R. (1983) *The Conflict of Tribe and State in Iran and Afghanistan*, Croom Helm: London.

Tarkowski, J. (1995). *Political Patronage, Politicus*. Bulletin of the Institute of Political Studies, Polish Academy of Sciences: Warsaw.

The Mediations of the Emperor Marcus Aurelius Antonius (2008). Hutcheson F., Moor J. (Trans.). Moor J. & Silverthorne, M. (Ed.). Liberty Fund: Indianapolis

The Social Capital Foundation", Citizendium, The Citizen Compendium,

Thomas Carothers (2000). Think Again: Civil Society. In *Foreign Policy*.

Tilley, J.J. (2000). Cultural relativism. In *Human Rights Quarterly*, Vol. 22, Nom. 2, May, p. 3.

Tocqueville, A. de (2000). *Democracy in America.* University of Chicago Press: Chicago.

Toshmuhammadov, M. (2004). *Civil War in Tajikistan and Post-Conflict Rehabilitation.* Hokkaido University Center of Slavic Researches.

Triands, Bontempo, Villareal, Asal &Luca (1988). Individualism and collectivism: Cross-Cultural Perspectives on Self Ingroup Relationships. In *Journal of Personality and Social Psychology.* Vol.54, No 2, 323-338.

Trice, H. M., Beyer, J. M. (1993). *The Cultures of Work Organizations.* Prentice Hall.

Tukmakov, D., Aleksandrov, V. (2003). *Tisyacha Vtoraya Noch. Jizn Posli Skazki* (One Thousond and Second Evening. Life After Fairy Tale). In *Zavtra* 10(485), Russian Federation. Retrieved from: http://zavtra.ru/cgi/veil/data/zavtra/03/485/451.html

Tusalem, R. F. (2007). A Boon or a Bane? The Role of Civil Society. In *International Political Science Review.* 28(3), pp. 361-386.

Universal Declaration of Human Rights adopted by General Assembly resolution 217 A (III) of December 10, 1948. Retrieved from http://www.un.org/en/documents/udhr/index.shtml#a1,25 December, 2010.

Usman Shah (2006). Livelihoods in the Asqalan and Sufi-Qarayateem Canal Irrigation.

Systems in the Kunduz River Basin. In *Field Report.*

Yankelovich D.(1981). *New Rules. Searching for Self-Fulfillment in a World Turned Upside Down.* New York.

Yusufbekov Y, Babajanov R & Kuntuvdiy N, (2007). *Civil Society Development In Tajikistan.* Aga Khan Development Network: Dushanbe.

Vahid Amani Zoeram; Jayum Anak Jawan; Lee Yok Fee (2010) The Epistemology of the Concept of Civil Society. In *The West and Iranian Interpretations.* Canadian Social Science Vol. 6 No. 4.

Wagner, J.A (1995). Studies of Individualism-Collectivism: Effects on Cooperation in Groups. In *The Academy of Management Journal,* Vol. 38, No. 1, Academy of Management, pp. 152-172. Retrieved from: http://www.jstor.org/stable/256731

Wardak, A. (n.d.) *Jirga - A Traditional Mechanism of Conflict Resolution in Afghanistan.* University of Glamorgan: UK.

Wardak, A. (2002). *Structures of Authority and Establishing the Rule of Law in Post War Afghanistan.* Paper Presented at Establishing the Rule of Law and Governance in Post conflict Societies, Conference Organized by Harvard University, the United Nations a ssociation – USA, and Koç University, Istanbul, July 11 - 14.

Warleigh, A. (2001). Europeanizing Civil Society: NGOs as Agents of Political Socialization. In *Journal of Common Market Studies.* 39(4), 619-639.

Whittington, K. E. (1998). Revisiting Tocqueville's America: Society, Politics, and Association in the Nineteenth Century. In *American Behavioral Scientist 42*, 21-32.

Wilson, J.F, (2002). *Hawala and Other Informal Payments Systems: An Economic Perspective.* JFW. Hawala: An Economic Perspective. Seminar on Monetary and Financial Law.

Zapaśnik, S. (1982). Kultura a filozofia Francii XVIII wieku (French culture and philosophy of the eighteenth century).

Zapaśnik, S. (2006) *Walczący islam w Azji Centralnej:* Problem społecznej genezy zjawiska (Fighting Islam in Central Asia: the social problem of the origin of the phenomenon)Wrocław.

Zickel, R. (1996). *Kazakstan, Kyrgyzstan, Tajikistan, Turkmenistan, Uzbekistan.* U.S. Library of Congress: USA. Retrieved from: http://countrystudies.us/tajikistan/

Zuzowski, R. (1992). *Political Dissent and Opposition in Poland. The Workers' Defense Committee "KOR".* Westport: Praeger.

Appendix

MAP OF THE REPUBLIC OF TAJIKISTAN

Field Research areas in Tajikistan.

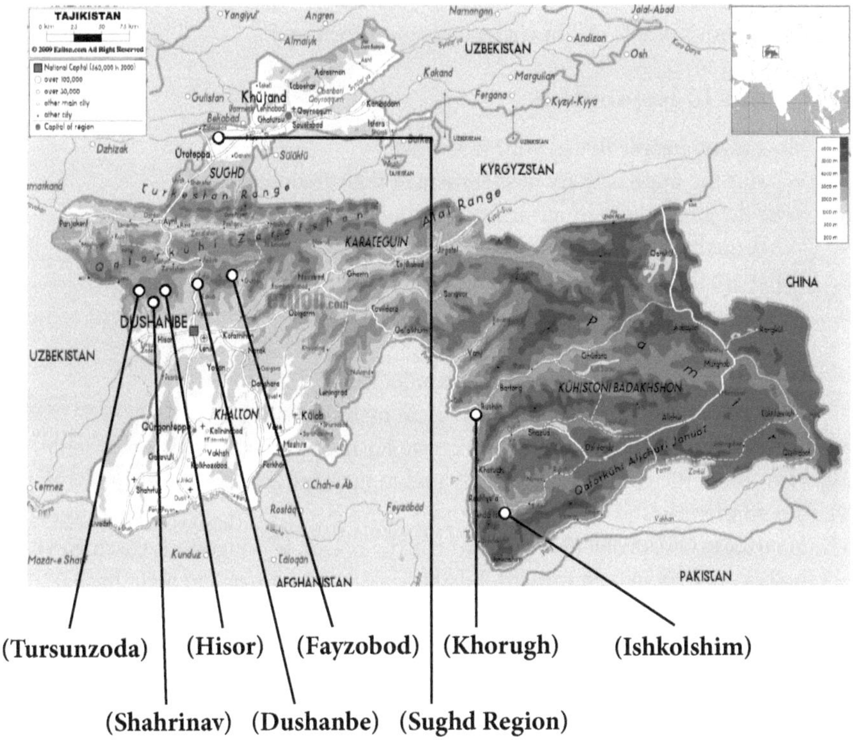

Source: http://www.ezilon.com/maps/asia/tajikistan-physical-maps.html

Questionnaire for interview with mahalla members

Introduction: My name is Saidbek Goziev. I am PhD student at Graduate School for Social Research in Institute of Philosophy and Sociology of Polish Academy of Sciences. In this meeting, I would like to have conversation about Your mahalla and daily life of mahalla members.

This meeting and conversation is made totally for scientific goals, and will be used only for my research. Results of interviews will be presented anonymously. During interview, you can refuse to answer a question. If in your opinion certain question is not suitable or not correct, please inform me.

Questions to respondent

1. How many people live in your mahalla?
2. What is the main activity of members of your mahalla?
3. Why do they owe their authority rais and members of council of elders?
4. What qualities should represent the ideal Rais?
5. What are the main problems of your mahalla?
6. In what way usually solves the problems of mahalla? Can you boast of some success?
7. What is the main source of your mahalla fund?
8. Who initiates the projects implemented by Mahalla?
9. Who makes decisions about organizing hashar?
10. How often the respondent participated in hashars?
11. Do all members of mahalla participate in hashars?
12. How solves the problem of persons who by reason of obligations outside mahalla (working in government, business, etc) cannot participate in hashar?
13. What are your responsibilities and duties as a member of mahalla?
14. What are the most important values in your life as mahalla member?
15. How would you characterize the ties between you with other members of Mahalla?
16. Would you agree with the opinion that Mahalla is like your extended family?
17. How are your relations with other mahallas? Do you have any cooperation?

Imprint

1. Sex __________ 2. Age __________ 3. Education ______________
4. Occupation ________________
5. Position in mahalla ________________

The list of mahallas in Jamoat Mirzo Rizo, Hisor region.

Name of mahalla	Number of housholds	Number of populations	Name and surname of the Head of mahalla
Tuda	690	5914	Haydarov T.
Tudai bolo	32	197	Yunusov M.
Nojii bolo	357	2793	Ortikov Sh.
Nurobod	181	1180	Eshonkulov A.
Dehi nav	104	681	Niyozov B.
Buyrobof	78	548	Kurbonov A.
Khojachildiyor	305	2478	Sharipov Kh.
Khokistarteppa	91	741	Bobokhonov G.
Jalolobod	132	973	Khalimov M.
Bolshewik	256	1961	Kulov A.
Surkhakchashma	257	1998	Niyozov U.
Noji	101	766	Sharipov B.
Chukurak	167	1235	Rahimov U.
Khjachildiyori bolo	140	1037	Sanginmurodov Kh.
Surkhakchashmai bolo	49	281	Akramov G.
Total in Jamoat	**2940**	**22783**	

Schools in Jamoat Mirzo Rizo

	Name and surname of Director of the schools	The number of schools	Number of pupils	Place of schools
1.	Kosimov Hamza	N:6	1214	Tuda
2.	Kabirov Yatim	N:23	559	Bolshewik
3.	Haydarov Amrikul	N:37	295	Khojachildiyori bolo
4.	Yuldoshew Haytali	N:38	303	Jalolobod
5.	Haydarov Nurali	N:41	616	Nojii bolo
6.	Sharipov Haybullo	N:47	732	Khojachildiyor
7.	Sattorova Gulghuncha	N:48	509	Surkhakchashma
8.	Buriev Khurshed	N:79	59	Surkhakchashmai bolo
9.	Salohov Rustam	N:83	207	Noji
10.	Ismoilov Chuponkul	N:86	236	Chukurak
11.	Sharipov Orzu	N:93	162	Dehi nav
12.	Sadulloeva Hafiza	N:112	76	Nurobod
	Total in Jamoa		**4968 pupils**	

Nations of Jamoat Mirzo Rizo

	The name of mahalla	Tajiks	Uzbeks	Russians	Afghans	Other nations
1.	Tuda	5890	15	8	2	1
2.	Tudai bolo	190	4	2	-	-
3.	Nojii bolo	2770	14	6	2	1
4.	Nurobod	600	580	-	-	-
5.	Dehi nav	670	7	3	1	-
6.	Buyrobof	96	452	-	-	-
7.	Khojachildiyor	2467	7	4	-	-
8.	Khokistarteppa	156	270	6	309	-
9.	Jalolobod	291	682	-	-	-
10.	Bolshewik	980	981	-	-	-
11.	Surkhakchashma	1990	5	3	--	-
12.	Noji	750	16	-	-	-
13.	Chukurak	247	988	-	-	-
14.	Khojachildiyori bolo	1030	4	2	-	-
15.	Surkhakchashmai bolo	281	-	-		
	Total in Jamoat	**18445**	**4006**	**207**	**314**	**2**

Respondent 1. The name of mahalla: Tuda

Imprint

1. **Sex**: male **2. Age**: 48 **3. Education**: high education
4. Occupation: Teacher
5. **Position in mahalla**: School teacher

Question: How many people live in your mahalla?
Answer: In our mahalla about 6000 people are living

Question: What is the main activity of members of your mahalla?
Answer: *The main activity of our mahalla members are to take active part in everyday life. People in our mahalla are working in different spheres depending on their professions. However, I think that majority of people in our mahalla working or in the land or in the market(doing small business). It does not matter who is working where the important thing for members that in everyday life we are together. After work usually we gather in mosque, chaykhana or in the streets and share information and discuss mahalla issues.*

Question: Why do you owe your authority to rais and members of council of elders?
Answer: *Because, we respect rais and council of elders. They are older than us and they have more experience of life in our society. We elect them in election of mahalla and their opinion and their advice is like unwritten law.*

Question: What qualities should represent the ideal Rais?
Answer: *Every person who is chosen for this position (I mean position of Rais) must be an Ideal rais. If rais –the head of mahalla- is not ideal and does not care about his community, people do not need him. Mahalla inhabitants immediately will change him. An ideal rais has to be like a caring father. He has to do all his best for his mahalla. He must be present in the happy days and in the bad days always with his people (I mean in the weddings and funerals). Rais has to be aware of the problems of mahalla and try to solve them. The head of mahalla must be equal and helpful in relation with rich people and poor people (with persons with high administration position and simple inhabitant). He has to work for developing of our mahalla. Together with council of elders he has to solve mahalla problems. We choose him as our rais; it means that he is our representative to government administration. He must support our interests in relation with the government.*

Question: What are the main problems of your mahalla?
Answer: *The main problems of our mahalla are water issues, the roads, construction of our school, building stadium for our youth and also we want to take land for our mahalla for poor households. We wrote zayawleniya and now we are waiting for their answer.*

Question: In what way usually solves the problems of mahalla? Can you boast of some success?
Answer: *For solving mahalla issues usually rais, council of elders, mulla and person with high authority in mahalla gather for meeting. They have meeting and discus problems and the way of solving them. Every mahalla has its financial funds from voluntary contributions and also some inhabitants of mahalla give their zakat to this fund. If the project is big and mahalla fund is not enough, we will do meetings with local businessman and everybody helps as much as he can.*
Concerning our successes, in autumn 2009 in our mahalla we have built the biggest mosque in our republic. People built it through hashar. All mahalla members and even people from other mahallas and other regions came and helped us. Also we reconstructed one building of our hospital and two buildings of our school. We also built sport complex and mini stadium. From voluntary contribution we have built 4 house for widows of our mahalla. In spring in the day of Nawruz we organized weddings for 25 families. Every year in Nawruz celebration we organize weddings for poor families. These are the main successes, except these every day we are doing something for our mahalla.

Question: What is the main source of your mahalla fund?
Answer: The main source of our mahalla is financial help through voluntary contribution from mahalla members.

Question: Who initiates the projects implemented by Mahalla?
Answer: Of course rais of mahalla and members of mahalla committee.

Question: Who makes decisions about organizing hashar?
Answer: *Usually council of elders and rais make decision about hashar. In hashar from every house at least one person must participate. However, usually from 2 up to 4 persons participate in hashar. I personally participate in all hashars (of course if I am in our mahalla during organizing hashar). If not then my sons will go instead of me. About the day of hashar rais or mulla announce in the mosque before or after performing prayer. There are hashars which everybody knows exactly its exactly days. For example, before Ramazan and Qurban holidays we go and clean cemeteries, streets and other public places. In these hashars all mahalla members*

gather without any announcement of hashar, because already from centuries it is part of their life and religion.
People who by reason of the obligation outside mahalla (for example working in the government or doing business) cannot participate in hashar, they will send somebody else instead of them. Sometimes they come in the morning to the place show them self and telling to Rais their obligations and they go to their jobs. In some other cases, if such people cannot participate in hashar, they provide food for workers during hashar.

Question: How often the respondent participated in hashars?
Answer: I try to participate in all hashars if I am here during it. If I am not here, for sure one person from our family participates in it. It is unwritten law and it is like our obligation towards our family members. Because mahalla members are our brothers and sisters.

Question: Do all members of mahalla participate in hashars?
Answer: From every house at least one person participates in hashar.

Question: How solves the problem of persons who by reason of obligations outside mahalla (working in government, business, etc) cannot participate in hashar?
Answer: People who are working outside of mahalla (for example in important governmental position) send one person from their house. If a person is working we know it but there are other members of family. Somebody else will come and participate. However, even in important hashars (before Ramazan and Kurban) for showing their respect they will come in the morning to hashar and after that they go to their jobs. People in mahalla everybody knows
each other and they observe who is come who did not come. It does not mean that with force we are gathering them or we are going because of their observation. It is a part of our life activity. We have to keep clean our mahalla.

Question: What are your responsibilities and duties as a member of mahalla?
Answer: *As a member of mahalla, I have to live according its rule. I have to participate in hashars, funerals, weddings and I have to help and respect all members like my own family. I have to respect people older than me. In happy days and in difficulty of mahalla members I have to be with them. These responsibilities are the most important for me as a mahalla member.*

Question: What are the most important values in your life as mahalla member?
Answer: *I have to keep the image of my family in my community. I have to be a good person and helpful to people. First of all I have to take care about my parents*

because I am living for them. They bring me to this world and they did all the best. My first duty is to help them and to take care of them. I want them to be happy. I do not want anything more than my parent's happiness.

Question: How would you characterize the ties between you with other members of Mahalla?
Answer: *The ties between me and other mahalla members is like ties between family. Mahalla is like an extended family. We know each other well and in everyday life we are together. All mahalla members are our brothers and sisters. We cannot live without each other separately. Throughout history we preserved our tradition together. We help each other in difficulties and share our happiness together. It's a part of our life. I cannot imagine my life without it.*

Question: Would you agree with the opinion that Mahalla is like your extended family?
Answer: Yes, of course. Because, mahalla in fact is like extended family not only for me but for everyone who is living in our mahalla.

Question: How are your relations with other mahallas? Do you have any cooperation?
Answer: *It is not possible to live without cooperation with other mahallas. Neighbor mahallas is like our personal members and relatives. We help them in their problems and also they help us. We support each other in difficulties and share our happiness. If they have hashar from our mahalla people go to help them and if we have hashar they come. We are living like this. Every mahalla has special transport for council of elders and other members of mahalla. If there is funeral in other mahalla Rais, Mulla and council of elders go with this transport to that mahalla and they will do the same. Our elders they have good relations with neighbor mahallas try to avoid any conflicts. We marry from neighbor mahallas and they merry from our mahalla. That's why we have very close relations with them.*

Respondent 2. The name of mahalla: Nojii bolo

Imprint

1. Sex: male **2. Age**: 56 years old **3. Education**: high education
4. **Occupation**: Farmer
5. Position in mahalla: Farmer

Question: How many people live in your mahalla?
Answer: *Approximately three thousand people are living in our mahalla.*

Question: What is the main activity of members of your mahalla?
Answer: *It depends who are where working. Our village is very famous in our country for its grapes. Majority of people have grape plantations and they are working there.*

Question: Why do they owe their authority rais and members of council of elders?
Answer: *Throughout history they were the leaders of our community. They are like our fathers- the fathers of community.*

Question: What qualities should represent the ideal Rais?
Answer: *The Ideal rais must take care about his mahalla. He is one of us and he has participate in mahalla life and he must represent interests to other mahallas and to Government. Because he is the face of our mahalla. It is well accepted in our region that mostly people looking at rais giving value to the mahalla. If Rais is not good people think that their leader is not good person that's why their mahalla members will be the same. He must be the best example. Of course, it does not mean that he must do everything. We – all mahalla member respect him and in every situation listen to his orders and advices and we will help him.*

Question: What are the main problems of your mahalla?
Answer: *The main problems of our mahalla are water and reconstruction of roads. We have water but it is far and because of its location it is not easy to provide water to our mahalla. During Soviet times provided pipes of water to our mahalla but now are not working. From mahalla fund and with the help of mahalla members we bought pipes and we are working on it. Another problem for now is buying new furniture and computers for mahalla school. All problems would be sold by mahalla members. Our country after facing civil war still has economic problems. Therefore, we will not sit and only wait for government help.*
Question: In what way usually solves the problems of mahalla? Can you boast of some success?
Answer: *Usually in majlis (mahalla meeting) we gather and discuss and solve mahalla problems. It happens usually on Friday after prayer or in any day it depends when rais or mulla announce the day of meeting. At first we discuss all sides of problems and the way of solving. The vise- rais concerning financial issues or some special expert tell the amount of money which we will need. He will tell us the amount money which we have in our fund and how much more we need. It is not compulsory for everybody(for example some mahalla members are not working and they are very poor). People will give as much as they can to vice rais. From those money we solve our problems. Internal problems (for example conflict between neighbors or between husband and wife) solves by rais, mulla and council of elders.*

About our success, I already mentioned that we are now buying pipes for providing water from 20 km distance. Another our success was our boarder and water disputes with neighbor mahalla. About two centuries we had this problem. However this year the council of elders of our mahalla met their council of elders and they solved this old dispute.

Question: What is the main source of your mahalla fund?
Answer: *Mainly through charitable contribution.*

Question: Who initiates the projects implemented by Mahalla?
Answer: *Rais, mula and mahalla committee.*

Question: Who makes decisions about organizing hashar?
Answer: *Rais, mula with the council of elders.*

Question: How often the respondent participated in hashars?
Answer: *Sometimes I am going to Russian Federation as a labor migrant for seasonal works. When I am here in my country, I participate almost in all hashars. However, if I am not here my sons or my Brother usually participate.*

Question: Do all members of mahalla participate in hashars?
Answer: *Yes, majority of people participate in hashars.*

Question: How solves the problem of persons who by reason of obligations outside mahalla (working in government, business, etc) cannot participate in hashar?
Answer: *We understand them, because they are working. However, one person participates from their house. From every Family at least one person participates. In most case such people come in the morning. Of course they will not work but in this way they show their respect to the community.*

Question: What are your responsibilities and duties as a member of mahalla?
Answer: *My responsibilities and duty to be a good mahalla member and to live according long history unwritten code of mahalla.*

Question: What are the most important values in your life as mahalla member?
Answer: *The most important values for me is to preserve the good name of my avlod (kin) and my family. I want to live according mahalla rule: respect for my parents, other mahalla members. Now my parents are not alive. I think that I tried to respect them and to keep their oburu (face) in our village(however as much as we do for our parents it is still nothing). Now, I have to take care of my children and to learn the most important values of Tajiks as adab, nomus, ehtirom and etc.*

Question: How would you characterize the ties between you with other members of Mahalla?
Answer: *Without any doubt it is like ties between family members.*

Question: Would you agree with the opinion that Mahalla is like your extended family?
Answer: *Of course, I am agree 100 per cent.*

Question: How are your relations with other mahallas? Do you have any cooperation?
Answer: *Our relations are god with other mahallas. Of course, we have cooperation. It is impossible to live without cooperation. We depend in each other. In our difficulties they are with us and in their difficulties, we are with them. Thanks to our cooperation now we are alive (because during civil war as you know the situation was very bad and we helped each other).*

Respondent 3. Dushanbe city- mahalla Zarafshon

Question: How many people live in your mahalla?
Answer: *In our mahalla, approximately three thousand people are living.*

Question: What is the main activity of members of your mahalla?
Answer: *The main activity of our mahalla members is related to mahalla issues. Their activity depends on problem of mahalla.*

Question: Why do you owe your authority rais and members of council of elders?
Answer: *They are representative of our community to other mahallas and in relation to government authority. They are doing all their best for us. Therefore, we respect them.*

Question: What qualities should represent the ideal rais?
Answer: *Rais has to be a person who is responsible over others in mahalla and must have a certain competence. He must have not only capacity to take responsibility but also the power to cause things to develop. He must be capable and talented, and he needs strong leadership ability. Rais must serve to his community and he must have much experience.*

Question: What are the main problems of your mahalla?
Answer: *The main problem of our mahalla now is reconstruction of mahalla boiler house.*

Question: In what way usually solves the problems of mahalla? Can you boast of some success?
Answer: *Usually, the problems of mahalla solves in mahalla meetings. About our success? In every problems we work together and help each other. We changed pipes*

in two building of our mahalla from first till 5 floor. We have built special house with several rooms, for organizing mahalla ceremonies and keep common things of mahalla (for example tables, chairs, carpets, plates and etc.).

Question: What is the main source of your mahalla fund?
Answer: *The main source of our mahalla is through charitable contribution.*

Question: Who initiates the projects implemented by Mahalla?
Answer: *The main projects of our mahalla initiate by mahalla committee in cooperation with people with high professional education as doctors, engineers, teachers and others.*

Question: Who makes decisions about organizing hashar?
Answer: *The members of mahalla committee make decision about organizing hashar.*

Question: How often the respondent participated in hashars?
Answer: *Almost all the time.*

Question: Do all members of mahalla participate in hashars?
Answer: *Yes, from every family one representative participates in hashars.*

Question: How solves the problem of persons who by reason of obligations outside mahalla (working in government, business, etc) cannot participate in hashar?
Answer: *They usually provide financial help or other important thing for hashar.*

Question: What are your responsibilities and duties as a member of mahalla?
Answer: *My responsibilities and duties are to take an active part in the life of mahalla and help mahalla members.*

Question: What are the most important values in your life as mahalla member?
Answer: *To keep the good reputation of me and my family.*

Question: How would you characterize the ties between you with other members of Mahalla?
Answer: *Our ties are like family members.*

Question: Would you agree with the opinion that Mahalla is like your extended family?
Answer: *Yes, of course.*

Question: How are your relations with other mahallas?Do you have any cooperation?
Answer: *Our relations are very good. It is impossible to live without cooperation with other mahallas.*

Studies in Social Sciences, Philosophy and History of Ideas

Edited by Andrzej Rychard

Vol. 1 Józef Niżnik: Twentieth Century Wars in European Memory. 2013.

Vol. 2 Szymon Wróbel: Deferring the Self. 2013.

Vol. 3 Cain Elliott: Fire Backstage. Philip Rieff and the Monastery of Culture. 2013.

Vol. 4 Seweryn Blandzi: Platon und das Problem der Letztbegründung der Metaphysik. Eine historische Einführung. 2014.

Vol. 5 Maria Gołębiewska / Andrzej Leder/Paul Zawadzki (éds.): L'homme démocratique. Perspectives de recherche. 2014.

Vol. 6 Zeynep Talay-Turner: Philosophy, Literature, and the Dissolution of the Subject. Nietzsche, Musil, Atay. 2014.

Vol. 7 Saidbek Goziev: Mahalla – Traditional Institution in Tajikistan and Civil Society in the West. 2015.

www.peterlang.com

www.ingramcontent.com/pod-product-compliance
Ingram Content Group UK Ltd.
Pitfield, Milton Keynes, MK11 3LW, UK
UKHW041828100926
8556IPUK00002B/77

9 783631 647240